M000312254

The Basics of Economics

for

a Modern Manager

Written by

Mikhail I. Melnik

Southern Polytechnic State University

Edited By

Victor J. Bellitto, Ph.D.

Copyright 2014 Mikhail I. Melnik

All rights reserved

Printed in the United States of America

ISBN: 978-1-934844-74-8
No part of this publication may be reproduced, stored in or introduced into a
retrieval system, or transmitted, in any form, or by any means without the prior
permission of the publisher.

Requests for permission should be directed to:
webmaster@teneopress.com, or mailed to:

Teneo Press
PO Box 349
Youngstown, NY 14174

Content

PREFACE

MOTIVATION

This work is a product of nearly fifteen years of teaching economics at the MBA level, and as such it serves as an expanded and updated collection of my lecture notes. Teaching economics at the MBA level is both an interesting and a challenging task. Although my opinion might be somewhat biased, I do think that teaching or studying economics is a very fascinating undertaking. Economics is a unique discipline that incorporates philosophy, history, mathematics, and statistics into its own unique mix that is aimed at making our lives better. Simply put, economics is all about efficiency. Understanding efficiency is the means to getting more out of limited resources whether this is at the level of an individual, a firm, or a society. Efficiency is the key to higher productivity of resources, greater returns, and a higher standard of living.

Managerial economics is particularly interesting as it unlocks the practical applications of economics. Economics is not just a theoretical discipline, but it is very much a practical field that can be applied in any setting where a resource allocation question arises, which includes practically any activity. In this sense, Economics is a decision science that is an essential component in business education. One of the objectives of this text is to achieve the ideal mix of theory and application. This book assumes a limited background in economics on the part of the reader and as a result puts a heavier emphasis on the fundamentals of economic theory.

Traditionally, managerial economics is considered as an applied micro field due to its focuses on the behavior of businesses and consumers, i.e. microeconomic agents. However, modern businesses increasingly find themselves having to continuously adapt and re-adapt to a changing macroeconomic environment. This dynamic nature of the macroeconomic environment that we are in requires a modern manager to have a basic understanding of macroeconomics. Consequently, this text contains two separate sections: the first focuses on the traditional microeconomics framework, and the second focuses on the basics of macroeconomics.

ACKNOWLEDGMENTS

I owe a debt of gratitude to several individuals who made this work possible. First, I would like to thank Victor Bellitto for the enormous effort he put into editing and polishing this work. His dedication made this project possible. I want to thank Phillip Freiji (Oglethorpe University) for his insightful review. I also would like to thank Paul Richardson of Teneo Publishing for all his help and support in producing this book.

I want to also thank all the students I had over the years as their experiences helped refine these lectures

Mikhail I. Melnik

Chapter 1
THE BASICS

"If a man does not know to what port he is steering, no wind is favorable to him."

Seneca (ca. 1 century)

EFFICIENCY AT WORK

As stated in the introduction, economics is all about efficiency. However, efficiency is not a straightforward concept, and in fact it is a multidimensional issue. This chapter begins with a quote by Seneca, an ancient philosopher and a teacher to the Roman Emperor Nero. The quote states a necessary condition for efficiency, knowing your objective. We can discuss efficiency only if we know our objective, for efficiency is simply the shortest path to reaching the objective. This seems like a simple issue, but it can be complicated. For example, when taking a class, students may have an objective to learn the material well or instead may have an objective to learn the material in a way that best prepares them for the exams. Depending on how the exams are structured, these may be two different objectives.

A more interesting example would be to examine the objectives of a firm. We almost want to jump to a logical conclusion that the objective of a firm is to maximize profits, after all that is why a firm is established by its shareholders in the first place. Lest we forget, the shareholders' income is directly derived from the profits of the business. However, profit maximization may not always be the objective since the shareholders are not the ones who usually run the day by day operations of the business. As a result, the firm may be trying to achieve the objectives of the management team instead.[1] Therefore, the objectives of these two groups may not coincide. In the event these objectives do not coincide, an economic issue develops, known as the Principal – Agent problem. The Principal-Agent problem emerges whenever we have a setting where one party is represented by another party and their objectives do not coincide.

---

[1] It is important to note here that although our discussion refers to the agent in the principal – agent problem as the manager, all employees of the firm act as the agents in this context, as they are employed by the employers, i.e. the shareholders, to act on their behalf.

The Principal – Agent problem is present in many settings, for instance, it might be present in your classroom. Your school is definitely interested in providing you with the best quality of education its resources can deliver, because you will serve as the living advertisement to the quality of your school after you graduate. However, you are not being taught by your school but rather by faculty hired by the school. Your professors may have other objectives in mind, such as to maximize their research, increase their own free time, and increase their consulting work, all of which may potentially have an adverse effect on the quality of service they provide in the classroom.

In the context of a firm, the Principal – Agent problem can be viewed as a conflict of interest between the principals of the firm (the shareholders) and the agents (the employees including the management team) hired by the shareholders to act on their behalf. The shareholders are likely to desire profit maximization, but the employees hired to represent the shareholders may be more concerned with their own pay, reduced work time, etc. If the objective of the firm is that of its owners and is defined as profit maximization, then the presence of the Principal – Agent problem creates inefficiency.

The Principal – Agent problem is likely to be a function of the size of the enterprise. For instance, a single proprietor who hires only himself is not going to have any Principal – Agent problem as the objectives of the principal and the agent fully coincide given that it's the same person. As the business expands and other individuals are hired to assist the owner, the Principal – Agent problem starts to emerge. Initially, it may not be a serious issue as the costs associated with monitoring a small group of workers may remain low but the problem expands as additional management layers are added. If not controlled, the principal – agent problem may become the Achilles heel of a large enterprise.

Controlling for the Principal – Agent problem can also be a costly undertaking. One commonly used method to reduce the magnitude of the efficiency losses due to the Principal – Agent problem is to make the interests of the workers coincide with those of the owners by making them shareholders of the business. This policy can also be modified to create a requirement that any such shares given to the employees cannot be sold for a certain time period. Such restrictions are aimed at incorporating the long-term interests of the firm into the interests of the employees. However, such policies can be rather costly as they dilute shareholder equity, i.e. the number of outstanding shares increases.

Alternatively, a stock option method can also be used. In this scenario, the manager receives call options typically with a strike price near the current stock price.[2] Thus, the manager only benefits if the price of the stock increases over time and exceeds the strike price. This policy also has no cost to the firm in the event of a decline in the stock price below the strike price, in which case the options become worthless.

Although both of these methods have been extensively used in the corporate setting, one can argue that in well-developed financial markets, the principal – agent problem may be limited in magnitude due to the threat of a possible takeover by another group of investors. If a business becomes inefficient, then its stock value declines, and yet this decline in value can be reversed by increasing its efficiency. In this case, another group of investors can take advantage of this reduced value, take over the business, replace the inefficient management team, and benefit from the gain in efficiency. The threat of this takeover can act as an incentive for the management team to maximize profits and therefore the stock value of the firm.

In addition, debt can establish a source of external monitoring. When a firm borrows money, it effectively establishes an outside monitoring entity in the form of a bond rating agency or a bank. Assuming that the objectives of this additional monitoring entity coincide with those of the shareholders, its presence helps reduce the magnitude of the Principal – Agent problem. Since the creditor's objective is to have the debtor be able to repay the debt, the ability of the debtor to generate future earnings to repay the debt enters into the decision making process of the creditor.

A FIRM AS A MULTI-PERIOD PROJECT

---

[2] A call stock option is a contract between two parties: the writer of the option (the issuer), and the holder of the option. The holder has the right to call on the writer to sell to the holder the underlying stock at the pre-specified price, called the strike price. The option specifies the price at which the transaction takes place (the strike price), the time period within which the option can be exercised (assuming American design) as the expiration period, and the quantity of shares subject to the transaction. The option derives its term from the fact that it is optional to the holder, although it is mandatory to the issuer, i.e. the holder has an option to exercise the option or let it expire, while the writer has to honor the decision of the holder. In the context of our discussion, the writer of the option is the firm while the holder of the option is the employee.

If a firm is a project established by its shareholders to generate income over time, then the value of a firm can be viewed as the present value of the future income stream that a firm is expected to generate over its existence. Note that the term income represents net income, i.e. inflows net of outflows. In finance, this is often defined as Net Present Value. The general formula for such a computation is:

$$1) \quad PV = \sum_{i=1}^{N} \frac{A_i}{(1+r)^i}$$

A_i represents the income in time period i, and r represents the discount rate.

For example, a project that is expected to generate an income of $1,000 a year from now and $2,000 two years from now if the discount factor is 3%, would have its net present value computed as:

$$2) \quad PV = \frac{\$1000}{(1+0.03)^1} + \frac{\$2000}{(1+0.03)^2} = \$2856.07$$

If the payoff amounts are the same in each time period (and there are N periods), as it would be in a fixed annuity, then the PV equation can be simplified to (for more details see Simon and Bloom, 1995):

$$3) \quad PV = \frac{A}{r}\left(1 - \left(\frac{1}{1+r}\right)^N\right)$$

In practice, this computation has two issues: the uncertainty about the value of future payments, hence they are entered as expected values, and the choice of the discount factor. Unless the stream of future payments is guaranteed, some estimation or even guesswork would have to be employed.

The discount factor is also an issue. In theory, the discount factor in economics refers to exactly as the term suggests, the discounting of future dollars. A dollar today is worth more to me than a future dollar, and not just because of inflation but also because I may value my consumption today more than my consumption tomorrow. Thus, in theory, the discount factor differs from person to person. Some people discount tomorrow at a very low rate and continue to invest into CD (certificate of deposit) accounts, even today, when the interest rate on these is around 1%. Other consumers are willing to incur credit card debt where the rate of interest might be as high as 15%, thereby placing a heavy discount on their

4

future consumption. Because of this personal nature of the discount rate, the use of this economic definition of the discount rate is not practical in business decisions. Therefore, one can use a measure such as the rate of return on an alternative investment project that is available to the firm. One option is to use the rate of return of a similar duration and low risk alternative that is available to the firm, which for a U.S. business would be a U.S. Treasury bond with equivalent maturity. For instance, for a two year project as discussed above, these could be the yields on a one and two year U.S. Treasury bonds. Later, we will define the cost of holding cash as the interest rate foregone, and we will use the Treasury bond yield as the rate used for that computation.

Let's consider an example where we have three investment projects. Project A is expected to return $1,000 a year from now and $2,000 two years from now; project B is expected to return $2,000 a year from now and $1,000 two years from now; and project C is expected to return $1,500 at the end of each of these two years. If the current one- and two-year bond rates are 3%, which of these projects would you recommend? Note that we also need to assume that the level of risk associated with these projects is the same; otherwise, we simply don't have enough information to make a recommendation.[3] Assuming that they carry equal risk, we can immediately conclude that project B is better than project A. Both projects pay the same total nominal return, but the return from B is shifted to the earlier period relative to A. The comparison between B and C is not as obvious and does require a computation. Table 1.1 presents the present value computations for these three projects. For comparative purposes, the computations are performed for two different discount rates: 3% and 1%. This is done to illustrate the impact a change in the discount rate has on the present value computation.

Comparison of the present value computations demonstrates that project B has the highest present value for both discount rates. One of the factors influencing the computation is the discount rate. As the discount rate declines, the present value of a project increases, making it more attractive. For example, if an investor has an objective to invest only in those projects that return above $2,951, then none of the projects are attractive when the discount rate is 3%. However, projects B and C become attractive when the discount rate declines to 1%. In a

	1y	2y
A	1000	2000
B	2000	1000
C	1500	1500

---

[3] This assumption is necessary because investors may have different preferences towards risk, e.g. such as risk aversion. Risk or uncertainty it creates helps disperse the distribution of payoffs but not change its expected value. However, investors averse to risk would prefer centered distributions to more dispersed ones.

	Project		
	A	B	C
Year 1	1000	2000	1500
Year 2	2000	1000	1500
PV	Discount Rate = 3%		
Year 1	970.87	1941.75	1456.31
Year 2	1885.19	942.60	1413.89
Total	2856.07	2884.34	2870.20
PV	Discount rate =1%		
Year 1	990.10	1980.20	1485.15
Year 2	1960.59	980.30	1470.44
Total	2950.69	2960.49	2955.59

Table 1.1

way, we just examined one of the basic effects of monetary policy on investment. As interest rates decline, investing into business projects become more attractive, naturally with all else being held constant.

PRICE TO EARNINGS RATIO

The preceding discussion formulated the value of a business as the present value of its future earnings. For publically held corporations, financial markets present us with a well-defined business valuation, a stock market capitalization. Although a stock market capitalization is a market assigned value to a business, a comparison between two different corporations based solely on the basis of their market capitalizations is rather uninformative as these measures do not convey any information about the earnings of these corporations. A more intuitive tool that is frequently used both to evaluate businesses and compare their valuations is the price to earnings ratio (P/E ratio). In this computation, the price refers to the price of a stock share, and the earnings represent the annual earnings per stock share. The price to earnings ratio can be computed with respect to the most recently reported earnings (sometimes referred to as the trailing ratio) or with respect to the expected future earnings (sometimes referred to as the forward ratio). Expected future earnings are unknown and therefore require some form of estimation. Current earnings may not be equal to future earnings but may serve as a predictor of future earnings. The price to earnings ratio based on forward looking earnings is similar to the present value approach developed in the preceding discussion. The price to earnings ratio defines the value an investor has to pay per dollar of earnings, and the ratio based on expected future earnings defines what an investor has to pay per dollar of future earnings. The ratio can also be interpreted as the number of years required to generate the nominal earnings needed to pay off the value of initial investment.

The price to earnings ratio enables a comparison of stock valuations across different companies. It also contains some additional information about the market expectation of the future profitability of companies. For instance, if the price to earnings ratio for company A is 10, while for company B it is 20, then this implies that investors in company A pay $10 per $1 of yearly earnings (10% rate of return), while investors in company B pay $20 per $1 of yearly earnings (5% rate of return). The question that is inevitably asked is why would investors accept a much lower rate of return on stock B? There are two possible explanations. One, investors expect the earnings of company A to decrease in the future and bring the two ratios on par with each other. Two, investors expect the earnings of company B to increase in the future and equalize the two ratios in that manner. Note that this discussion assumes that these two investments are otherwise identical (in terms of risk, industry, etc.).

DEFINING RESOURCES IS ECONOMICS

Resource, input, and factor in production are practically all synonymous terms in economics and represent any entity that can be used in a production process to produce output. The term resource tends to be used in a more general way describing the fundamental resources, while the other two terms tend to be used in the context of a production process. Resources include land (with all its natural resources), labor, human capital, and physical capital. Note that money is not a resource in economics. Money is a form of "claim" on something but not an economic resource. Money fulfills a multitude of important functions in our economy but being a resource is not one of them. Money is a medium of exchange, a store of value over time, and a unit of measurement. What disqualifies money as a resource is the fact that money itself cannot be used to produce output. This also means that financial capital is not a resource in economics, but real physical capital (buildings, machinery, etc.) is a resource.

Since the process of formation of physical capital requires savings, the health of the financial system becomes an essential ingredient for economic growth.

The financial system, including the banking sector and the financial markets, pools together the savings of many and transforms them into investments that generate physical capital formation. In the process, it serves as the brain of a capitalist economy. It is the financial markets that fundamentally decide which capital investment projects are undertaken and which are not. The health and the functionality of this mechanism of transforming financial capital into physical capital is one of the key components in achieving economic prosperity.

In fact, capitalism, as an economic system, derives its name from the way it assigns the ownership rights to productive capital. In capitalism, productive capital stock belongs to private individuals.

OPPORTUNITY COST

In economics, cost is defined as a foregone benefit. Since every activity consumes resources and those resources have alternative uses, undertaking an activity precludes other uses of the resources. Thus, the cost of an activity is the loss of an opportunity to undertake another activity. Obviously, there may be many alternative uses of the consumed resources, but it is the next best alternative use, the one that would have been alternatively selected, which becomes the opportunity cost.

Economics studies the behavior of people, and therefore it is important to account for all cost factors that influence our behavior. This is where the economic definition of cost begins to differentiate from the accounting definition. We can define some costs as explicit; these typically constitute the accounting cost. Explicit costs arise whenever we have to use resources that we do not own and therefore have to compensate their owners (suppliers) for their use. However, not all costs are explicit. Sometimes we employ our own resources and therefore do not have to compensate anyone for their use. In these instances, we incur no monetary costs, and yet there is still an alternative use of those resources, making these costs implicit. Since both explicit and implicit costs, enter into our decision making process, we can't ignore either of them. Perhaps a better way to understand the difference between these types of cost is to examine an example.

EXAMPLES OF OPPORTUNITY COST

The Economic Cost of your class to you   The course you are taking consumes resources and as a result has a cost. The logic here is simple; all costs that would not have occurred, had you not taken the class, become a part of the cost of the class. We can qualify some of the cost you incur as explicit and some as implicit. Explicit costs occur when you employ the resources of others. For example, in taking the class you utilize the resources of your school, and therefore you have to pay the tuition. There are many explicit costs involved in taking your class; these might include the cost of your textbook, parking, gasoline and so on. Recall that what constitutes an explicit cost is an instance that you have to pay someone else for the use of their resource. In essence, these are your accounting costs of the class; however, these do not represent the total cost of the class. There is another resource that is being consumed as a result of your decision to take the class – your time. Because this resource is your own, and therefore you do not have to pay anyone for its use, it constitutes an implicit cost. The fact that you do not have to compensate anyone for the use of this resource does not make it costless. Your time has an alternative use, and by directing your time to the class, you sacrifice any alternative use of this time.

For instance, instead of taking the class, you could have used this time to take another class, work, take a vacation, sleep, watch TV, and so on. You have a number of alternative uses of your time, and whatever would have been the next best alternative use of your time becomes its opportunity cost. In practice, however, we frequently use the market value of your time to evaluate the cost of time. There are two reasons for this method. One, the market value of your time, your current market wage, is available to you as an alternative. And two, it is defined in monetary terms, and since your explicit costs are also defined in monetary terms, it simplifies the computation of the total (monetary) cost of an activity.

Thus, for someone with a higher wage, the use of their time becomes more costly. This is a very important observation. For instance, if one were to visit a typical college classroom, one would notice that most students tend to be young, in their late teens early twenties. That is not a coincidence but rather a direct consequence of the cost-benefit analysis of education. The economic cost of college education tends to be lower for people in their teens and early twenties as opposed to people in their 30's or 40's. This is due to the difference in their market wages. On-the-job training and accumulated experience tend to increase workers' wages during the first couple of decades of their careers; thus all else held constant, it makes the cost of time spent studying in college higher for older students. Note that both groups of students face the same explicit, or accounting costs of education, but their implicit costs are different.

Let's assume that the class makes each student allocate 100 hours to study. The tuition cost of the class is $1,000 dollars, the cost of the textbook is $100, and the cost of the commute to school is another $100. Let's further assume that these costs are identical for every student in the class. Thus, the explicit cost of the class is $1,200, and it is the same for everyone. Now, let's assume that we have two students: an 18 year old who works at a fast food restaurant and makes $8/hour, and an older student who works in a business office and makes $20/hour. Since each student is forced to sacrifice 100 hours studying for the class, the cost of that time to the first student is $800, making their implicit cost $800, and their total economic cost of the class $2,000. For the second student, the implicit cost is $2,000, making the cost of the class $3,200. Since people respond to costs, we must conclude that the average classroom will have fewer older students.

Note that there is also an increased benefit to obtaining education at an earlier point in one's life since the effect of education on wages is captured over a longer period in the labor market. However, it is important to differentiate between the cost of an activity and its benefit. A possible positive effect of education on one's wage is a benefit of education and has nothing to do with its cost. Whether an activity is to be undertaken will depend on the difference between its benefit and its cost. However, each of these needs to be identified separately.

It is important to keep in mind that everything we do uses resources, and since resources have alternative uses, everything we do has an opportunity cost. Since people respond to costs, these costs alter our behavior.

Another interesting illustration would be the potential relationship between the level of economic development and the fertility rate. During the XX century, fertility rates in developed economies declined sharply (for a further discussion of the relationship between economic development and birth rates see Ray, 1998). The decline of fertility rates was observed during a period when incomes and labor force participation rates increased (see Mishra and Smyth, 2010). Opportunity cost may offer some partial explanation to the phenomenon of demographic transition, a relationship between the birth rate and economic development (see Shultz, 2001). What can be deduced is that as incomes and labor participation rates of the parents increased, the cost of having a child also increased. One of the components of the cost is the interruption of work resulting in the loss of possible wages (the opportunity cost of the interruption).

The economic cost of home ownership Consider a scenario where you purchase a house for $200,000 and pay for it with cash. You also incur additional expenditures during the first year of homeownership including: $2,000 in property taxes and $1,000 in insurance. Also, assume that during the first year of homeownership, the market value of the house decreases by $5,000 to $195,000. Then, what is the economic cost of homeownership in the first year?

First, it is important to distinguish between price and cost. A price is just a measure of valuation. A cost is a loss, a reduction in wealth. The purchase price does not represent the cost of the house at all. When you purchase the house your net wealth does not change; all that happens is that some of your wealth is rebalanced from cash (a liquid form) into the house (a real estate asset) but the net effect on your wealth is zero. Before purchasing the house, you had $200,000 in liquid wealth and zero in real estate assets; after the purchase, you have zero in liquid wealth but $200,000 in real estate assets. Note that if there were any additional expenditures such as closing costs, appraisal, inspection, etc., then those would be considered costs as they would represent a reduction in your wealth.

In this example, you do incur several costs in the first year of homeownership such as taxes ($2,000), insurance ($1,000), and the change in the market value of the house (-$5,000). In the first year, the house saw its market value decline by $5,000, thereby reducing your net wealth by $5,000. Changes in market value are defined in economics as economic depreciation and are a part of the economic cost of homeownership. It is also possible to have the house appreciate in value, in which case this cost component would become negative and reduce the cost of homeownership for that time period.

In addition to these, there is one more cost component, and that is the foregone interest you could have earned if you had invested the cash. Imagine that as an alternative use of the cash, you would have invested it into a CD account that pays 5% interest a year. Then by purchasing the house, you lost the opportunity to earn $10,000/year in interest (the purchase price of the house times the interest rate). This is also a cost of the house to you since you would have earned an additional $10,000 had you not purchased the house. Thus, the cost of homeownership in the first year is $3,000 (insurance and taxes) plus $5,000 (economic depreciation), plus $10,000 (foregone interest), for a total of $18,000.

Interest as the economic cost of cash   Holding cash has an economic cost. If your checking account pays 0.5 percent interest, then by holding cash in your pocket you forgo the opportunity to keep those funds in your checking account and earn interest. For instance, if on average you keep $50 in your pocket, then during the course of one year you incur the economic cost of $0.25, given the interest rate on your checking account.

Many U.S. corporations select to hold their cash holdings in short-term U.S. Treasury bonds. Short-term U.S. Treasury bonds offer a rate of return, and at the same time, their short-term nature makes them relatively liquid.

The economic cost of physical capital   Consider a scenario where you purchase a computer for $1,000, and you pay for it with cash. Alternatively, the cash could have been invested into a one year CD account at a 3% rate of return. Also assume that the computer is expected to last for four years. The table below represents the market value at the start of each year.

Year	Market Value at the start of the year	Market Value at the end of the year
1	1000	600
2	600	300
3	300	100
4	100	0

Table 1.2

Based on the information in Table 1.2, we can conclude that the economic depreciation in year 1 is $400, in year 2 it is $300, and so on. Economic depreciation is defined as a change in market value. The reason why market value is used is because it is the market value that can be obtained in the event the capital unit is liquidated. Clearly, economic depreciation constitutes a part of the cost of physical capital. As the computer undergoes economic depreciation, the asset you have loses value, thereby causing you to incur a cost. However, economic depreciation is just a part of the cost. Because you paid cash for the computer, you lost the opportunity to invest the cash into the CD account and receive interest. In the first year, you could have invested $1000 into the CD instead of purchasing the computer, thereby earning $30 in interest. These $30 dollars constitute an additional cost to you, making the total cost of the ownership of the computer in the first year equal to $430 (economic depreciation plus the foregone interest payment).

At the start of the second year, you have a choice to either continue the ownership of the computer or to liquidate it and invest the proceeds into the CD account. Since the market value of the computer at the start of the second year is only $600, the foregone interest payment (assuming the interest rate of 3%) would be only $18. This results in the total cost of the ownership in the second year of $318. Similarly, if we continue to assume the same interest rate on the CD account for the other years, we can compute the economic cost of the ownership of the computer for the four years, as shown in Table 1.3.

Year	Market Value at the start of the year	Market Value at the end of the year	Economic Depreciation	Foregone Interest (at 3%)	Economic Cost
1	1000	600	1000-600=400	1000*0.03=30	400+30=430
2	600	300	600-300=300	600*0.03=18	300+18=318
3	300	100	300-100=200	300*0.03=9	200+9=209
4	100	0	100-0=100	100*0.03=3	100+3=103

Table 1.3

If we were to assume that the computer rental market is competitive, then a brand new computer should rent for about $430/year, a one year old computer should rent for about $318/year, a two year old computer should rent for about $209/year, and a three year old computer should rent for about $103/year.

If the purchase of the computer was financed and you had to make an interest payment to someone, then it would be this interest payment that would be used instead of the foregone interest payment. This would also make the interest expense an explicit cost.

The computer example is convenient since the capital unit has a short life span, and therefore its entire life can be represented in a rather short table. It is however, a rather bad example because it does not reflect what happens with the bulk of the value of physical capital used in production. If you look around your classroom, you will notice that there are several pieces of equipment that do depreciate quickly and have a rather short life span. These include the computer, the projector and so forth. The combined value of these items is not very large relative to the value of the room itself, and yet the rate of economic depreciation of the room is rather low. This suggests that the bulk of the value of our capital stock undergoes a rather slow economic depreciation, making the interest payment the largest component in the cost of capital. For example, an office condo tower may have the market value of $50,000,000 and undergo the economic depreciation of only 1% a year, $500,000. However, the foregone interest payment even at a mere 3% would be $1,500,000/year.

The large role that the interest rate plays in the economic cost of capital often makes some simply equate the cost of capital to that of the interest rate. Although this may make sense under some circumstances, it nevertheless is a big approximation as it ignores the economic depreciation and other forms of costs such as property taxes, insurance, etc.

The fact that the interest rate is a significant factor in the cost of capital also demonstrates the important role monetary policy plays in affecting the costs of production in an economy. However, this is a topic for a much later discussion.

References

Mishra, V., Smyth, R., 2010, Female labor force participation and total fertility rates in the OECD: New evidence from panel cointegration and Granger causality testing, *Journal of Economics and Business [P]*, vol 62, issue 1, Elsevier Inc, USA, pp. 48-64.

Ray, D., 1998. Development Economics, Princeton University Press.

Schultz, T. Paul. 2001. *The fertility transition: Economic explanations.* New Haven, CT: Yale University.

Simon C. P. and L. Bloom, 1994, *Mathematics for Economists.* W. W. Norton and Company, NY.

APPENDIX A

EFFICIENCY IN ECONOMICS

As stated earlier in the chapter, efficiency is a multi-dimensional concept. Efficiency can be defined by addressing the following three fundamental economic questions: What to produce? How to Produce? For whom to produce?

What to produce? This question asks where economic resources should be allocated, hence it addresses resource allocation. For instance, is it efficient for MBA students to take a course in economics, or instead would they be better served by using the resources allocated to the economics course in another management course? The resource allocation question arises when any activity is undertaken, and efficiency requires the undertaken activity to generate the greatest benefit compared to any other alternative use of the resources.

How to Produce? This question addresses productive efficiency, or productivity of resources. Once we decide on what to produce, the next question is how to produce it using the least costly methodology.

For whom to produce? This question addresses output allocation. Once output is produced, the next question is how to distribute it. For instance, should it be provided to those who need it the most, who value it the most, or who are capable of paying the most for it?

Addressing the fundamental questions in a market economy The question of "what to produce?" is answered by consumer demand. Firms in a market economy produce those products and services for which consumers are willing to pay more than the cost of production. The question of "for whom to produce?" is answered by prices and incomes. Those consumers who are willing and able to pay the price are the ones who end up acquiring the product or service. The most interesting answer is provided to the question of "how to produce?" This last question deals with productive efficiency, which is not even an economic but rather a technological question. However, if we assume competition, we can assure ourselves that the technological process would continuously improve and evolve, resulting in the most cost effective use of economic resources.

Chapter 2

MARKETS

"There are three things that matter in property:

Location, Location, Location."

Frequently attributed to Lord Harold Samuel

A MARKET AS AN INSTITUTION

Perhaps nothing is more affiliated with economics than the demand-supply model, which is used to analyze markets. However, before we formulate the model, we need to understand what a market is.

In economics, a market can be viewed as a set of arrangements that can be used to facilitate the exchange between a buyer and a seller of a given product or service. Historically, such a set of arrangements mainly consisted of a physical location where sellers and buyers gathered to conduct their exchange. These centralized places of commercial exchange were one of the two fundamental reasons for the development of cities in agricultural (feudal) societies.[4]

In a modern setting, defining a market as a physical place where the exchange is being conducted is insufficient, and that is why today we define a market as a set of arrangements, effectively as an institution that facilitates the exchange. One example of this is eBay, a platform for an online community of buyers and sellers from across the world who utilize the eBay website for their commercial exchange. One can still think of eBay as just a place or location in the virtual world of the internet, or one can recognize that eBay is a well-developed tool, an arrangement that is used to facilitate the exchange. In this second setting, we define eBay as a market mechanism that enables buyers and sellers from different geographical locations to participate in the exchange.

---

[4] National defense is a pure public good and is the other of the two key reasons for the development of cities in the pre-industrial era. The industrial revolution created another important reason for the need of city development and that is to have a concentrated labor pool.

INTERNET AND GEOGRAPHICAL SCOPE

The commercial adaptation of the internet in the 1990s has transformed the internet into a market mechanism, which in turn altered the geographical scope of many markets. Historically speaking, the commercial adaptation of the internet is a relatively recent event, and its effects on the economy have not yet been fully understood. The extension of the geographical scope of the market is just one of such effects. In the context of brick and mortar commerce, the geographical scope of the market is relatively well defined. For instance, a shopping mall attracts buyers from its surrounding geographical area. However, in the case of online commerce, this need not be. For example, consider the implications of the internet on the labor market. In the pre-internet era, the costs associated with a job search, outside of one's geographical area, were higher. The internet has effectively reduced the job search costs and perhaps even the relocation costs as it made it easier to obtain information about a perspective area. These lower costs may have made the labor force more geographically mobile. This may seem like a minor thing, but it may actually have significant implications on matching workers with jobs, reducing duration of unemployment, harmonizing unemployment rates across various locations, etc.

PRODUCT DIFFERENTIATION

In addition to the geographical scope of a market, another criterion by which we can narrow our view of a market is product differentiation. For example, both Harvard and MIT are in the higher-education market. They are located near to one another, so geographically it would be difficult to argue that they are in two different markets, and yet they are in some sense. Both of these schools have high overall reputations, but MIT has defined its image as a science and technology oriented school, while Harvard has emphasized its image in law and business disciplines. This becomes especially interesting when we compare schools from different tiers. In the higher-education market, students who apply to tier 1 schools may not even consider tier 3 schools. Can we argue that tier 1 schools are in the same market with tier 3 schools? If they are not, then they can have different pricing behavior.

Product differentiation effectively segments what seems to be one market into different markets. Just as MIT and Harvard appear to specialize in certain fields, the same happens across all businesses. A possible example of this would be the U.S. shipping industry. The industry is dominated by three major players: FedEx,

UPS, and USPS. And it seems like it is a competitive industry with three large competitors; however, USPS tends to be perceived to focus primarily on letters and general mail, while UPS tends to be perceived to focus on parcel deliveries and FedEx on express mail.

Perhaps one of the best illustrations of product differentiation can be seen in the housing market where, at times, two adjacent properties can have very different prices. Imagine a resort condominium building where one side faces the beach, while the other side faces inland. It is quite possible that these two sides of the building will end up with significantly different prices for the same size units, given that consumers who want to purchase a beach view property would not consider the inland facing units as an alternative.

There are examples where it makes sense not to differentiate your product and in fact underscore the similarities. This is specifically the case if the objective is to enter into the market for the other product. For instance, in 2011 Hyundai Corporation used a TV commercial in the U.S. in which the company tried to underscore the similarities between its models and those of BMW. In this case, the objective seemed to be to enter the luxury car market, whether it succeeded or not is up to the consumer. It is the consumer who ultimately decides the market definition.

Generally speaking, we can consider two products to be in the same market if the consumer considers them as perfect or near perfect substitutes for each other and therefore is indifferent between them. In this case, the two products will end up having similar prices and similar price dynamics.

THE HOUSING MARKET

Since 2008, the term "housing market" has practically become the subject of nearly every single news report covering the U.S. national economy, and yet there really is no such thing as the national housing market. Here, the geographical scope is just too serious a constraint. Sometimes housing prices differ sizably in neighboring jurisdictions. For instance, when one visits the Niagara Falls area in New York, one usually does not consider the housing market, and yet it is a rather interesting market. In 2008, one could have purchased a 3 bedroom house less than a mile away from the falls for about $40,000. However, if one were to travel down the Niagara River for just about seven miles one would enter the town of Lewiston, where the average price for a

3 bedroom house would have exceeded $120,000. This is a sizable difference within a very short distance, suggesting that these are two different housing markets. Individuals who look for homes in Lewiston may not consider properties in Niagara Falls as alternatives.

During the most recent period of correction in housing prices, 2007 – 2009, most areas of the country experienced declines in prices, although some parts of the country managed to post price increases. The National Association of Realtors in the U.S. monitors and reports home prices for about 161 metropolitan areas across the country on a quarterly basis (for more information on these reports please see: www.realtor.org).[5] In addition, the Federal Housing Finance Agency, established in 2008, reports various housing price indices. Table 2.1 reports a summary of the purchase-only housing price index (purchase based) for three individual metropolitan areas and the U.S. overall.

Metropolitan Area	Change in House Price Index, Purchase-Only		
	2007	2008	2009
Buffalo, NY	0.40%	1.30%	2.28%
Columbia, SC	2.56%	-3.35%	2.17
Dallas, TX	2.36%	-0.02%	0.76%
USA	-2.45%	-9.77%	-2.21%

Table 2.1.[6] Source: U.S. FHFA.

Although, on average, home sales prices declined during this period and in some metropolitan areas such declines were severe, in some areas we saw a steady increase in prices. It seems that the areas with strong price performance of the housing market between 2007 and 2009 were unaffected by the housing boom that took place between 2002 and 2007 (see David Robinson, 2008). Table 2.1 clearly demonstrates that the housing market is always local.

MARKET PARTICIPANTS

Any market will have two distinct participant groups: buyers and sellers. These two groups have different interests when it comes to price, although on the part

---

[5] The number of covered metropolitan areas varies slightly across the quarterly releases.
[6] The underlying data is obtained from the Federal Housing Finance Agency (http://www.fhfa.gov/Default.aspx?Page=87). Computations are performed by the author.

of quantity their interests tend to coincide. Both buyers and sellers would prefer to have a greater quantity of product traded, but on price, their preferences differ. Buyers prefer the price to be low, while sellers prefer it to be high. In economics, we attempt to model the behavior of these two groups with the help of mathematics and statistics. We use demand to represent the behavior of buyers, and supply to represent the behavior of sellers. Both demand and supply are structured as functions that mathematically describe the behavior of the market participants. The following two chapters will develop and present the model of supply/demand. Although we construct these two functions separately, we typically don't observe them directly since we only observe a market outcome, the result of an interaction between the two functions. We will refer to this outcome as the market equilibrium that contains two pieces of information: the market price and the market quantity of output.

For example, on any given trading day, the NYSE, a major U.S. stock market, produces two pieces of valuable information: the movement of the index and the volume of exchange. Since the index is a form of a weighted price average, changes in the index represent changes in the weighted average price. The volume of exchange is the quantity of shares of stocks traded. These two indicators provide us with information about what happened in the market during the trading session. However, they don't define for us the demand for shares or the supply of shares during that trading session.

THE ROLE OF PRICES

Prices play a number of very important roles in our economy. First of all, it is through prices that our economy answers the fundamental economic question of output allocation: what to produce? This makes prices act as the rational of distribution in a market-based economy.

Prices also act as signals by which markets communicate with one another. For example, in the 1980s and 90s we saw a sizable increase in the salary of software engineers. Since salary acts as the price for that specific type of labor, the increase in the average pay for software engineers acted as an incentive for future workers to study computer science. This rise in the demand for software engineering skills induced more colleges to expand their computer science programs. In essence, the U.S. economy did not have enough trained software engineers, so the price of software engineers in the market (i.e. their salary) increased. The rise in the salary was the signal that encouraged more people to obtain the necessary skills to become software engineers, which in turn induced producers of those skills to expand their production.

In economics, we define prices in three forms: nominal, real, and relative. It is important to understand all three of these representations of price because they each convey different information.

Nominal Price A nominal price is the price measured in the current currency unit. This is the price we typically observe. For example, at the time of writing this discussion, the price of gasoline in the city of Atlanta averaged around $3.45/gallon. This was the nominal price of gasoline at the time. Nominal prices change for a variety of reasons, which affect the demand and the supply functions, but nominal prices also change due to inflation.

Real Price A real price is measured in some "constant" currency unit. For instance, we can measure the prices of everything sold during 2000 – 2010 using constant dollars from 2000. When we say "constant" dollars, we mean the dollar with a constant purchasing power over time. This enables us to take the effect of inflation on prices out of the picture for the examined time period. For example, if we assume that the nominal price of gasoline was $3.20/gallon a year ago and today it is $3.45/gallon, and if the rate of inflation during these past twelve months was 3%, then we can compute the price of gasoline today using the last year's dollars:

$$1) \quad Preal = \frac{Pnominal}{price\ index} = \frac{\$3.45}{1.03} = \$3.35$$

The use of real prices is essential when making comparisons across different time periods. This is because the monetary unit we use to measure the value of goods and services itself is not constant over time.

Relative Price Perhaps the most important representation of price is conveyed by relative price. Relative prices measure the changes in the relative importance of products. These prices serve as the signaling mechanism between markets. Relative prices are not measured in monetary units but rather in terms of a quantity of another product and thus represent the opportunity cost of one unit of a product in terms of the quantity foregone of another. For instance, if we assume that the price of gasoline today is \$3.45 and the price of milk is \$2.50, then the relative price of gasoline in terms of milk would be computed as follows:

$$2) \quad P \text{ relative price of gasoline} = \frac{P \text{ gasoline}}{P \text{ milk}} =$$
$$= \frac{\$3.45 / \text{gallon of gasoline}}{\$2.50 / \text{gallon of milk}} = 1.38 \frac{\text{gallons of milk}}{\text{gallon of gasoline}}$$

In this example, we have the price of gasoline being equal to 1.38 times the price of milk. This means that we forego the opportunity to purchase 1.38 gallons of milk when we purchase one gallon of gasoline. Our prior example of the salary changes of software engineers, is an illustration of a relative price change and its effect on human behavior.

References

Federal Housing Finance Agency, The, *House Price Indexes*, available online at: http://www.fhfa.gov/Default.aspx?Page=87.

Robinson, David. "Feel pinched? It could be a lot worse." The Buffalo News 17 August, 2008. Print and online at: http://www.buffalonews.com/article/20080817/BUSINESS/308179948.

Chapter 3

DEMAND

"A horse, a horse, my kingdom for a horse."

From William Shakespeare's *Richard III*, 1592

DEMAND AS A FUNCTION

In economics, we use functional forms to describe the behavior of various economic agents. Demand is one such function used to represent the behavior of a buyer or buyers. A demand function is structured as quantity demanded as a function of price and other relevant factors to the consumption decision and thus is written as:

1) $Q_X^D = f(P_X, \text{other relevant factors})$

$Q^D{}_X$ reads as quantity demanded of good X, and P_X represents the price of X.

A demand function serves as the algebraic representation of consumer behavior. A demand function is used to capture the relationship between price and quantity demanded. However, price is not the only determinant of quantity demanded; other factors, such as consumer income, price of related goods in consumption, expectations, and etc. influence consumer behavior. Although the previously listed factors seem to be present in most demand functions, each demand can contain product specific factors. For instance, consider the demand for coffee on your campus. Clearly, the quantity of coffee purchased would depend on the price charged, but it would also depend on the time of day, the classroom temperature, the difficulty of courses offered at the time, the price of soft drinks on campus, etc. Ignoring these relevant factors potentially leads to a serious misspecification of the demand function.

We will primarily focus on the most commonly used factors such as income, prices of goods related in consumption, and expectations. However, every demand function can have a set of factors specific to its own market that need to be identified and included.

INCOME

Prior to purchasing any good or service, one needs to obtain the means to pay for it. This can come from the current period income or from previously accumulated savings that form wealth. Note that income and wealth are two different things. Income represents earnings *during* a given time period, while wealth simply represents the net worth of assets *at* a given point in time. One is a flow variable that takes time to earn (income), whereas the other is a stock variable representing a value at a given point in time (wealth). Wealth can also be an important determinant in a demand function.

We naturally tend to assume that the income effect on demand is positive, i.e. demand increases with income, as is represented in equation 2:

$$2) \quad Q_X^D = a - bP_X + cI$$

I represents income, and *c* is a positive coefficient, representing the effect of income on the demand for *X*. However, not all goods will have a positive sign in front of *c*. For some goods, demand may be lower at higher income levels. In economics, we refer to such goods as inferior goods.

Fundamentally, our demands are derived from other factors, such as wants and preferences. For instance, I may have a preference to dine out, and my preferred restaurant might be Outback Steakhouse; however, if my income declines, I may choose to substitute with a lower cost establishment such as a fast food restaurant. In this case, the fast food restaurant acts as an inferior alternative to Outback Steakhouse. I would prefer to go to Outback Steakhouse, but given a decline in my income, I end up substituting with a less liked but cheaper alternative.

Formally, a normal good is defined as one where a rise in consumer income leads to a rise in demand, and a decline in consumer income leads to a decline in demand. An inferior good is one where the opposite is observed: A rise in consumer income causes demand to decrease, and a decline in consumer income causes demand to increase. We should not view inferior goods as bad goods as they are still economic goods. Inferior versus normal are simply terms used to describe the income effect on demand. Both constitute economic goods. An economic good is anything that is in shortage when the price is zero.

In is important to note that the relationship itself is a function of income, i.e. what might be a normal good for one income group may be an inferior good for

24

another. Imagine the following simple scenario where you just graduated from high school and entered college. Your income is nonexistent and you might be using a public bus to commute to school. While riding the bus, you might be dreaming of having your own car. This suggests that any car would be a normal good for you at this point. Now, imagine you graduate from college and get your first job paying $50,000/year. As a result of this, you purchase a new Honda Civic. Your purchase decision demonstrates that for someone with an annual income of $50,000, a Honda Civic is a normal good, while public transportation appears as an inferior service. Let's now assume that you go back to college and obtain your MBA degree, and as a result your income increases to $100,000/year. If you decide to purchase a new Acura after the rise in income instead of continuing to drive your Honda, then you would effectively indicate that a new Acura is a normal good, and a new Honda Civic is an inferior good for you when your income level is $100,000. Let's say you become the CEO of a major company, your annual income increases to $10,000,000, and as a result you decide to purchase a limousine and hire a chauffeur. This would indicate that when your income is $10,000,000, a new Acura is an inferior good, and in fact, driving is an inferior service to riding (which is actually quite ironic since at the start of this discussion and prior to your new found income you were riding a bus to campus).

The inferior versus normal status of a good has a serious implication on how the demand for that good is affected by the business cycle. Normal goods tend to be pro-cyclical, whereas inferior goods may potentially be countercyclical. If recessions are characterized by declining average incomes, then recessions may have a positive effect on the demand for an inferior good.

It is also important to underscore one other advantage of the algebraic approach. In Equation 2, we clearly separate the terms Px and I. This enables us to identify their individual effects (the derivatives of the function with respect to each of these variables). In Equation 2, b represents the effect of a change in the price of X, and c represents the effect of a change in consumer income. This approach allows us to control for the other variables while measuring the effect of any one of the variables on quantity demanded. We can interpret the coefficient b as the effect on quantity demanded of X from a one dollar change in the price of X while holding all other factors constant (in this case that includes income). In economics, this refers to the Ceteris Paribus assumption (all else remains unchanged).

PRICES OF GOODS RELATED IN CONSUMPTION

Two goods are related in consumption when changes in the price of one of these goods have an impact on the demand for the other good. Goods may be related as substitutes or complements in consumption. If two goods are substitutes in consumption, then the same want can be satisfied by either one of these goods. Driving and public transportation are examples of substitutes in consumption. Complements in consumption are goods that are used together in order to satisfy the same want, like a car and gasoline. The demand in Equation 3 illustrates the cases of related in consumption goods:

$$3) \quad Q_X^D = a - bP_X + cI + dP_Y - eP_Z$$

The demand in Equation 3 includes two additional variables, the prices of two other goods (P_Y and P_Z). If the coefficients d and e are different from zero, then these two goods are related to X in consumption. Another way to examine the equation is to recognize that the consumer considers the prices of Y and Z when making the decision to purchase X. In Equation 3, Py has a positive effect in the demand for X, implying that as the price of Y increases the demand for X also increases ($\Delta Qx = d\Delta Py$). This positive effect of the price of Y on the demand for X makes X and Y substitutes in consumption (competing goods). A simple example would be Coca-Cola versus Pepsi. As the price of Pepsi increases, the demand for Coca-Cola increases; thus, the price of Pepsi must have a positive sign of the coefficient multiplying the price of Pepsi in the demand for Coca-Cola.

On the other hand, Pz has a negative effect on the demand for X in Equation 3. As the price of Z increases, the demand for X decreases. This implies that goods X and Z are complements in consumption. Examples would be vehicles with high fuel consumption and fuel. As the price of fuel increases, the demand for such vehicles declines, all else held constant.

EXPECTATIONS

Expectations of future prices play a very important role in both demand and supply functions (to be defined later). Just imagine if you could go back in time to the early 1990s, before the stocks of Microsoft, Intel, and many other companies took to the sky, would you not purchase those stocks knowing that their prices were about to skyrocket? Of course, knowledge and expectation are two different things, but the effects are similar. If you expect the price of something to go up tomorrow, you will try to purchase it today, effectively increasing your demand for it today. Interestingly, a rise in demand can bring about a price increase, thus making expectations a self-fulfilling prophecy. In economics, we often argue that expectations of inflation can bring about inflation. The mechanism through which this inflation is created is in part explained by the effect of expectations on demand.

For instance, it can be argued that the Federal Reserve in its monetary policy rounds of 2008 – 2013 has attempted to create expectations of moderately higher future inflation with its commitment to maintain low interest rates far into the future. If successful, these expectations can motivate households and businesses to increase their spending on those items that are expected to see price appreciation in the future. This could motivate households to purchase homes, businesses to acquire land and physical equipment, and so forth. Inflation effectively penalizes holding onto cash, and therefore inflationary expectations might induce spending. One of the most prominent economists today and a Nobel Prize winner, Paul Krugman, seems to have advocated an increased tolerance for inflation on the part of the Federal Reserve (Krugman, 2012).

Obviously, expectations can also bring down prices. If we expect the price of something to decrease tomorrow, we will reduce our demand for it today. If we can employ the assumption of *ceteris paribus*, then such a decline in the demand today will cause the price to decrease, once again fulfilling our expectations. The reason to employ the *ceteris paribus* assumption here is because we need to assume that the supply is not simultaneously decreasing.

IDENTIFYING MARKET SPECIFIC FACTORS

A simple survey of consumers can reveal many relevant factors involved in consumption decisions. Although, basic logic can frequently help to identify these factors, sometimes an empirical investigation and/or a consumer survey is needed. Consider the factors that are relevant to the demand for higher education from a particular university. For instance, Atlanta has several major universities including: Georgia State University, Georgia Institute of Technology, Emory University, Kennesaw State University, and several others. Although there appear to be many universities in the area, over time they have been able to differentiate themselves by establishing a strong reputation in specific fields. For instance, Georgia Institute of Technology appeals to science and engineering students. Emory has established a strong reputation for its school of public health and its business program, while Georgia State University and Kennesaw State University seem to serve as institutions with a broader scope in their programs. From this, we can assume that Kennesaw State University (KSU) and Georgia State University (GSU) may be competitors. If we are interested in estimating the demand for education at GSU, then we should include the cost of tuition at KSU. We should probably include the cost of attending Emory and Georgia Tech as well into our regression analysis, and let the regression determine for us which of the schools happen to be competing with GSU.

However, tuition is not the only factor why students attend a given school. Its reputation also matters because it affects the expected earnings potential of its graduates. If wage data are available, then the relative wage of the average GSU graduate can be used in the estimation. Otherwise, the school's reputation may serve as an instrument for the relative wage. The overall population around Atlanta, where GSU is located, would also serve as an important variable. Since one of the key cost components of education is time, we should include the area's unemployment rate and the average wage for individuals with no college education, as these could serve as measures of the opportunity cost of time.

Alternatively, we could conduct a survey of perspective students (high school seniors) to see what factors they consider important when identifying schools to apply to.

The preceding discussion demonstrates that there are potentially many market specific factors in the demand for higher education.

LAW OF DEMAND

The law of demand simply states that price has a negative effect on quantity demanded. As price increases, quantity demanded decreases. Algebraically we can state it in the following form: [7]

4) $Q_X^D = a - bP$

---

[7] Although a more proper way would be to express it as: $Q_X^D = a + bP$ and state that b<0.

Intuitively, we all understand the law of demand, but we may wish to explain it theoretically. The coefficient on P in the demand equation captures two effects: the income effect and the substitution effect.

The Substitution Effect Changes in the nominal price of a product, all else held constant, cause changes in the relative price, i.e. the product becomes relatively less or more expensive compared to other goods. As a result, consumers alter their behavior by "substituting" with a cheaper alternative when the price of a product rises. All else held constant, as the price of product X increases, X becomes more expensive relative to other products, and the consumer responds to this rise in the relative price of X by purchasing less of X. The consumer substitutes away from a product that becomes relatively more expensive. Note that the substitution effect works in only one direction; consumers substitute away from a product with a rising price. This causes quantity demanded to decrease with price, i.e. negative sign on the price coefficient in demand.

The Income Effect The income effect is yet another consequence of a change in the price of a product. All else held constant, as the price of X increases, it effectively reduces the purchasing power of the consumer's income, as a result the consumer feels like their real income decreases. If X is a normal good, then this decline in the real income should cause quantity demand of X to decrease. However, if X is an inferior good, this loss in the purchasing power would actually cause quantity demand of X to increase. Thus, in the case of a normal good, both the income and substitution effects work in the same direction, whereas for an inferior good they work in opposite directions. For virtually all inferior goods, the magnitude of the substitution effect surpasses that of the income effect, resulting in the law of demand still applying. Theoretically, it is feasible to have an inferior good scenario where the magnitude of the substitution effect is less than that of the income effect in which case the demand becomes upward-slopped. Such goods are referred to as Giffen goods, named after Robert Giffen who formulated this scenario.

ESTIMATING DEMAND

We can create a simple example that illustrates the process of estimating demand using Excel. Excel has a pre-programmed command for regression. To access this command in Excel 2010, you would need to install the Analysis ToolPak add-in. Once the add-in is installed, the command will become available under the Data tab, see Figure 3.1.

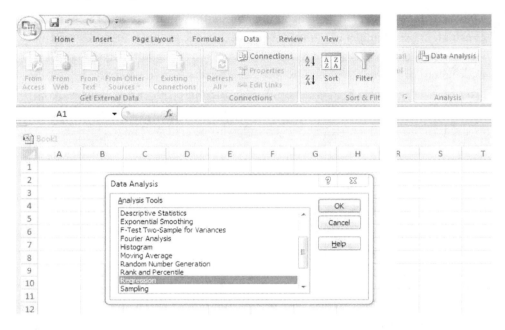

Figure 3.1

In our fictional example presented in Table 3.1, we have data from a local gas station for the entire month of October that includes the average price charged each day and the quantity of gasoline sold that day. We also assume that there are two other gas stations located within half a mile from our station (gas stations A and B). Since the demand for gasoline might be a function of the day of the week, we also need to consider differentiating between weekend and workday sales. We also attempt to control for the weather, by recording whether it rained or not on that day, since our customers may not wish to get out of their cars on a rainy day.

	Day of week	Rain	Q-sold	Price	Price(A)	Price(B)
1-Oct	Monday	no	263	3.40	3.50	3.44
2-Oct	Tuesday	no	258	3.41	3.50	3.45
3-Oct	Wednesday	yes	227	3.41	3.48	3.45
4-Oct	Thursday	no	259	3.44	3.49	3.47
5-Oct	Friday	yes	227	3.46	3.49	3.46
6-Oct	Saturday	yes	177	3.47	3.50	3.49
7-Oct	Sunday	no	201	3.55	3.60	3.52
8-Oct	Monday	no	261	3.53	3.61	3.54
9-Oct	Tuesday	no	258	3.49	3.55	3.49
10-Oct	Wednesday	no	259	3.45	3.52	3.44
11-Oct	Thursday	no	260	3.41	3.47	3.43
12-Oct	Friday	no	258	3.38	3.46	3.40
13-Oct	Saturday	no	205	3.36	3.40	3.35
14-Oct	Sunday	yes	174	3.36	3.38	3.34
15-Oct	Monday	yes	229	3.36	3.37	3.33
16-Oct	Tuesday	yes	228	3.35	3.37	3.33
17-Oct	Wednesday	no	257	3.39	3.40	3.35
18-Oct	Thursday	yes	226	3.40	3.42	3.40
19-Oct	Friday	no	259	3.41	3.42	3.40
20-Oct	Saturday	no	204	3.48	3.45	3.45
21-Oct	Sunday	no	205	3.49	3.50	3.51
22-Oct	Monday	no	260	3.50	3.51	3.50
23-Oct	Tuesday	yes	221	3.48	3.50	3.50
24-Oct	Wednesday	yes	223	3.48	3.47	3.47
25-Oct	Thursday	no	255	3.45	3.45	3.44
26-Oct	Friday	no	256	3.40	3.41	3.42
27-Oct	Saturday	yes	177	3.39	3.41	3.41
28-Oct	Sunday	yes	176	3.39	3.39	3.39
29-Oct	Monday	yes	226	3.38	3.39	3.37
30-Oct	Tuesday	no	257	3.36	3.38	3.37
31-Oct	Wednesday	no	257	3.35	3.37	3.33

Table 3.1

	Day of week	Rain	Q-sold	Price	Price(A)	Price(B)	Rain	Weekend
1-Oct	Monday	no	263	3.4	3.5	3.44	0	0
2-Oct	Tuesday	no	258	3.41	3.5	3.45	0	0
3-Oct	Wednesday	yes	227	3.41	3.48	3.45	1	0
4-Oct	Thursday	no	259	3.44	3.49	3.47	0	0
5-Oct	Friday	yes	227	3.46	3.49	3.46	1	0
6-Oct	Saturday	yes	177	3.47	3.5	3.49	1	1
7-Oct	Sunday	no	201	3.55	3.6	3.52	0	1
8-Oct	Monday	no	261	3.53	3.61	3.54	0	0
9-Oct	Tuesday	no	258	3.49	3.55	3.49	0	0
10-Oct	Wednesday	no	259	3.45	3.52	3.44	0	0
11-Oct	Thursday	no	260	3.41	3.47	3.43	0	0
12-Oct	Friday	no	258	3.38	3.46	3.4	0	0
13-Oct	Saturday	no	205	3.36	3.4	3.35	0	1
14-Oct	Sunday	yes	174	3.36	3.38	3.34	1	1
15-Oct	Monday	yes	229	3.36	3.37	3.33	1	0
16-Oct	Tuesday	yes	228	3.35	3.37	3.33	1	0
17-Oct	Wednesday	no	257	3.39	3.4	3.35	0	0
18-Oct	Thursday	yes	226	3.4	3.42	3.4	1	0
19-Oct	Friday	no	259	3.41	3.42	3.4	0	0
20-Oct	Saturday	no	204	3.48	3.45	3.45	0	1
21-Oct	Sunday	no	205	3.49	3.5	3.51	0	1
22-Oct	Monday	no	260	3.5	3.51	3.5	0	0
23-Oct	Tuesday	yes	221	3.48	3.5	3.5	1	0
24-Oct	Wednesday	yes	223	3.48	3.47	3.47	1	0
25-Oct	Thursday	no	255	3.45	3.45	3.44	0	0
26-Oct	Friday	no	256	3.4	3.41	3.42	0	0
27-Oct	Saturday	yes	177	3.39	3.41	3.41	1	1
28-Oct	Sunday	yes	176	3.39	3.39	3.39	1	1
29-Oct	Monday	yes	226	3.38	3.39	3.37	1	0
30-Oct	Tuesday	no	257	3.36	3.38	3.37	0	0
31-Oct	Wednesday	no	257	3.35	3.37	3.33	0	0

Table 3.2

The *Q-sold* column reports the quantity of gallons of gasoline sold that day, while the *Price* column reports the average price charged by our gas station. *Price(A)* and *Price(B)* represent the prices charged by the gas stations, A and B. Note that the variable *Rain* is either "yes" or "no" depending on whether it rained or not that day. By looking at this data, it is rather difficult to deduce if there are any relationships.

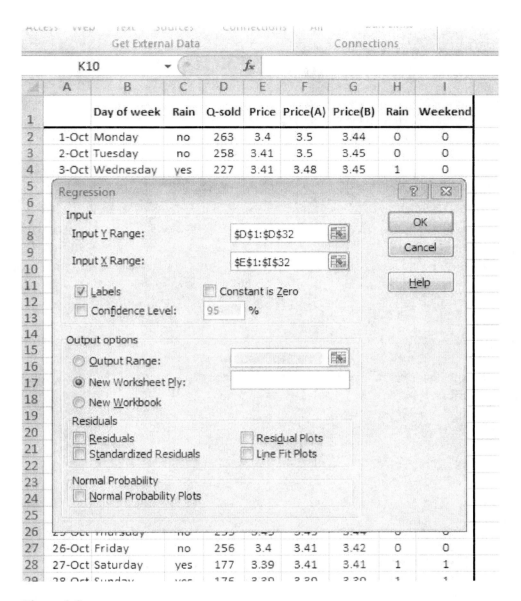

	A	B	C	D	E	F	G	H	I
1		Day of week	Rain	Q-sold	Price	Price(A)	Price(B)	Rain	Weekend
2	1-Oct	Monday	no	263	3.4	3.5	3.44	0	0
3	2-Oct	Tuesday	no	258	3.41	3.5	3.45	0	0
4	3-Oct	Wednesday	yes	227	3.41	3.48	3.45	1	0
26	25-Oct Thursday	no	255	3.43	3.43	3.44	0	0
27	26-Oct	Friday	no	256	3.4	3.41	3.42	0	0
28	27-Oct	Saturday	yes	177	3.39	3.41	3.41	1	1
29	28-Oct Sunday	yes	176	3.39	3.39	3.39	1	1

Figure 3.2

First, we need to convert the variables *Day of week* and *Rain* into binary variables. We will create a new variable, *Weekend,* which will assume the value of one if the day is a Saturday or Sunday and zero otherwise. We will also recode *Rain* to one if "yes" and to zero if "no". In Excel, these procedures can be easily accomplished with the help of the "if" operator (e.g. for the *Rain* variable, we can use the following command: =if(C2="yes", 1, 0)). Table 3.2 represents the updated dataset.

33

Now we are ready to regress the following model:

5) $Q\ sold = f(\text{Price, Price(A), Price(B), Rain, Weekend})$

Figure 3.2 shows the regression command screen in Excel 2010. Note that our dependent variable is located in the D column (Q-sold), whereas columns E-I contain the regressors. The *Labels* option is also checked because the first row of our dataset contains the names of the variables.

Figure 3.3 presents the output worksheet of the regression estimation. The estimated equation coefficients are contained in column B rows 17 through 22. Prior to writing the equation, we need to examine its statistical significance. The goodness of fit of this model is extremely high as is indicated by the adjusted R-square. The model effectively explains 99.48% of the variability in the dependent variable. The F-test reported by the ANOVA allows us to determine the joint statistical significance of our coefficients. Columns C, D, and E for rows 17-22 can be used to evaluate the statistical significance of the individual coefficients. We see that all coefficients but one exhibit statistical significance at or above the 90% confidence level. The coefficient that fails to demonstrate any meaningful statistical significance is the coefficient on *Price(B)*. Here, the level of statistical significance is only about 45%, suggesting that we fail to reject the hypothesis that it is different from zero at 90% level of confidence.

The economic interpretation of the lack of statistical significance of the coefficient on *Price(B)* is that gas station B is not a competitor to our gas station. In other words, the gasoline sold by gas station B and the gasoline sold by our gas station are not related in consumption goods. As a result, we should rerun the model excluding *Price(B)*. Figure 3.4 reports these results, from which we see that excluding the statistically insignificant variable helped to improve the overall goodness of fit and the F-test results. In our basic discussion, we will not perform any diagnostics on the data to verify the validity of the use of the OLS model; instead, we will just focus on the interpretation of the results (assuming that they are correct).

	A	B	C	D	E	F	G	H	I
1	SUMMARY OUTPUT								
2									
3	*Regression Statistics*								
4	Multiple R	0.99778							
5	R Square	0.995565							
6	Adjusted R Square	0.994678							
7	Standard Error	2.174861							
8	Observations	31							
9									
10	ANOVA								
11		*df*	*SS*	*MS*	*F*	*Significance F*			
12	Regression	5	26544.85	5308.969	1122.399	1.47E-28			
13	Residual	25	118.2505	4.73002					
14	Total	30	26663.1						
15									
16		*Coefficients*	*Standard Error*	*t Stat*	*P-value*	*Lower 95%*	*Upper 95%*	*Lower 95.0%*	*Upper 95.0%*
17	Intercept	294.3895	25.36172	11.60763	1.46E-11	242.156	346.6229	242.156	346.6229
18	Price	-51.4998	20.49709	-2.51254	0.018806	-93.7143	-9.28524	-93.7143	-9.28524
19	Price(A)	28.17071	16.553	1.701849	0.101189	-5.92084	62.26226	-5.92084	62.26226
20	Price(B)	12.35715	22.17114	0.557353	0.582243	-33.3052	58.01948	-33.3052	58.01948
21	Rain	-31.0442	0.874526	-35.4984	6.53E-23	-32.8454	-29.2431	-32.8454	-29.2431
22	Weekend	-51.7368	0.940117	-55.0323	1.3E-27	-53.673	-49.8006	-53.673	-49.8006

Figure 3.3

Once again, our equation is presented in column B rows 17 - 21 and is estimated to be:

6)
$$Q\text{-sold} = 293.31 - 44.14\, Price + 33.43\, Price(A) - 30.96\, Rain - 51.75\, Weekend$$

Now we can interpret the economics of our results. We see that the law of demand is satisfied in this case because the coefficient on *Price* is negative. From the magnitude of the coefficient, we can conclude that for every increase of 10 cents in the price of gasoline at our station, all else held constant, our sales should be expected to decline by 4.417 gallons per day.

	A	B	C	D	E	F	G	H	I
1	SUMMARY OUTPUT								
2									
3	*Regression Statistics*								
4	Multiple R	0.997752							
5	R Square	0.99551							
6	Adjusted R Square	0.994819							
7	Standard Error	2.145835							
8	Observations	31							
9									
10	ANOVA								
11		*df*	*SS*	*MS*	*F*	*Significance F*			
12	Regression	4	26543.38	6635.844	1441.131	4.2E-30			
13	Residual	26	119.7198	4.604609					
14	Total	30	26663.1						
15									
16		*Coefficients*	*Standard Error*	*t Stat*	*P-value*	*Lower 95%*	*Upper 95%*	*Lower 95.0%*	*Upper 95.0%*
17	Intercept	293.3065	24.94969	11.75591	6.6E-12	242.0216	344.5913	242.0216	344.5913
18	Price	-44.1371	15.46323	-2.85433	0.008357	-75.9222	-12.352	-75.9222	-12.352
19	Price(A)	33.43106	13.41721	2.491655	0.019421	5.851588	61.01052	5.851588	61.01052
20	Rain	-30.9592	0.849607	-36.4394	7.56E-24	-32.7055	-29.2128	-32.7055	-29.2128
21	Weekend	-51.7483	0.927344	-55.8027	1.34E-28	-53.6545	-49.8421	-53.6545	-49.8421

Figure 3.4

We also see that gasoline sold by gas station A is a substitute to our gasoline as implied by the positive sign of the coefficient of *Price(A)*. If gas station A were to reduce its price by 10 cents, our sales would decline by 3.343 gallons a day.

The results demonstrate that *Rain* also has a negative impact on our sales. We are expected to sell 30.96 gallons less on a rainy day. We are also expected to sell less on a weekend day than on a work day by 51.75 gallons.

Regression analysis allows us to identify each regressor's effect separately. The power of this approach is that now we can forecast what our sales would be if any of the regressors were to change. For instance, the equation enables us to model our response to a price change by our competitor, in this case gas station A. For example, if the gas station A reduces its price by 5 cents and our objective is to keep the quantity sold the same, then we would need to reduce our price by about 3.8 cents:

$$7) \quad \Delta \text{Price} = \frac{33.43 \times \Delta \text{Price (A)}}{44.17} = \frac{33.43 \times (-0.05)}{44.17} = -0.038$$

GRAPHICAL REPRESENTATION OF DEMAND

In our discussion, we formulated demand as a relationship where quantity demanded is a function of price. However, when we plot demand, we place price on the Y-axis and quantity on the X-axis, see Figure 3.5. Even though we label the curve as demand, it is actually the inverse demand that is being plotted. There are several justifications for this mislabeling and some of which are listed in the next section.

Since the demand diagram only contains two dimensions (price and quantity), all other independent variables in the demand equation have to be combined with the constant term. This implies that changes in those non-price independent variables, such as income, prices of goods related in consumption, etc., become factors that shift the demand curve.

For example, assume that a demand function is represented by the following relationship:

8) $Q_X^D = 100 - 10P_X + 0.01I$

Note that this function contains three variables (quantity, price, and income) but our two-dimensional diagram only has two. In order for us to plot the demand, we need to combine the income term with the constant, and this can only be done by evaluating the income term at a given level. For instance, let's assume that the average household income is $10,000, then the demand equation simplifies to:

9) $Q_X^D = 100 - 10P_X + 0.01 \times 10,000 = 200 - 10P_X$

This demand is plotted in Figure 3.5. We can shift the demand by changing the consumer's income. For instance, if we increase the income to $12,000, then the expression in Equation 9 becomes:

10) $Q_X^D = 220 - 10P_X$

The increase in the consumer's income shifts the demand curve outwards in our diagram. This is an illustration of an increase in demand. The reason the demand increases in this case is because X is a normal good, which is seen by the positive sign of the income coefficient in Equation 8. This is an increase in demand because, at any price level, quantity demanded is now higher. Another way to phrase it would be to say that the consumer is willing to pay more for any level of quantity.

In practice, it makes little sense to combine variables like income with the constant term. Any such step reduces the information presented by the demand equation. For example, Equations 9 and 10 contain less information than Equation 8. However, this is a necessary step to construct a demand diagram, and diagrams can serve as an intuitive and simple learning tool. They will become especially important when we start discussing the concept of equilibrium.

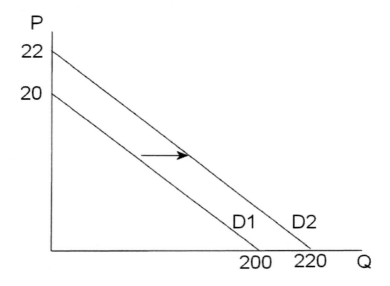

Figure 3.5

WILLINGNESS TO PAY

In the previous discussion, we asked the question of how quantity demanded depends on the product price. Structuring quantity as the dependent variable frequently makes sense, especially since a firm typically has the choice of what price to ask. However, an equally interesting question is, how much is a consumer willing to pay for a given unit of output? This question is also rather practical in an auction setting where the product quantity is fixed, and it is the price that becomes the dependent variable. To answer this question, we simply need to invert the demand and structure it as the price as a function of quantity. If we start with Equation 4, then we can construct the inverse demand as:

11) $P = \dfrac{a}{b} - \dfrac{1}{b} Q_X^D$

An inverse demand represents a willingness to pay, which is the maximum price that the consumer is willing to pay for the marginal unit of output.

For instance, if our demand function happens to be:

12) $Q^D = 200 - 10P$

Then the inverse demand function will be:

13) $P = 20 - 0.1Q^D$

From this, we can conclude that the consumer is willing to pay up to $19.90 for the very first unit of output, up to $19.80 for the second unit, up to $19.70 for the third, and so on.

Willingness to pay and auctions   In a rising price auction setting (sometimes referred to as an English auction), we actually do not know the willingness to pay of the auction winner, as the bidding stops when the bidder with the second highest willingness to pay stops bidding. However, we do know the willingness to pay of the second highest bidder.

In this case, it is suitable to estimate the willingness to pay function. Note that even though a typical auction is for a fixed quantity of a product, the willingness to pay is still a function of the quantity supplied in the market. As the quantity of the product being auctioned increases, the marginal willingness to pay declines (see Melnik and Alm, 2005).

References

Bank for International Settlements, 2010. Triennial Central Bank Survey of Foreign Exchange and Derivatives Market Activity in 2010 - Final results. Available online at: http://www.bis.org/publ/rpfxf10t.htm

Federal Reserve Bank of St. Louise, 2013. Trade Weighted U.S. Dollar Index: Broad. Available online at: http://research.stlouisfed.org/fred2/series/TWEXB

Krugman Paul. 2012. Inflation Expectations: A Feature, Not A Bug. NY Times, Paul Krugman's blog. Available online at: http://krugman.blogs.nytimes.com/2012/09/18/inflation-expectations-a-feature-not-a-bug/

Melnik, Mikhail and James Alm. 2005. Seller Reputation, Information Signals, and Prices for Heterogeneous Coins on eBay. *Southern Economics Journal*. Vol 72 (2): 305-328.

APPENDIX A

THE BASICS OF ORDINARY LEAST SQUARES (OLS)

Regression analysis is used to statistically establish the relationships between the independent variables and the dependent variable. For example, earlier in the chapter, we represented algebraically a demand function as:

1A) $\quad Q_X^D = a - bP_X + cI + dP_Y - eP_Z$

The objective of regression analysis is to estimate the coefficients a, b, c, d, and e. The following discussion uses a very simple scenario where there is only one regressor (independent variable). The discussion offers a simplified and hopefully somewhat intuitive illustration of linear regression. Please note that due to this simplification, the discussion ignores the Central Limit Theorem by limiting the dataset to only three observations. In practice, a dataset must contain enough observations to satisfy the Central Limit Theorem.

When there is just one regressor and only two observations, establishing the relationship between the regressor and the dependent variable is rather simple. As there is only one line that goes through the two points, defining the relationship is straight forward (see Figure 1A).

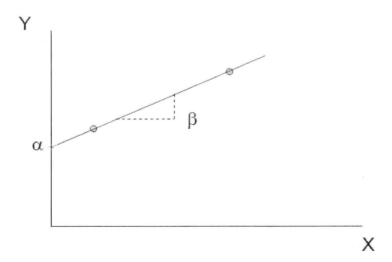

Figure 1A

2A) $Y = \alpha + \beta X$

The above equation represents the line in Figure 1A. Here, the relationship between X and Y is defined with the help of parameters α and β.

However, if we introduce just one more observation, then it would be a strong coincidence to expect that all three observations would lie on a straight line. If the observations do not form a straight line, then we need to find a line that best represents the dataset (the best fit line). It is the job of regression analysis to construct the equation for this line.

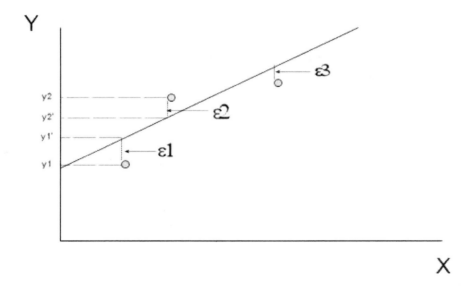

Figure 2A

In Figure 2A, the values that are primed (') indicate the values predicted by the regression line of Y for the observations. Thus, y1' represents the predicted value of Y when X is equal to x1 (x1, x2, x3, y3, and y3' are not shown for clarity but self-evident). However, we have the actual value of Y when X is equal to x1 and that is simply the value from observation 1. Because the best fit line represents the dataset, the actual observation 1 does not need to lie on it. As a result, there is an error, $\varepsilon 1$, defined as the difference between the estimated value (y1') and the actual value (y1). Similarly, the line predicts the values for the other observations (y2' and y3'). Since those values do not have to equal the corresponding observation values of Y, we also have the error terms $\varepsilon 2$ and $\varepsilon 3$.

Thus, for every observation we have a predicted value:

3A) $y_i' = \alpha + \beta x_i$

Since the error is defined as the difference between the predicted value and the observed value, we can define the observed value as:

4A) $y_i = y_i' + \varepsilon_i = \alpha + \beta x_i + \varepsilon_i$

Now, for illustrative purposes, we will employ one further simplification to make our algebra easier; we are going to suppress the constant term, thus requiring that the best fit line go through the origin. This simplifies the number of parameters we need to estimate and define algebraically in our discussion. Thus, Equation 4A simplifies to:

5A) $y_i = \beta x_i + \varepsilon_i$

Equation 5A represents the computation for each observation i. Since we have multiple observations, we can replace this notation with vectors where the number of rows is equal to the number of observations. In our three observation data set it would look like this:

6A) $$\begin{bmatrix} y_1 \\ y_2 \\ y_3 \end{bmatrix} = \beta \begin{bmatrix} x_1 \\ x_2 \\ x_3 \end{bmatrix} + \begin{bmatrix} \varepsilon_1 \\ \varepsilon_2 \\ \varepsilon_3 \end{bmatrix} \Leftrightarrow Y = \beta X + \varepsilon$$

The capital letters Y, X, and ε represent vectors. In fact, this is exactly how the data looks in Excel where each column represents a vector.

The three values for variable Y in Figure 3A constitute a vector with three values of Y. Similarly, the X column also represents a vector with three values of X.

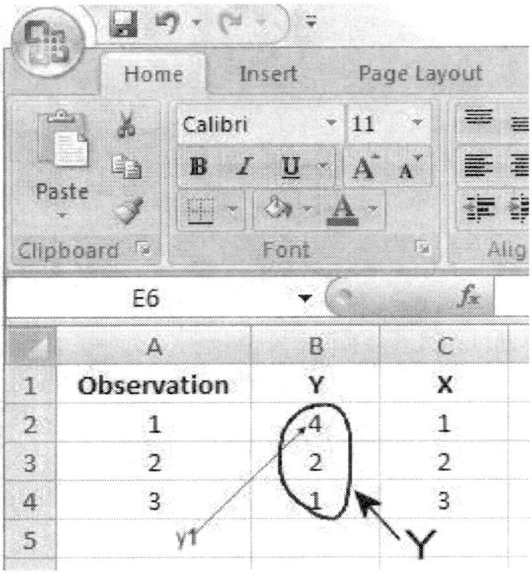

Figure 3A

Ordinary Least Squares selects the coefficient by simply minimizing the sum of squares of the error terms. The individual error terms can be positive or negative depending on whether the observation lies above or below the line. Since we are interested in the magnitude of the sum of the error terms, we need to convert all error terms to positive values. This is accomplished by squaring the error terms, hence the name of the method. Summing up these squared error terms provides us with an overall measure of the error of the estimation. The objective is to minimize this combined error. From Calculus, we know that minimization or maximization of a function requires its differentiation with respect to the variable used in the computation of minimization or maximization. The second order condition is then used to determine whether it is a maximum (in the case of a concave function), or a minimum (in the case of a convex function). In our discussion here, we will not bother with the second order condition but recommend to those readers interested in examining this further to read any statistical text at the upper undergrad level and higher that covers regression analysis. However, we will construct the first order condition, as it is necessary to obtain the regression coefficient. Since we are dealing with vectors, the multiplication of a vector by itself will require taking a transpose (T). Equation 7A presents the computation of the square of the error term:

7A) $\quad \varepsilon^T \varepsilon = \left(Y - \beta X\right)^T \left(Y - \beta X\right) = Y^T Y - \beta Y^T X - \beta X^T Y + \beta^2 X^T X =$
$= Y^T Y - 2\beta Y^T X - \beta^2 X^T X$

44

We compute the first order condition by differentiating 7A with respect to β:

8A) $\qquad \dfrac{\partial(\varepsilon^T \varepsilon)}{\partial \beta} = -2Y^T X - 2\beta X^T X$

Setting the optimization condition from 8A to zero (to find the minimum) and solving it for β provides us with:

9A) $\qquad \beta = \dfrac{Y^T X}{X^T X}$

Equation 9A represents the solution for the slope parameter. It is this solution that is reported to you when you perform a regression in Excel. Using the values from Figure 3A, we will compute the solution here from the linear algebra Expression in 9A. First, let us compute the numerator:

10A) $\quad Y^T X = \begin{bmatrix} 4 & 2 & 1 \end{bmatrix} \begin{bmatrix} 1 \\ 2 \\ 3 \end{bmatrix} = 4 + 4 + 3 = 11$

Now, let us compute the denominator of Expression 9A:

11A) $\quad X^T X = \begin{bmatrix} 1 & 2 & 3 \end{bmatrix} \begin{bmatrix} 1 \\ 2 \\ 3 \end{bmatrix} = 1 + 4 + 9 = 14$

At this point, we have everything we need to compute the optimal choice of the slope parameter:

12A) $\qquad \beta = \dfrac{11}{14} = 0.785714$

For comparison, let's compute the regression in Excel using the data from Figure 3A. First, don't forget to check the "Constant is Zero" option to suppress the constant term in the estimation as it is shown in Figure 4A.

Then run the regression. The results of the estimation are reported in Figure 5A. As you can see, our computation of the coefficient is identical to what is reported by Excel.

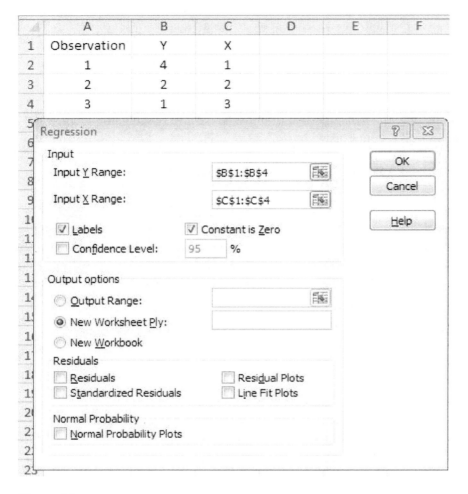

Figure 4A

	A	B	C	D	E	F	G	H	I
1	SUMMARY OUTPUT								
2									
3	*Regression Statistics*								
4	Multiple R	0.641533							
5	R Square	0.411565							
6	Adjusted R Square	-0.08844							
7	Standard Error	2.485673							
8	Observations	3							
9									
10	ANOVA								
11		*df*	*SS*	*MS*	*F*	*gnificance F*			
12	Regression	1	8.642857	8.642857	1.398844	0.446829			
13	Residual	2	12.35714	6.178571					
14	Total	3	21						
15									
16		*Coefficie nts*	*Standard Error*	*t Stat*	*P-value*	*Lower 95%*	*Upper 95%*	*Lower 95.0%*	*Upper 95.0%*
17	Intercept	0	#N/A	#N/A	#N/A	#N/A	#N/A	#N/A	#N/A
18	X	0.785714	0.664324	1.182727	0.358467	-2.07264	3.64407	-2.07264	3.64407

Figure 5A

Chapter 4

SUPPLY AND MARKET EQUILIBRIUM

"Corpus omne perseverare in statu suo quiescendi vel movendi uniformiter in directum, nisi quatenus a viribus impressis cogitur statum illum mutare."

"Every body persists in its state of being at rest or of moving uniformly straight forward, except insofar as it is compelled to change its state by force impressed."

Newton's First Law, Sir Isaac Newton 1687.

SUPPLY – ESTABLISHING THE RELATIONSHIP

The previous chapter focused on demand, and defined it as quantity demanded as a function of the product price and other factors relevant to the consumption decision. At this point, to complete our discussion of the market, we need to introduce the supply function. This function needs to be introduced in a consistent format to the demand function constructed in the previous chapter:

1) $Q_X^S = f(P_X, \text{other relevant in production factors})$

The supply function is defined as quantity supplied as a function of the product price and other factors relevant to the production process. Stating quantity as a dependent variable is consistent with our formulation of the demand function, which models the decision to produce/sell as a function of the product price. The price acts as the incentive to produce, and therefore higher prices would justify higher quantities supplied. In fact, this observation of a direct relationship between price and quantity supplied is referred to in economics as the law of supply. One plausible illustration of this can be found in the U.S. residential housing investment.

Figure 4.1 shows the level of residential housing permits (source: U.S. Department of the Census) and the Case-Shiller 20-City Home Price Index (source: Federal Reserve Bank of St. Louise) over a period of five years in the

U.S. (source: U.S. Census), and the Case-Shiller housing price index (source: Federal Reserve Bank of St. Louis).[8] The Case-Shiller index is set to 100 for January of 2000. The Case-Shiller values reported in Figure 4.1 are for the month of January in each of the years. The figure illustrates a sharp decline in the number of permits during the 2008-2009 price meltdown as illustrated by the Case-Shiller price index. Lower housing prices act as a disincentive to homebuilders, resulting in a lower quantity of homes being supplied/build. This provides an illustration of the law of supply.

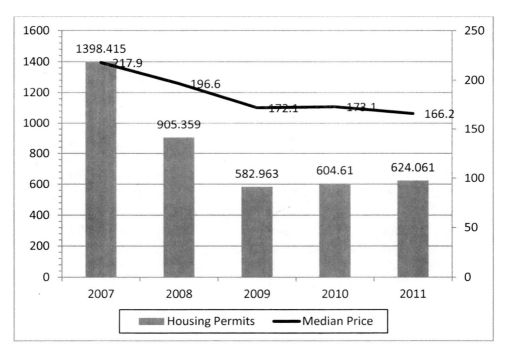

Figure 4.1 U.S. Housing Permits (in thousands) and S&P Case-Shiller 20 Cities Housing Price Index.

The law of supply implies that the coefficient of the price in the supply function is positive as illustrated in Expression 2:

2) $Q_X^S = c + dP_X$

[8] Additional information on housing prices, including median home prices for various US metropolitan areas, is available through the National Association of Realtors at www.realtor.org.

However, there are still other factors relevant to the supply decision that need to be considered. For instance, in the case of the housing market, it is important to note that there may be other factors at work that account for some of the reduction in the quantity of new housing being supplied. These factors may include: input costs (labor, construction equipment, materials, etc.), the productivity of those inputs, expectations about the future housing prices, and so on.

Unlike in the case of demand, the supply factors are simpler and can be summarized by costs of production. The decision to construct a housing unit is based on the difference between the expected benefit from the sale of the unit, i.e. the price, and the costs of building the unit. If this difference is positive, then the unit of housing will be supplied, and if it is negative, then the unit won't be. Thus, a comparison is made between the price (the benefit of selling a unit of output) and the production costs of the unit (the marginal cost of production).[9] The marginal cost of production is simply the cost of the next unit to be produced or the last unit produced, which depends on whether the decision is to expand or contract the level of output. Thus, the marginal unit is simply the decision unit.

The cost of production is not merely a function of input prices, such as wages, rental rates for equipment, etc., but it also depends on the productivity of those inputs. Consider the following simple scenario: Your school decides to develop an economics program and begins by hiring one instructor who teaches just one course per semester. Since there is only one course offered per semester, scheduling it is rather easy (e.g. finding a convenient time period and a large classroom). Let's assume that the capacity of the classroom is 50 students, and the cost of the instructor to the school is $10,000 for this class.

At this point, we have all the information needed to establish the marginal product of this first unit of labor for the economics program and the corresponding marginal cost. In this case, the marginal product of labor (the contribution of the marginal unit of labor) can either be defined in terms of classes offered (one class) or in terms of students trained (50 students). If we define the output as the number of students trained, then the marginal product is 50, and the cost of production is $10,000 (assuming the cost of room, utilities, and so on is zero - a very unrealistic assumption but one that helps us simplify things for now). In this case, we have the marginal cost of the class being well

---

[9] The proper comparison is not between the price of output and the marginal cost but between the marginal revenue and the marginal cost. As we will see later, marginal revenue equals marginal cost in perfectly competitive markets only.

defined. However, in practice we measure the output by the number of students not classes. After all, schools sell credit hours, which is another way to represent enrollment. In this formulation, we can't compute the precise marginal cost of each additional student. In fact, once the class is offered and the first student is enrolled, the marginal cost of each of the next 49 students is zero. Nevertheless, we can compute the "average" marginal cost as the cost of the class divided by the number of students in the class ($10,000/50 = $200). This means that the school would be willing to charge at least $200 in tuition for the class. This gives us the first point on the supply curve (Q=50, P=$200).

At this point, we can expand our program and hire another instructor to teach one additional class per semester. Chances are that the marginal product of labor will start to decline. One possible explanation is an overutilization of other (other than labor) inputs. We may have to utilize a room with a lower capacity (once again, the larger room is already being used by the first class). Let's assume that we offer the second course, and it has an enrollment of 40 students. Let's continue to assume that the cost of labor remains $10,000. The marginal product of the second unit of labor is the enrollment of only 40 students. The marginal cost is now $10,000/40 = $250. In order for the school to offer this class, the tuition cost has to be at least $250. This provides us with another observation for the supply function (Q=90, P=$250).

If we were to assume that the relationship is linear, then we could also express it algebraically as:

$$Q_X^S = 0.8P_X - 110$$

To get the above equation, we first had to computed the slope, which is the change in quantity over the change in price, $(90-50)/(250-200) = 0.8$. After the slope was obtained, we computed the Q-axis intercept using the coordinates of anyone of these two points. Using the coordinates of the first point, we would obtain the intercept value of -110 ($50-0.8*200 = -110$). Figure 4.2 depicts this supply function as S1. Since it makes no sense to think of negative quantities of output, only the part of S1 to the right of the price axis and above the quantity axis is relevant. Note that our supply function is consistent with the law of supply as the coefficient on the price is positive (S1 is upward slopped). This is the result of a declining marginal productivity, a point we will discuss further at a later time.

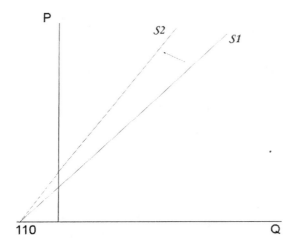

P

S2   S1

110   Q

Figure 4.2

We can also illustrate shifts in the supply function. For instance, we can demonstrate how the supply function is affected by a change in the cost of labor. Assume that the cost of each instructor to our school increases from $10,000 to $15,000 per class (wage inflation). The marginal cost for the first 50 students now averages at $300 ($15,000/50=$300), and for the next 40 students it averages at $375 ($15,000/40=$375). This changes the supply equation to:

$$2) \quad Q_X^S = \frac{40}{75} P_X - 110$$

Graphically, we have a rotation of the supply around its Q-axis intercept (see Figure 4.2). This represents a decline in the supply as at any price level (greater than zero) the quantity supplied is now lower. Alternatively, for any level of quantity supplied, the price would have to be higher to justify higher costs of production. Note, we could have also reduced our supply by reducing the marginal productivity of labor. For instance, if the sizes of the first and second classes were 40 and 30 students, respectively, then the supply function would be (assuming the instructor salary of $10,000/class):

$$3) \quad Q_X^S = 0.36 P_X - 50$$

We could also illustrate a parallel shift of the supply function by changing other factors, such as the fixed costs of production, introducing additional cost components, etc. For instance, let's introduce a simple overhead cost of $50/student. This might be the costs of running the administrative offices on campus. This will result in a parallel shift of the supply function to the left in the diagram (a reduction of the supply).

Note that a shift to the left, sometimes referred to as an inward shift, represents a decline in supply, whereas a shift to the right, an outward shift, represents a rise in supply. A decline in supply is characterized by a higher price associated with every level of output, while a rise in the supply is characterized by a lower price associated with every level of output.

With the $50 per student overhead cost, we have the cost of the first class at $12,500 ($250 per student), while the cost of the second class is $12,000 ($300 per student). Note, the slope of the supply function remains unchanged relative to equation 3, (90 - 50)/(300 - 250) = 0.8. However, the intercept shifts to -150 (50 - 0.8*250 = -150), which results in the supply function shifting to the left:

4) $Q_X^S = 0.8P_X - 150$

You may be tempted to ask why the intercept in Equation 6 did not change by 50 as that was the cost increase on per student basis. However, an intercept did change by $50, but along the P-axis. The intercept we see in the supply equation above is the Q-axis intercept. If we invert the supply function and obtain the inverse supply, we will notice that it changed by exactly the increase in the cost of production on per unit basis:

3') $P = \dfrac{Q_X^S}{0.8} + 137.5$

6') $P = \dfrac{Q_X^S}{0.8} + 187.5$

Expression 3' is the inverse of Expression 3, the original supply function, while Expression 6' is the inverse of Expression 6, the supply function after the $50 increase in the cost of production on per student basis. Unlike an inverse demand function, which economists often refer to as the Willingness to Pay function, an inverse supply function has no additional interpretation in our discussion and is just a way of rephrasing the same information. Sometimes it might be intuitively useful to pose the question, what would the price need to be in order for sellers to supply a given quantity of output? This is a question that can be directly answered by inverse supply.

Related in Production Goods   Goods can also be related in production if the price of one of the goods is a determinant in the supply function of the other. One possible relationship is where two goods are substitutes in production. This requires that the same resources be used to produce either one of the two goods. For instance, a managerial economics course is a substitute in production to another economics course. The same faculty and classroom can be used to produce either one of these two courses. If the enrollment in the managerial course is expected to be higher than that in the alternative econ course, then the school would prefer to offer the managerial course instead, assuming all else is held constant (including tuition rates). This determinant of the supply can still be considered part of costs of production because the managerial course serves as part of the opportunity cost of the other economics course. If the other economics course is offered, then the school forgoes the opportunity to offer the managerial economics course and receive the benefit of its enrollment.

Perhaps a more interesting example is the competition between various agricultural commodities for the use of agricultural inputs. When the U.S. government further encouraged the use of a corn produced ethanol additive in gasoline, it caused a rise in the relative price of corn. Over time this induced U.S. farmers to shift more of their production efforts to corn, but that meant reduced production activity in other agricultural commodities, such as wheat. All else held constant, this shift resulted in a reduced supply of these other commodities.

Another possible relationship is one where goods are related as complements in production. This is a scenario where one product becomes a by-product of another product's production process. In this case, as the price of one product increases, the supply of the other product also increases. For instance, gold mining companies usually report their results on by-product and on net of by-product basis (for illustrative purposes see Gold Corporation). This is done because production of gold results in production of several by-products, such as silver and copper. These metals are contained in the same ore. It also implies that higher prices of gold not only induce an increase in the quantity supplied of gold but also in the supply of the other by-products.

Expectations As stated in the discussion about demand, perhaps nothing is more important than expectations! Expectations also play a crucial role on the supply side. The logic here is rather simple; if a seller expects the price to increase in the future (and it is not a quickly perishable product), then the seller will withhold the product from the market until the price increase materializes. This action will indeed help to increase the price and cause the materialization of the expectation. The opposite is also true; if a seller expects the price to fall in the future, they will attempt to sell more now, prior to the decline in the price.

One example of this would be the behavior of the Japanese Yen in the ForEx[10] market in December 2012 -January of 2013. On December 16, the Liberal Democratic Party led by Mr. Shinzo Abe won the general elections in Japan. One of the key points in the economic platform of Mr. Shinzo Abe was the desire to weaken the Japanese Yen. Immediately after the elections, in the absence of any actual policy implementation (the first post-election policy meeting of the Bank of Japan was held on January 21, 2013), the Japanese Yen started a rapid decent. According to the Federal Reserve, the Japanese Yen went from 82.3700 Yen per Dollar on December 7, 2012 to 89.9000 Yen per Dollar on January 18, of 2013 (U.S. Federal Reserve). This was a response to the expectation that the Central Bank of Japan would embark on a massive money printing and induce a depreciation of the Yen. Effectively, the supply of the Yen in the ForEx market increased between December 16 of 2012 and January 20 of 2013 on the expectation of future monetary policy.

GENERAL ALGEBRAIC FORM OF SUPPLY

Generally, a supply function can be represented as:

5) $\quad Q_X^S = aP_X + bP_{Input} + cP_Y + dA + eExpectations + \text{intercept}$

- The law of supply requires a to be positive. As the price of the product increases, the quantity supplied of the product should also increase. A higher output price justifies higher marginal costs of production and therefore creates an incentive to increase quantity supplied. Note that this is the only factor that is responsible for moving along a supply curve. All other factors, including the ones listed below, cause a supply curve to shift.

---

[10] ForEx stands for Foreign Exchange.

- The input price(s) coefficient, b, is expected to have a negative sign. As the index of input prices increases, the supply should decrease. We saw that in the previous example where we increased the cost of economics faculty to the school and saw a reduction in the supply.
- Goods can be related in production. This can be determined from the sign of the coefficient on the price of a related in production good. If two goods are substitutes in production, then coefficient c should be negative. If two goods are complements in production, then c should be positive.
- A represents the state of productivity or production technology. With higher productivity, there should be higher supply. Therefore, coefficient d should be positive.
- Expectations play a significant role in the supply function. Usually, when we refer to expectations, we make a reference to the expectations about the future price of the product for which the supply function is constructed. Depending on how this is structured algebraically, the sign of the coefficient may be different. For example, instead of *Expectation*, we can include the expected future price of x. In this formulation, the higher the future price of x is expected to be, the lower the level of supply will be in the present. Thus, it makes e a negative coefficient. There are many ways of trying to capture the expectations about the future. We can survey market analysts or production managers and ask them about their expectations of the future price. We can also survey production managers and ask them about their confidence about the future.

QUANTITY SUPPLIED VERSUS SUPPLY

At this point it is important to make a theoretical distinction between these two concepts. When a reference is made to a change in quantity supplied, the interpretation is that a movement occurs along a stationary supply function. The only way this can occur is if the product price changes, while all the other decision factors relevant to the production remain unchanged. Therefore, a change in quantity supplied can only occur if the demand shifts. A change in supply is a change induced by any one of the other factors relevant to the production decision. A change in supply refers to a shift in the supply curve, which leads to a different quantity supplied for any price level.

MARKET EQUILIBRIUM

Market equilibrium is a concept borrowed by economists from physics. In physics, an object at rest remains at rest if all forces applied to it add up to zero. For instance, while you are reading your class notes on your computer, your computer remains in equilibrium. The force of its own weight is completely balanced by the support offered by the table. The same exact logic is used in economics. In a market, we have two forces: demand and supply. They pull on the product price in different directions where buyers prefer lower prices and sellers prefer higher prices (ironically, a rise in demand causes the price to increase, whereas a rise in supply causes it to decrease). Equilibrium emerges when the two forces are exactly balanced and there is no net pressure on the price (and the corresponding equilibrium quantity).

Equilibrium represents a market clearing, a situation where quantity supplied is equal to quantity demanded. In this case, we have no pressure on the price to move and we say that the market clears. Clearing implies that that there is no shortage or surplus. In fact, if either shortage or surplus is present, the market is not in equilibrium and there is pressure on the price to adjust.

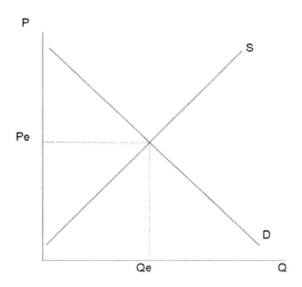

Figure 4.3

Figure 4.3 illustrates the concept of equilibrium graphically. Here, *Pe* and *Qe* represent the equilibrium price and quantity. Note that when a market is in equilibrium, then the equilibrium quantity, the quantity demanded, and the quantity supplied are all equal. Consider what would happen if we were to deviate from equilibrium. Figure 4.4 provides a basic illustration of how a market adjusts to a shock and moves from one equilibrium to another.

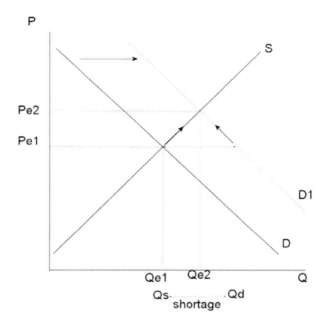

Figure 4.4

Figure 4.4 illustrates the following setup:

Consider a market that is initially in equilibrium at *Qe1* and the corresponding *Pe1*. Then assume that there is a positive shock applied on the demand side. The shock is graphically represented by an increase in the demand from D to D1. From the diagram, we conclude that the price will have to adjust upwards, but the market does not see the diagram. So how does the market know what to do? The rise in the demand causes a shortage to develop, which typically translates into a depletion of inventories. The shortage is the difference between the new quantity demanded (*Qd*) at the original price (*Pe1*) and the original equilibrium quantity (*Qe1*) where the quantity supplied still remains (*Qs*). This shortage encourages the sellers to start increasing the price. As the price increases, the shortage starts to diminish. It does so for two reasons. First is the law of supply, as the price

58

increases, the quantity supplied increases. Second, is the law of demand: as the price increases, the quantity demanded decreases. The process of this upward move in the price continues as long as the shortage remains in the market. The shortage will disappear when the market reaches *Pe2* where, once again, we have the quantity demanded equal the quantity supplied.

Can a market overshoot in this adjustment process and move the price above the new equilibrium price, *Pe2*? Yes, but that will only be temporary. As the price exceeds *Pe2*, the market will develop a surplus (quantity supplied will exceed quantity demanded) and the pressure on the price will reverse.

We started this chapter with an illustration form the U.S. housing market (see Figure 4.1), which is an illustration of a market correction. What is evident is a reduction in the quantity supplied as a response to a dropping price due to a pullback in the demand. This is a normal market response as it attempts to adjust to a shock. In this case, the shock came from a decline in demand. We don't see demand in the figure, but we do see its effect as both the Case-Shiller Home Price Index and the quantity supplied are lower. This is your typical consequence of a decline in demand, which is just the reverse of the example in Figure 4.4.

Shocks can come from the supply side, the demand side, or both. A demand increase, as seen in Figure 4.4, puts pressure on both the price and the quantity to increase. Since the price is a measure of product scarcity, a rise in demand increases the product price. A decline in demand would cause the opposite effect and reduce both the price and quantity. A supply increase would cause the price to decline, whereas it would cause the quantity to increase. This is because a rise in the supply of a product reduces the scarcity of the product. A supply reduction would actually increase the scarcity of the product and therefore increase the price. A supply reduction would also naturally reduce the quantity of the product in the market. All of these shocks should be analyzed under the Ceteris Paribus assumption.

What if two shocks occur simultaneously? For instance, what if both supply and demand increase at the same time? Then the outcome would depend on the magnitudes of these shocks. A rise in demand would cause both the equilibrium price and quantity to increase, whereas a rise in supply would cause the quantity to increase and the price to decrease. In this setting, we know that the equilibrium quantity will definitely increase because these two shocks coincide in their effect on the quantity. However, in terms of the price, unless we know which shock dominates, we are uncertain of the effect. This is because the two forces pull on the price in opposite directions. A good example of this would be the market for software engineers during the 1990s. At the start of the decade, the salaries of software engineers were relatively high compared to most other engineering fields. This was in part because of a shortage of skilled workers and a sharp increase in the need for their skills. These high wages induced more students to pursue an education in the field and thereby increased the demand for software engineering education. The response by the U.S. colleges was enormous as many schools opened IT programs, and several new colleges emerged that would almost entirely focus on the development of these skills. By the end of the decade, the salary advantage of software engineers decreased. What this illustrates is that during the course of the 1990s, the demand for software engineers continued to increase, but the supply increase outpaced the rise in the demand.

The market for gold during the course of the first 12 years of this millennium provides another illustration. At the start of the decade, one ounce of gold traded below $200. At the end of 2012, the price was around $1650. Yet, during these twelve years, the production of gold increased. We saw many gold mining companies, including the previously mentioned Gold Corporation, expand their mining activities. Unlike the IT case, the gold market presents an example of a rise in demand that causes the quantity supplied to increase. In a later chapter, we will show that the costs of production of gold increased during this time. The rise in the demand for gold was induced by a number of factors including a significant increase in purchases of gold by emerging economies. For instance, some of the BRICS economies saw a rise in the demand not only from their Central Banks (China, India, and Russia) but also from the general public as the demand for jewelry increased with higher incomes.

A similar example can be seen in the market for oil. According to Statistical Review of World Energy 2012, a publication by BP (British Petroleum, 2012), the world's consumption of oil increased by 14% between 2001 and 2011, while the global production of oil expanded by only 11.8%. Given the relatively price insensitive nature of the demand for oil (the elasticity of the demand for oil is relatively low in absolute value), this resulted in a sizable increase in the price of oil from about 15 dollars a barrel to 90 dollars. Again, here we had the demand and the supply increase at the same time, but the rise in the demand outpaced the rise in the supply.

Consider a scenario where the supply increases while the demand decreases. A rise in the supply causes the scarcity to decrease, and so the price decreases while the quantity increases. A drop in the demand causes the scarcity to decrease leading to a decline in both price and quantity. Therefore, scarcity is reflected in the price. In this case, the two shocks coincide in their effect on the price as they both reduce it; however, they differ in the direction of the effect on the quantity. We know with certainty that the price will decrease, but the impact on the quantity is ambiguous. A plausible illustration of such an example is the U.S. housing market for existing homes in 2007-2009. First the demand pulled back due to higher interest rates (2007). Later, due to the recession and the liquidity crunch within the lending sector (2008), the demand for housing continued to decline. These declines in the demand put pressure on the price to decrease. On the supply side, the picture was more complicated. Construction of new housing declined, but at the same time a spike in the supply of existing homes occurred as a result of a rise in foreclosures. As homeowners were forced into foreclosure, their properties were placed on the market by the foreclosing entities. This rise in the supply of foreclosed properties expedited the meltdown of the price.

Housing

ALGEBRAIC COMPUTATION OF EQUILIBRIUM

Let's assume that the following equations summarize the demand and the supply in the market for X:

6) $Q_X^D = 1000 - 10P_X - 5P_Y + 0.01 Income$

7) $Q_X^S = 20P_X - 20ECI - 50P_z - 200$

ECI stands for the Employment Cost Index in the industry.[11] *Px, Py,* and *Pz* represent the prices of *X, Y,* and *Z. Income* represents the income of the consumer. From these equations, we can already make several observations:

- *X* is a normal good since the coefficient on *Income* in the demand is positive.
- *X* and *Y* are related in consumption as complements. As the price of *Y* increases, the demand for *X* declines given the negative sign of the coefficient on *Py* in the demand for *X*.
- The law of demand is satisfied, which is seen in the negative coefficient on *Px* in the demand.

---

[11] For the US economy as a whole, this statistic is available on the BLS website at www.bls.gov.

- The law of supply is satisfied, which is seen in the positive coefficient on *Px* in the supply.
- *X* and *Z* are related in production as substitutes. As the price of *Z* increases, the supply of *X* decreases, meaning that the resources are being diverted to the production of a relatively more lucrative *Z* (relative to the situation with a lower price of *Z*). This is seen in the negative sign of the coefficient on *Pz* in the supply of *X*.

To solve this system of equations for equilibrium, we need to introduce values for all the variables except *Px* and *Q* (the equilibrium quantity of x). Let's assume that the average consumer income is currently $100,000, the *ECI* is 1.5, the price of *Y* is $20, and the price of *Z* is $4. With these values, we can simplify the equations in 8 and 9 to a two-variable model (*Px* and *Q*):

8) $Q_X^D = 1900 - 10P_X$

9) $Q_X^S = 20P_X - 430$

In equilibrium, the quantity demanded equals the quantity supplied. Thus, in equilibrium these two equations can be set equal to each other:

10) $1900 - 10P_X = 20P_X - 430$

At this point, we have one equation and one unknown (*Px*), so we simply solve for *Px*:

11) $1900 + 430 = 20P_X + 10P_X \Rightarrow P_X = \dfrac{2330}{30} = 77.667$

To obtain the equilibrium quantity of output, we need to plug the computed equilibrium price of X into either the demand or the supply equation. If we did everything right, we should get the same result no matter which of these two equations we use:

12) $Q_X^D = 1900 - 10 \times 77.667 = 1123.33$

13) $Q_X^S = 20 \times 77.667 - 430 = 1123.34$

The difference is due to our rounding in the computation of the price. At this time, we can begin to model the effects of various shocks on the equilibrium. For example, if the labor union increases the cost of labor and the *ECI* increases to 2.0, then what would be the resulting effect on the market?

The demand remains unaffected as it is a supply side variable. Although one could argue that the *ECI* affects the consumer income, the demand function does not contain *ECI*. Nothing is stated about *Income* being affected by the *ECI*. Therefore, under the Ceteris Paribus assumption, one can't assume that the *ECI* affects the demand in this case. However, the *ECI* does enter on the supply side. A different value of the *ECI* requires a recomputation of the intercept in the supply function, which causes the supply to shift. The new supply becomes:

14) $Q_X^S = 20P_X - 440$

Note that our supply curve shifted to the left (decreased) by 10 units for every price level. This constitutes a decline in supply, which means that the equilibrium moves along a stationary demand curve resulting in a change in quantity demanded. Solving for the equilibrium still requires setting quantity demanded equal to quantity supplied:

15) $1900 - 10P_X = 20P_X - 440 \Rightarrow P_X = 78$

The corresponding equilibrium quantity is:

16) $Q_X^D = 1900 - 10 \times 78 = 1120$

Note that the suppliers were able to pass some of the increase in the Employment Cost Index onto the consumer, and the price increased from 77.667 to 78. We also saw a reduction in the quantity sold. As our firm attempted to pass the cost increase, some consumers exited the market or reduced their consumption, and as a result the producers also absorbed some of the cost increase. This is an important observation that costs generally get shared.

LEGAL VERSUS ECONOMIC INCIDENCE

We often hear arguments for tax reforms or regulatory changes that promise to improve the fairness of the tax system. Sometimes we see commentators argue in the news that corporations pay less than what they should or more than they should. The interesting point is that a corporation or a business is merely a legal entity, and economically, it practically does not exist. What exists is an arrangement between three groups of individuals: shareholders, workers, and consumers. These three groups in a way compete with each other. The workers prefer a higher pay, the shareholders prefer to see a higher profit, and the consumers prefer to see a lower price. These three preferences are somewhat contradictory to one another.

Economically, a business is merely an arrangement between these three groups of individuals. Businesses, including large corporations, are owned by individuals (shareholders), are run by individuals (workers), and serve individuals (consumers). Therefore, businesses do not pay taxes, only people do. If we tax a business, it will be these three groups that will feel the burden of the tax. It is important to understand how this burden gets shared between the groups, and this will depend on the relative flexibility of each of the three groups. Generally, whoever is most flexible ends up with the least burden.

For instance, any tax, including a business tax, has a well-defined legal incidence. Legal incidence defines which party is responsible for paying it. However, the legally responsible party may be able to shift the economic burden, or economic incidence, onto another party. An example would be the luxury tax introduced by President Bush in 1990, which was supposed to generate nearly $300 million in revenues but failed to provide even half of that as the purchases of luxury items declined. The buyers of luxury items demonstrated that they had flexibility in their purchasing decision and simply reduced their spending on the U.S. produced items (their demand was relatively elastic). As a result, the tax reduced employment in the industries that produced the luxury items. This meant that the burden of the tax fell on the producers (both the shareholders and workers), many of whom were not in the high income groups who were originally targeted by the tax. In fact, there was plenty of anecdotal evidence collected to support the notion that the luxury boat tax, which was targeting the high income consumers ended up producing unemployment among the low and middle income group of workers; therefore, the burden of this luxury tax fell on the low and middle income groups (see Kwame Holman, 1996). Ultimately, the tax was repealed by the U.S. Congress in 1993.

REGULATING AWAY FROM THE EQUILIBRIUM

Government has the power to regulate markets. In some instances, regulation and even outright provision by the public sector may be necessary. Such instances include: public goods, markets with externalities, and other forms of market failures. In a managerial class, we have no desire to focus on these cases, but we do want to point out some cases that fit into our discussion. One such case is a simple price control instituted by government in the form of a price floor.

Price controls can be used to restrict the price from moving into a range not desired by the government. A price floor is a simple control that effectively sets the lowest price permissible in the market. One example of a price floor is the minimum wage. The objective of the minimum wage is to ensure that no one is paid below a certain standard. However, depending on the elasticities of supply and demand, and on where the minimum wage is introduced, we may have less than desirable effects.

First of all, the minimum wage may or may not be a binding constraint on the current equilibrium. If the minimum wage is introduced below the current market equilibrium wage, then effectively it will produce no effect. For instance, if low skilled labor is being paid $9/hour and the government specifies a minimum wage of $6/hour, then the effect of this constraint is practically nonexistent on the market as the market equilibrium wage is legally permissible. However, if the government introduces a minimum wage above the market equilibrium wage, then the constraint becomes binding and impacts the market. At a minimum wage rate set above the equilibrium, a surplus of labor will emerge (unemployment). This surplus can come from both a change in the quantity demanded and a change in the quantity supplied.

On the demand side, we are likely to see a reduction in the quantity demanded as the cost of employing workers moves higher. Depending on the wage elasticity of demand for labor, we may see a very large or a very small level of layoffs. What factors would determine this elasticity of demand? One such factor would be the ability of firms to substitute away from labor to other inputs. For instance, as labor becomes more expensive, firms look to capital stock and automatization. Automated cashier lines at grocery stores are such an example. Another would be the ability of businesses to pass the cost increase onto the consumer. If the consumer of the product is not very price-sensitive, then the demand for labor will also likely show limited flexibility. Recall that the demand for labor is a derived demand; it is derived from the demand for the output that labor produces.

On the supply side, the contribution to the unemployment will come from the rise in the quantity supplied. A higher wage would encourage more individuals who previously had been out of the labor market to enter it and start looking for work. Again, the elasticity of supply will play the key role here in terms of determining the size of this entry into the labor market.

Price floor

minimum wage

Depending on these elasticities, we can see two very different scenarios as Figure 4.5 illustrates. The unemployment produced by D1 and S1 is considerably larger than the unemployment produced by D2 and S2, D1 and S2, or D2 and S1.

This illustration clearly shows that it pays to be flexible; employers comprising D1 are capable of substituting away from the now relatively more expensive labor, while employers comprising D2 are not as capable. As a result, the cost of labor (sometimes referred to as the wage bill), increases by a larger amount for employers in D2.

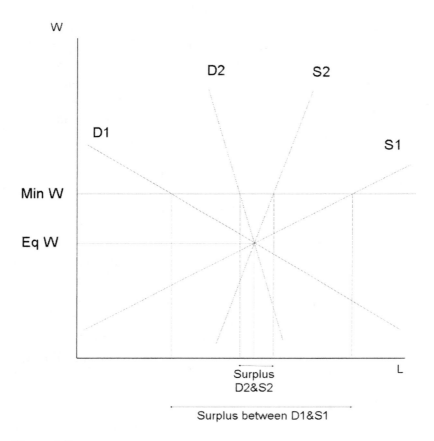

Figure 4.5

References

British Petroleum Corporation (2012), *Statistical Review of World Energy 2012*, available online at:
http://www.bp.com/sectionbodycopy.do?categoryId=7500&contentId=7068481

Gold Corporation, *Investor Resources, Financial Highlights*, available online at:
http://www.goldcorp.com/English/Investor-Resources/Financial-Highlights/default.aspx

Holman, Kwame (1996), *Effects of Repeal of the Federal Luxury Tax on Boats*, PBS, available online at:
http://www.pbs.org/newshour/bb/government_programs/jan-june96/budget_01-01.html

National Association of Realtors, *Median Home Prices*, available online at:
www.realtor.org

U.S. Census Department, *Housing Permit Data*, available online at:
http://www.census.gov/construction/nrc/

U.S. Federal Reserve, *Foreign Exchange Rates – H10*, available online at:
http://www.federalreserve.gov/releases/h10/current/

U.S. Federal Reserve Bank of St. Louis, S&P Case-Shiller 20-City Home Price Index, available online at:
http://research.stlouisfed.org/fred2/series/SPCS20RSA/

APPENDIX A

In this appendix, we examine algebraically the economic incidence of additional costs in a market. This analysis would apply to any setting where an additional cost is present. Examples of such additional costs include: sales taxation, real estate commission or any other third party commission, shipping costs, and any other types of fees imposed by the government or a third party.

Let's begin with a simple scenario where the demand and the supply are represented by the following equations:

1A) $\quad Q^D = 1000 - 10P$

2A) $\quad Q^S = 20P - 200$

From these two equations, we can compute the equilibrium in the market to be: Q=600 and P=40.

Now let us introduce a fee of $5 applicable on per unit basis to every transaction. This can be a sales tax, or a fee imposed by a market maker (such as eBay when someone sells an item on their site), or a shipping charge, etc. At this point, we have two ways to incorporate it into our framework, and it does not matter which of these we undertake. One is to incorporate it into the demand equation, and the other is to include it into the supply equation. For the purpose of our discussion, we will include it into the supply equation. Since it is a fee, it is similar to a cost and that intuitively is accounted for on the supply side.

Since the fee is in dollar terms, it can't just be added to the supply function stated in its current form (dollars do not add up to units of output). Thus, we would first proceed with inverting the supply, or solving it for the price:

$20P = Q + 200$
$P = \frac{Q}{20} + \frac{200}{20}$

3A) $\quad P = \frac{Q^S}{20} + 10$

At this point, we can just add the fee to the right hand side of the equation (note that the units on the right hand side of the equation are the same as those of the price, dollars):

4A) $\quad P = \frac{Q^S}{20} + 10 + 5 = \frac{Q^S}{20} + 15$

Graphically what we have done up to this point is effectively added a per unit cost component of $5 to the supply. Thereby shifting the supply "upwards" or to the left, which is a negative shock or a reduction of the supply, see Figure 4.1A.

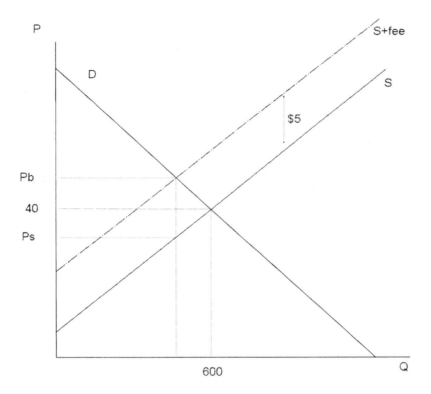

Figure 4.1A

However, there is now a different equilibrium that is determined by the new supply (S+fee) and the demand. That equilibrium will provide us with two important pieces of information: the new equilibrium quantity and the price that the buyer pays (Pb). To obtain the price received by the seller, we will simply need to subtract the fee ($Ps = Pb - fee$).

Now, let us solve for this new equilibrium by setting the new supply equation equal to the demand equation, but first we need to invert the inverse supply equation back to its original supply form (quantity as a function of the price because that is the way demand is defined):

5A) $\quad P = \dfrac{Q^S}{20} + 15 \Rightarrow Q^S = 20P - 300$

Now set the quantity demanded equal to the quantity supplied:

6A) $\quad 1000 - 10P = 20P - 300 \Rightarrow P = 43.33$

By plugging the price back into the demand function, we obtain the equilibrium quantity of 566.6. Now we can compute the price the seller receives by simply subtracting the fee ($43.33 - 5 = 38.33$).

Note that the imposed fee of $5 per unit in this market was shared between the two market participants. The seller absorbed $1.67 per unit of the $5 fee, which can be observed from the comparison between the price the seller receives now ($38.33) and the pre-fee price of $40. This is the economic incidence of the fee to the seller. To the buyer, the economic incidence is a bit higher in this case. Before the fee, the buyer paid $40/unit, but now they end up paying $43.33, which means that the incidence is $3.33 per unit. In this case, the buyer absorbs the bulk of the fee. This difference in economic incidences is rooted in the price flexibilities of the two parties. The price flexibilities can be examined by computing the point elasticities of demand and supply at the original equilibrium:

7A) $\quad \varepsilon^D = slope \dfrac{P}{Q} = -10\dfrac{40}{600} = -\dfrac{4}{6} = -0.67$

8A) $\quad \varepsilon^S = slope \dfrac{P}{Q} = 20\dfrac{40}{600} = \dfrac{8}{6} = 1.33$

These computations clearly demonstrate that the seller is more flexible; in fact the elasticity of supply is twice the magnitude of the elasticity of demand (note that the fee incidence is twice as large on the buyer relative to the seller). The conclusion is that flexibility is the key!

APPENDIX B

FOREIGN EXCHANGE MARKET

This appendix provides a simple illustration of the ForEx (Foreign Exchange) market using the supply-demand framework developed in Chapters 3 and 4. The foreign exchange market is one of the largest and most dynamic markets in existence today. According to the Bank for International Settlements, the average daily volume of exchange in April of 2010 was almost four trillion dollars (Bank for International Settlements, 2010). However, even such a large market can be analyzed using a simple supply-demand framework.

First, we must narrow our definition of the market by focusing on a single currency, the USD (U.S. dollar). Second, we need to identify the forces behind each of the two functions. In order to understand the forces behind the functions, we need to answer the following two questions:

- Who would supply the USD in the ForEx market and why?
- Who would demand the USD in the ForEx market and why?

These two questions will identify the forces that move the supply of and the demand for the USD in the ForEx market.

The Supply Side   Anyone who holds U.S. dollars and wants to convert them into another currency will contribute to the supply of the USD in the ForEx market. One group of people who supply U.S. dollars consists of U.S. consumers who wish to purchase foreign goods or services. When a U.S. consumer purchases an imported product, they effectively sell a fraction of the price (that covers the import value) in the ForEx market. This implies that a rise in U.S. imports would lead to an increase in the supply of the USD. Another group of people who supply U.S. dollars includes those Americans who wish to invest overseas. In addition to these private entities, there are also official participants in the ForEx market, central banks. Any central bank that holds U.S. dollars can choose to sell them and therefore contribute to the supply of U.S. dollars in the ForEx market. Of course, only the U.S. central bank would have potentially an unlimited supply of U.S. dollars as all foreign central banks would be limited by their holdings of U.S. dollars.

The Demand Side   The same factors that impact the supply side can be found on the demand side. Since the supply side included the value of U.S.

imports, the demand side includes the value of U.S. exports. When a foreign consumer purchases a product or service made in the U.S., a purchase of U.S. dollars occurs in the ForEx market. This is because U.S. factors of production require payments in U.S. dollars. Thus, a rise in U.S. exports would cause the demand for the USD to increase. We listed capital outflow (investment) from the U.S. as a factor on the supply side. Similarly, we can list capital inflows (foreign investment into the U.S.) as a factor on the demand side. When foreign investors increase their investments into the U.S., they cause the demand for the USD to increase. Naturally, central banks can also participate on the demand side since any central bank may choose to purchase U.S. dollars.

Market Equilibrium   The market reaches its equilibrium when the quantity demanded equals the quantity supplied. Like any market, the ForEx market may experience changes in demand and supply over time. For example, during the course of 2008, the USD appreciated in value. The trade weighted broad index for the currency, created and reported by the Federal Reserve, showed an 8.1% appreciation (Federal Reserve Bank of St. Louis, 2013). Because 2008 was a rather bad year for the U.S. and global financial markets, it caused a spike in the level of fear. This fear forced investors to seek the safety of U.S. Treasury bonds, thereby causing the demand for the USD in the ForEx market to increase.

Chapter 5

ELASTICITY AND REVENUE

PRICE ELASTICITY OF DEMAND

Although elasticity in economics is computed for both supply and demand, we will focus exclusively on the measures of elasticity of demand. Elasticity is merely a way of presenting the information already captured by demand. As the term suggests, elasticity is a measure of the responsiveness or flexibility of demand. Since the flexibility of demand can be measured with respect to a number of various factors, there are numerous elasticities. We will focus mainly on one type of elasticity, the own-price elasticity of demand. The own-price elasticity of demand is frequently referred to as the price elasticity of demand and sometimes simply as just the elasticity of demand. We will refer to it as the price elasticity of demand.

The price elasticity of demand measures the sensitivity of demand with respect to changes in the price of the product. Given that the price elasticity of demand measures the response in demand to a change in the price, the response represents a change in quantity demanded, or a movement along a demand curve. Since we are moving along a demand curve, we must assume that all other (other than the price) factors relevant to the consumption decision remain unchanged so that the demand curve remains stationary.

Unlike the slope of a demand curve, which measures the response of quantity demanded to a change in the price in units of output per dollar, elasticity represents the sensitivity of a demand function. The price elasticity of demand measures the sensitivity with respect to the own-price of the product and evaluates both the price change and the quantity demanded response in percentage terms. This formulation is particularly useful as it enables us to directly connect the price elasticity of demand to revenue, which is not immediately visible from the slope. Expression 1 introduces the price elasticity of demand:

1) $\quad \varepsilon = \dfrac{\%\Delta Q}{\%\Delta P}$

CONNECTING ELASTICITY TO REVENUE

To understand the convenience of the price elasticity of demand, we need to expand the discussion to include total revenues. Revenue is generated by a demand function. This can be a market demand, in which case the price elasticity of demand will enable us to compute the impact of a price change on the level of total sales in the market. This can be a demand faced by a particular firm, in which case the price elasticity of demand will enable us to compute the impact of a price change on the total revenue (sales) of the firm. Recall that total revenue is simply a product of price and quantity demanded:

Total Revenue = Price × Quantity demanded

$$2) \quad TR = P \times Q$$

The total revenue impact from a change in the price can simply be viewed as the sum of the percentage changes of price and quantity demanded. To gain insight into this, we need to differentiate the total revenue function. Since total revenue is a product, first we convert the product into a sum by taking the natural log of both sides of the equation:

$$3) \quad \ln TR = \ln P + \ln Q$$

This step allows us to separate the P and Q terms. Then we use the rule of natural log differentiation:

$$4) \quad \frac{d \ln x}{dx} = \frac{dx}{x} = \frac{\Delta x}{x} = \%\Delta x$$

Expression 4 demonstrates natural log differentiation. Since a derivative represents a small change, we can approximate the derivative sign with a difference sign. A change in a variable divided by the value of the variable is just a percentage change. Note that by definition, differentiation assumes a very small change (one that is approaching zero), so the approximation in Equation 4 applies only for such small changes. Applying this logic to the total revenue function, we can conclude that for very small changes in the price the following approximation would hold:

$$5) \quad \%\Delta TR = \%\Delta P + \%\Delta Q$$

Due to the law of demand, the two right-hand terms in Equation 5 have opposite signs. A rise in the price will lead to a decline in the quantity demanded and vice-versa. This implies that any magnitudinal comparison between these two terms would have to be done of their absolute values. Depending on the demand's response, the impact of a price change on total revenue can be classified in three broad categories: Elastic, Unit Elastic, and Inelastic.

- *Elastic.* This category describes a flexible (or price-sensitive) consumer. In this scenario, described by Equation 6a, the magnitude of the response in quantity demanded exceeds the magnitude of the change in the price. One example would be a situation where a 5% increase in price leads to a 10% drop in quantity demanded.

6a) $|\%\Delta Q| > |\%\Delta P|$

In this case, a small price increase would lead to a decline in total revenue, while a small price decrease would increase total revenue.

- *Unit Elastic.* This category describes an equal response on the part of the consumer. In this scenario, depicted by Equation 6b, the magnitude of the response in quantity demanded is equal to the magnitude of the change in the price. An example would be a situation where a 5% increase in price leads to a 5% decline in quantity demanded.

6b) $|\%\Delta Q| = |\%\Delta P|$

Here, a small change in the price leaves revenues unaffected.

- *Inelastic.* This category describes a price insensitive consumer. Equation 6c illustrates a situation where the magnitude of the response in quantity demanded is less than the magnitude of the change in the price. An example would be a 5% increase in price leading to a 2% decline in quantity demanded.

6c) $|\%\Delta Q| < |\%\Delta P|$

In this case, a small price increase would lead to a rise in total revenue. A small decline in price would cause total revenue to decrease.

Expressions 6a – 6c constitute logical operations. The price elasticity of demand simply combines these three logical operations into one convenient measure. For instance, if we are in a world defined by 6a, then the value of elasticity from equation 1 will range from just under negative one to negative infinity. This is defined as the elastic range of demand. If we are in a world defined by 6b, then the price elasticity of demand will assume the value of exactly negative one. If the relationship in 6c applies, then the value of the price elasticity of demand will be between just above negative one and zero. Since price elasticity of demand is always negative, the acceptable practice is to take the absolute value. In this case, the ranges of price elasticity of demand can be stated in positive values:

$$7) \quad |\varepsilon| = \left| \frac{\%\Delta Q}{\%\Delta P} \right| \Rightarrow \begin{array}{l} > 1 \Rightarrow \text{elastic range} \\ = 1 \Rightarrow \text{unit elastic} \\ < 1 \Rightarrow \text{inelastic range} \end{array}$$

The next step is to define the process of computing the percentage changes (the percentage changes in quantity demanded and price). Generally, when we think of a percentage change in any variable, we think of the change as a percentage of the starting value. For instance, if a worker's current salary is $40,000 and the worker receives a $4,000 pay increase, the conclusion would be that their pay increased by 10%. However, if someone with a starting salary of $44,000 has their pay cut by $4,000, would see their pay decline by 9.1%. This computational approach to percentage change is direction dependent. Most of the time, we actually want a direction dependent computation of a percentage change. Examples of this are numerous in economics, suffice it to say that inflation and growth in output are approached in this manner. However, in the case of elasticity, we prefer to use a direction independent formula. This is because we want a constant measure of the sensitivity of demand between any two given points no matter whether we move from a lower price point to a higher price point or vice-versa. To address this issue, we simply need to use the midpoint approach, i.e. compute the average value between the two levels and compute the percentage change with respect to the average value. In our example, the average value would be $42,000, so we would obtain the same result whether we move from $40,000 to $44,000, or from $44,000 to $40,000, a 9.5% change ($4,000/$42,000).

To understand the convenience and simplicity of elasticity, consider a simple scenario where we operate a gas station. Let us assume that during the past week the price of gasoline has remained stable at $3.00 a gallon at our station. We can conduct a brief experiment by offering a small discount for a few hours and observe how it affects the quantity demanded. Let us assume that the price discount was just 3 cents per gallon. Let us further assume that the level of sales during the few hours while this discount remained in effect was 400 gallons. Let us also assume that the quantity sold one week prior, on the same day of the week and during the same time period was 392 gallons. If all the other factors relevant to the consumer decision remained the same, then we can argue that these two observations lie on the same demand curve. Note that we don't know how the other relevant factors influence the demand, but luckily for the purpose of our computation, we don't need to know that. All we need to do is to make sure that the change in the quantity sold represents a change in the quantity demanded and not a change in the demand (movement of the demand curve). Given that our experiment is conducted on the same day of the week, during the same time period and with only seven days apart, we can assume that the behavior of drivers is exactly the same, which would allow us to attribute any change in the quantity sold to the discount. For this case, we can compute the price elasticity of demand using the midpoint formula:

$$8) \quad \varepsilon = \frac{\dfrac{8}{\left(\dfrac{400+392}{2}\right)}}{\dfrac{-0.03}{\left(\dfrac{2.97+3.00}{2}\right)}} = \frac{0.0202}{-0.0101} = -2.00$$

Note that the discount is entered with a negative sign as it represents a decline in the price. The value of the price elasticity of demand falls into the elastic range of the demand. This implies that a price discount would increase the total revenue. In our example, the revenue increased from $1176 to $1188, demonstrating that the consumer behavior is price-sensitive.

One important condition for our price experiment is that it should be unanticipated. If consumers anticipate a discount at a future point in time, they will likely postpone their consumption. This would bias our results because the demand would actually shift. Do firms ever conduct unannounced discounts? Most of the time retailers announce their discounts in advance. It is important to understand that when retailers announce upcoming sales, they are not interested in gathering the data on elasticity but rather advertise their competitive pricing strategies. However, there are unannounced temporary price decreases, and those are typically done to obtain data for demand and elasticity estimation. Examples of such experiments have been performed by eBay. Historically, eBay would conduct a one day discount on certain fees charged to sellers, and such discounts would only be announced via email the moment they commenced (see Melnik et al, 2009). In this case, the company would be able to conduct a controlled price experiment to see the response of the consumer.

POINT PRICE ELASTICITY OF DEMAND

It is important to understand that elasticity is just a way to present information on the demand flexibility. The richest source of information about consumer behavior is the demand function itself. If the demand function can be estimated, then all questions relevant to the revenue side can be answered. Elasticity can indeed be computed directly from the demand equation. Recall that the general form of demand is:

9) $\quad Q = a - bP$

Expanding Equation 1 using the midpoint formula leads to:

10) $\quad \varepsilon = \dfrac{\%\Delta Q}{\%\Delta P} = \dfrac{\dfrac{\Delta Q}{Qaver}}{\dfrac{\Delta P}{Paver}}$

If we assume the change is infinitely small such that the two points on the demand function are practically indistinguishable from each other, we can compute what is known as the point (price) elasticity of demand. In the case of the point price elasticity of demand, the average values in Equation 10 are replaced with the values at the point on the demand curve for which the elasticity is being computed:

11) $\quad \varepsilon = \dfrac{\dfrac{\Delta Q}{Q'}}{\dfrac{\Delta P}{P'}} = \dfrac{\Delta Q}{\Delta P} \times \dfrac{P'}{Q'}$

Note that the first term in Equation 11 is the slope of the demand function, and the ratio of P' to Q' is just a ratio of the coordinates of the point on the demand curve.

Consider a scenario where the demand is known to be represented by Equation 12:

12) $Q = 10 - 1P$

We can compute the point price elasticity of demand for any point on this demand curve. Figure 5.1 presents these computations.

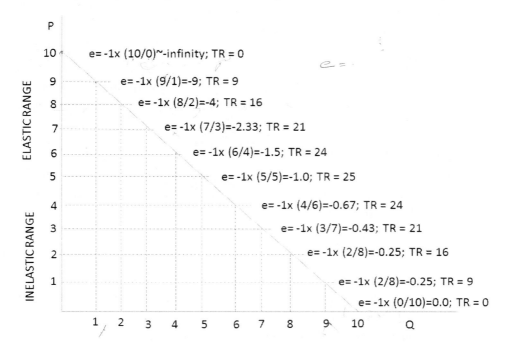

Figure 5.1

The demand depicted in Figure 5.1 has a constant slope of negative one, but the point price elasticity value varies from zero to negative infinity. A linear demand curve that is consistent with the law of demand (downward-slopped) will have all three ranges of price elasticity of demand: inelastic, elastic, and unit elastic. The last of these, unit elastic, is actually not a range as it consists of a single point on a linear demand curve. For a given downward-slopped linear demand, the higher the price, the more elastic the consumer's response. Graphically, this is easy to see from Figure 5.1 since higher prices correspond to lower quantities demanded. Thus, as the price increases, the same unit change in quantity demanded generates a larger percentage change, while the same unit change in the price constitutes a smaller percentage change. However, economists have a better explanation for this phenomenon, which we will discuss in the Determinants of Price Elasticity of Demand section.

Figure 5.1 also presents the computations for total revenue. Note that in the inelastic range, a price increase causes the total revenue to increase. As the price continues to increase, the rise in the total revenue decreases but remains positive as long as it continues to remain in the inelastic range. This process continues until the unit elastic point is reached. In Figure 5.1, the unit elastic point corresponds to five units of output and the price of five dollars at which time the total revenues are maximized. As the price increases above the unit elastic price level, we enter the elastic range of the demand. In the elastic range, a price increase causes the total revenues to decrease. This allows us to connect the price elasticity of demand to total revenue. The total revenue maximization occurs at the unit elastic point.

In Figure 5.1, the unit elastic point on the demand curve corresponds to five units of output. Note that the range of this demand is ten units of output. The unit elastic point appears to be exactly half way through the quantity range of this (linear) demand. This is not a coincidence since in the case of a linear demand curve, the unit elastic point is always located halfway through the quantity range of the demand.

Despite the fact that we have not yet discussed costs of production, we can already say something about profit maximization. If the cost of producing an additional unit of output is greater than zero (if it is zero, then profit maximization and revenue maximization are the same), then a profit maximizing firm would always find itself operating in the elastic range of demand. For example, let's begin with a price of $1 and a quantity demanded of 9 units. If the firm increases the price to $2, it will not only increase the total revenue from $9 to $16, but also reduce its costs of production since it reduces the output level from 9 to 8, assuming that the cost of an additional unit of output is positive. Thus, this price increase will result in a higher profit. This rise in profits due to price increases will continue throughout the inelastic range. Therefore, a profit maximizing firm will continue to increase the price until it exits the inelastic range. Once the elastic range is entered, more information is required to determine the profit maximizing price. For instance, if the firm were to increase the price from $5 to $6, it would reduce its revenue by $1. Whether this price rise increases the profits or not, will depend on the cost of the 5th unit of output. Without knowing the costs of production, we are not certain where in the elastic range the firm should operate; however, it is clear that when the cost of producing an additional unit is positive, a profit maximizing firm will find itself operating in the elastic range of the demand.

MARGINAL REVENUE

The total revenue computations shown in Figure 5.1 are simply the product of price and quantity demanded:

13) $TR = P \times Q$

Recall that economics is a decision science that studies how various economic agents make resource allocation decisions. Total revenue is an important function, but its slope, marginal revenue, is far more relevant in the context of output decisions and therefore relevant to input decisions. Marginal revenue is defined in economics as a change in total revenue that is caused by a change in production by one more (or less) unit of output. The marginal unit of output is the decision unit. If the firm is considering expanding its output level, then the decision unit is the next or additional unit to be produced. However, if the firm contemplates reducing its output level, then the marginal unit of output becomes the last unit produced because the next production cycle will be reduced by that unit. Algebraically, marginal revenue is represented by Equation 14:

14) $MR = \dfrac{\Delta TR}{\Delta Q}$

In Expression 14, the change in output is not defined as a single unit because this may not always be technologically feasible. For example, if a firm cannot vary output in the increments of single units, then the marginal revenue will be computed as an average over the range of the change in output. An example of this is your classroom. The school is unable to vary its output in single credit hours, and yet it is the unit of output for a college. Even though the output is measured in credit hours, the variation in the output is achieved by offering more or fewer classes. Each class produces a change in the school's output that is more than one credit hour. For instance, a one credit hour course with the seating capacity of ten students, if filled to capacity, would change the output by ten credit hours (ten students each purchasing one credit hour).

Figure 5.1 presents a simple example of a marginal revenue computation. This example is simple because the output varies in single unit increments. For instance, the marginal revenue of the first unit of output is $9. This is because when no output is sold, the total revenue is zero. Increasing the output level from zero to one unit, results in the total revenue increasing from zero to nine dollars. Therefore, the sale of the first unit of output (the change in output is that first

81

unit) results in a $9 increase in the total revenue. Similarly, the marginal revenue of the second unit is $7 because the rise in the output from one to two units causes the total revenue to increase from $9 to $16. Note that each additional output unit results in a lower marginal revenue value. This is because the demand is downward slopped, and to sell more units of output requires the price to be reduced on all units to be sold.

It is important to note that marginal revenue is positive in the elastic range of demand. While in the inelastic range of demand, marginal revenue is negative. This implies that at the unit elastic point marginal revenue is zero, connecting the concept of marginal revenue to revenue maximization. Revenues are maximized when the absolute value of the price elasticity of demand is one, which corresponds to zero marginal revenue. For an algebraic derivation of marginal revenue in the context of a linear demand function see Appendix A at the end of this chapter.

DETERMINANTS OF PRICE ELASTICITY OF DEMAND

The price elasticity of demand measures consumer sensitivity to price changes. We can identify three factors that influence consumer price sensitivity: availability of substitutes in consumption, percentage of the overall spending allocated to the product, and time.

Availability of substitutes in consumption   The easier it is for a consumer to substitute away from the product, the more flexible or price-sensitive the consumer will be. For example, contrast the demand for gasoline as a commodity with the demand for gasoline from a particular seller, such as a given gas station. As a commodity, gasoline has very few substitutes; however, gasoline sold by a gas station has many alternatives. If we compare the two demands, we would find that the demand for gasoline as a commodity would be relatively more inelastic than that for gasoline from a gas station. Another example would be the demand for air travel between Atlanta and Los Angeles. There are very few substitutes to air travel between these two destinations, resulting in a relatively inelastic consumer demand. However, the demand for air travel between Atlanta and Los Angeles by a specific carrier is more price-sensitive as there are more substitutes, other carriers. Figure 5.2 depicts two demands, where D1 is relatively more elastic than D2. Note we define D1 as relatively more elastic and not more elastic because every linear demand will have an elastic and inelastic range.

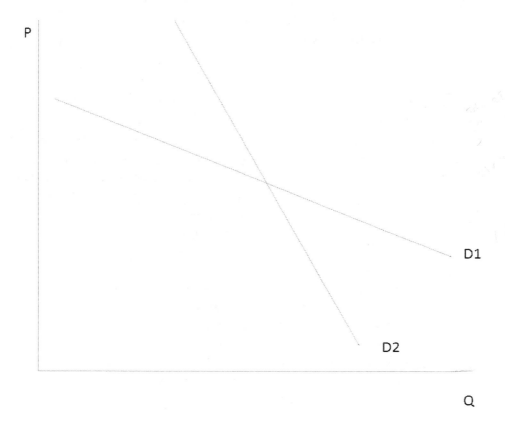

Figure 5.2

From a practical business stand point, it is better to face a relatively more inelastic demand. Since greater availability of substitutes makes a demand relatively more elastic, one way to make the consumer's demand less flexible is by reducing the number of available substitutes. One common practice is to differentiate the product or service. For instance, do Harvard and MIT sell the same services? Both of these schools are not only scholastically excellent and known throughout the world, but they are also located within walking distance of each other. Yet they are different in more than name only. They differ in terms of what disciplines they emphasize and excel in. They differ in research concentrations and program development. Sometimes product differentiation is rather difficult to do when your competitor sells the exact same product, and yet firms can be creative enough to find ways to differentiate themselves even then. One example can be found in the retail sector. For the most part, BestBuy, h.h. gregg, and Fry's sell the exact same products; nevertheless, they still manage to differentiate themselves. Some retail chains provide an on-site maintenance service, some provide different types of extended warranty plans, and others attempt to make the shopping experience different.

Percentage of the overall spending allocated to the product   As the percentage of consumer spending allocated to the product increases, so does the absolute value of the price elasticity of demand. Consumers simply become more price-sensitive as the importance of the product in the overall consumer expenditures increases. Would you ever consider reducing your consumption of pencils if the price of a box of pencils were to increase by 20%? Would you do the same thing if the price of a new car were to increase by 20%? One conclusion might be that items with higher sticker prices are likely to have relatively more elastic demands, but that is not always the case. Note that we define this determinant of elasticity of demand as the percentage of the overall spending, which makes it depend on the income of the consumer. For example, for someone with an income of $50,000, a $20,000 Honda Accord may constitute a sizable percentage of their overall spending, making them price-sensitive and encouraging them to seek discounts or special event sales. On the other hand, for a consumer with an income of $1,000,000, a $200,000 Ferrari may constitute a smaller percentage of their spending, resulting in a lower degree of price sensitivity on the part of the consumer.

Time   Time is the most mysterious of the three determinants of elasticity of demand. The problem with time is that its effect depends on the nature of the good. In many cases, over time, consumers become more flexible as they can substitute away from the product more easily. One example is the demand for gasoline. With time the demand for gasoline becomes more price-sensitive because time allows consumers to switch to other sources of energy. The saying that "high prices are the cure for high prices" applies here. In the short-run, a consumer's response to a rise in the price of gasoline is rather limited. At best, the consumer can try to limit their driving by combining trips or carpooling. In the long-run, the consumer has more choices. The consumer can relocate closer to their workplace, purchase a more fuel efficient vehicle, and so on. The rise in condominium and high-rise developments in U.S. cities at the start of the XXI century in part represents an adjustment to higher commuting costs from suburbia. Thus, we can conclude that over time the number of available substitutes in consumption increases for such goods, and therefore the demand for these goods becomes relatively more elastic.

However, there are goods where the opposite applies. This is the case for many types of capital equipment where with time the need to replace equipment increases, which causes the demand to become relatively less elastic. For example, consider the decision to purchase a new car. In the short-run, the consumer may need to be persuaded by a price discount. This is because the consumer still has a functioning car, and the need to replace the car is not as severe. With time, as the car gets older, it begins to exhibit higher maintenance costs, and as a result the consumer becomes more motivated to purchase a new car. This is because in the short-run there is still a viable substitute, but in the long-run that substitute disappears.

We can see the same behavior in the business sector as well. During economic downturns, capital spending decreases. However, businesses can postpone capital spending (on equipment) only for a while as the need to increase worker productivity ultimately forces capital spending recovery. Even in prolonged economic downturns, the demand for capital equipment can rematerialize. Possible beneficiaries of such behavior include firms like Intel and Cisco.

EXTREME CASES

Two extreme cases are possible: perfectly elastic and perfectly inelastic demands. Figure 5.3 demonstrates both of these cases graphically. A perfectly elastic demand has the elasticity value of negative infinity at any point on the demand curve. This implies that a tiny increase in price would result in sales dropping to zero, and a tiny drop in price would result in sales increasing to infinity. In a later chapter, we will argue that a perfectly competitive firm faces a perfectly elastic demand.

A perfectly inelastic demand is one where the consumer has to have a certain quantity of the good no matter the price. This characterizes the demand for a necessity with no substitutes. For instance, how much are you willing to pay to renew your driver's license if you live in an area with no public transportation? Would you pay the renewal fee if it were doubled or tripled? If your answer is yes, then chances are you have a perfectly inelastic demand for a driver's license renewal.

Figure 5.3

SIMPLE APPLICATIONS OF PRICE SENSITIVITY

In the 1990s, BestBuy introduced a rewards program that since has been replicated by many firms including more recently eBay. The BestBuy rewards program was simple as it allowed its members to accumulate points on each purchase from BestBuy. These points were later exchanged for coupons that could be used on future purchases from BestBuy. The BestBuy rewards program is still around today and allows its members to receive a 2% future discount rate from their purchases (see the program rules online at: https://myrewardzone.bestbuy.com/about/). This program has two important effects on the consumer demand. The first effect is that it lowers the price sensitivity as the consumer feels that they pay only 98% of the price. This rotates the demand making it a little less elastic (for further discussion of this see the health care insurance example below). The second consequence is that since the coupon is redeemable for a future purchase from BestBuy, it generates a repeat demand. Rewards programs are very common, and they tend to serve the two objectives discussed above.

Reducing Price Sensitivity of Demand: HealthCare Insurance   One of the side effects of any insurance is moral hazard. Moral hazard is a situation where one of the parties to a transaction changes their behavior after entering into the transaction, in such a way that it negatively impacts the other party. Moral hazard is common in the insurance industry. For instance, if you have no fire hazard insurance, you are less likely to use your fireplace. Once you obtain the fire hazard insurance, you may change your behavior and start increasingly using your fireplace. This change in your behavior exposes the insurer to a greater risk. The irony is that your prior behavior (when you had no insurance) cannot be used as an indicator of your future behavior, making it difficult for the insurer to adequately measure the risk specific to you.

Health care demand is affected by health care insurance in a similar manner. We will build this example on the demand depicted in Figure 5.1; to bring it more in line with the cost of a doctor's appointment, we will multiply the price by 10. Figure 5.4 represents this demand in the absence of healthcare insurance (D1), and the corresponding demand with healthcare insurance (D2).

In the D1 case, the consumer pays the full price of a medical appointment. D1 is consistent with the law of demand, as the price decreases, the number of annual appointments increases. Note that our quantity demanded is capped at 10 visits a year when the price is zero; most people would not prefer to spend most of their time at a medical office even if the cost were zero. Let us now provide our consumer with a healthcare insurance plan that offers a 50% copay, i.e. the consumer pays 50% of the price of the appointment and the other 50% is paid by the insurer. Let us also assume that the plan does not cost anything to the consumer. This second assumption is just for simplification purposes. If there was an annual insurance premium, it would affect the consumer's income and therefore create an income effect. Depending on the nature of the good (normal versus inferior), the demand for medical appointments may shift outwards (if a medical appointment is perceived as an inferior good) or inwards (if a medical appointment is perceived as a normal good).

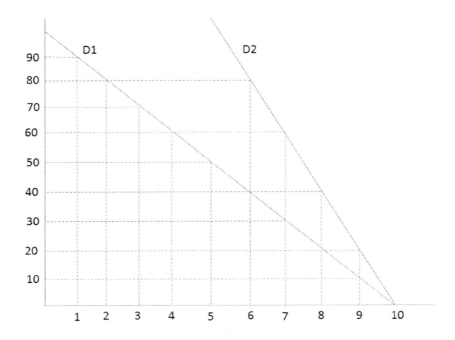

Figure 5.4

The 50% copay plan causes the demand curve to rotate to D2. To understand this rotation, consider the implications of the plan on the consumer's decision. For instance, if the price of an appointment were $80, then under D1 the consumer would purchase two appointments a year. However, with a 50% copay the consumer would only pay $40 when the price is $80. At the price of $40, the consumer would demand six appointments (this is determined by D1). The same logic applies to every price level. This results in the demand curve rotating around the quantity axis intercept, causing the new demand to be relatively less elastic than the original demand.

If we assume that the supply of medical services is consistent with the law of supply, then this has two interesting implications. One is that when the consumer obtains insurance coverage, the quantity of appointments purchased (and their price, given the applicability of the law of supply) increases. This causes a rise in the level of healthcare spending. As a result, the insurer's expenditures increase. This illustrates moral hazard as the behavior of the consumer changes in a way that now causes an increase in spending by the insurer. Two, it is easier for firms to raise their prices if the absolute value of the price elasticity decreases. Thus, the presence of the insurance makes our consumer less sensitive to the price of appointments.

OTHER TYPES OF ELASTICITY OF DEMAND

We started this chapter by stating that elasticity is merely a measure of sensitivity, and as such it can be applied in a variety of settings. For instance, one can compute the price elasticity of supply. One can even measure the sales tax elasticity of demand to determine the sensitivity with respect to sales taxes. This chapter's discussion has been centered on the own-price elasticity of demand, but there are two other popular measures of elasticity in the case of demand: cross-price elasticity and income elasticity.

CROSS-PRICE ELASTICITY OF DEMAND

As the term suggests, this elasticity measures the sensitivity in the demand for one product with respect to changes in the price of another product:

$$15)\ \varepsilon_{X,Y} = \frac{\%\Delta Q_X}{\%\Delta P_Y}$$

X and Y are the two products, and the elasticity measure can have a positive or negative sign based on how the two goods are related in consumption. If X and Y are substitutes in consumption, the sign of the cross-price elasticity will be positive. This is because a rise in the price of Y will lead to an increase in the demand for X. Since substitutes in consumption can be perceived as competing goods, the cross-price elasticity of demand can be used to illustrate the degree of competition between the two goods. The higher the value, the greater is the substitutability.

If two goods are complements in consumption, then the sign of the cross-price elasticity between these two goods will be negative. A rise in the price of one of the goods results in a decline in the demand for the other good.

INCOME ELASTICITY OF DEMAND

The Income elasticity of demand measures the income sensitivity of demand and is defined as:

$$16)\ \varepsilon_I = \frac{\%\Delta Q}{\%\Delta I}$$

The Income elasticity can assume positive or negative values depending on whether the good is normal or inferior. For a normal good the sign of the income elasticity will be positive. The greater the magnitude of the income elasticity, then the greater is the sensitivity of demand to changes in consumer's income.

ELASTICITY, A WAY TO PRESENT INFORMATION

All types of elasticity are simply ways of presenting information that is already captured by the relevant function. As such, elasticity offers no additional information, but it is a convenient way to present information relevant to the revenue side. For example, if the value of the own-price elasticity of demand at the current price is said to be negative two, then we immediately know:

- The firm operates in the elastic range of the demand.
- A price increase would lead to a decline in revenue.
- A price decrease would lead to an increase in revenue.
- A 1% increase in the price would lead to a 2% decline in quantity sold.

All of the above information is captured in a single value.

References

Best Buy, 2013. Rewards Policy. Available online at:
https://myrewardzone.bestbuy.com/about/

Melnik, M., J. Alm, and Y. Xu. 2009. "The choice of opening prices on eBay." The Manchester School 77 (4): 411-429.

APPENDIX A

In this appendix, we algebraically derive marginal revenue. Since revenue is generated by demand, we need to start with a demand function:

1A) $Q = a - bP$

Note that we treat b as a positive number. However, the presence of the negative sign in front of b in Equation 1A satisfies the law of demand. At this point, we are going to solve the equation for price, i.e. express as price as a function of quantity. This is performed in order to express the total revenue function generated by the demand as a function of output. The obtained inverse demand function is:

2A) $P = \dfrac{a}{b} - \dfrac{1}{b}Q$

Now, we can construct the total revenue function by simply multiplying the inverse demand from 2A by output:

3A) $TR = P \times Q = \left(\dfrac{a}{b} - \dfrac{1}{b}Q \right) Q = \dfrac{a}{b}Q - \dfrac{1}{b}Q^2$

Since marginal revenue is defined as a change in total revenue over a change in output, it represents the derivative of the total revenue function with respect to output:

4A) $MR = \dfrac{\Delta TR}{\Delta Q} = \dfrac{dTR}{dQ} = \dfrac{a}{b} - \dfrac{2}{b}Q$

Note the similarities between the marginal revenue function in 4A and the inverse demand in 2A. Both functions have the same price axis intercept of a/b. The slope of MR is twice that of the inverse demand. This last observation is what causes the marginal revenue to equal zero exactly half way through the output range of the demand.

Chapter 6

PRODUCTION AND COSTS: SHORT-RUN

MEASURES OF OUTPUT

Firms serve a very important function in an economy; they combine various resources or inputs (also sometimes referred to as factors of production) to produce output. Production of output in economics is described by a production function. The role of the function is to mathematically represent the process by incorporating the inputs used and the state of production technology.

In practice, the number of inputs can be relatively large. The main inputs include labor, capital (physical capital), human capital, and land. This problem is made more complicated by the fact that these inputs do not need to be homogeneous. For instance, an economist is not a substitute for an accountant. While both are units of labor, it is their human capital that makes them different. In order for us to adequately examine the fundamentals of a production process, we will employ some strict assumptions. First, we will assume that our firm employs only two inputs: labor (L) and capital (K). Second, we will assume that both of these inputs are homogeneous, meaning that one unit of a resource is not different from any other unit of a resource. Under these assumptions, we can state the general algebraic form of the production function as:

1) $Q = f(L, K)$

It is easy to conclude that there are as many production functions as there are production processes, but luckily for us, we can simplify these into three major categories depending on the relationship between inputs.

PERFECT COMPLEMENTS IN PRODUCTION

One way in which inputs can be used is in fixed proportions to one another. There are numerous examples of such a production process. For instance, to make a delivery, a shipping company needs a truck (a unit of capital) and a driver (a unit of labor). There is no need to have two trucks and one driver, or two drivers and one truck as any one of these combinations would result in one delivery (a unit of output). In this case, we say that the inputs are perfect complements in production as they perfectly complement each other. Mathematically this is actually not a function but rather a logical operation:

$$2) \quad Q = \min[aL, bK]$$

Note that a and b refer to the productivity coefficients of labor and capital, respectively. In our delivery example, a and b are each equal to 1. This production process is rather simple to analyze as the firm is always required to use the inputs in a constant ratio. These processes are relatively common. For instance, our class is such an illustration. To have a class, the school needs to hire an instructor and use a classroom. So, at any given point in time, the number of instructors should match the number of classrooms. In this case, the ratio is one unit of labor for one unit of capital, but our function is capable of accommodating any ratio. For instance, an airline carrier that offers a flight also has to employ labor and capital at a given ratio, but that ratio may not need to equal one. To have a flight, the company may need one plane, one pilot, and one co-pilot. In this case, we see two units of labor and one unit of capital required to produce one flight (defined here as output):

$$3) \quad Q = \min[0.5L, 1K]$$

Note, in order for us to have one flight, we need $L=2$ and $K=1$. If $K=1$, then it does not matter how many pilots we have; as long as that number exceeds or is equal to two, we will only be able to produce one flight. And if that number falls below two, then there is no output at all (we assume that the number of flights is a discrete number).

In practice, we rarely measure output in terms of the number of classes or flights, but rather in terms of students (or student credit hours) or passengers (or passenger miles). We can redefine our production function from Equation 3 to represent the output in terms of passengers. Let's assume that the passenger capacity of a plane is 100. Let's also assume that the number of planes is a discrete number. Under these assumptions, we can restate the production function as follows:

4) $Q = \min[50L, 100K]$

Here we increased the productivity coefficients on each input, but alternatively we could have added a different overall coefficient to describe this production technology:

5) $Q = 100 \times \min[0.5L, 1K]$

In this case, the optimal combination of inputs is predetermined by the state of production technology and the firm has little control over it. If the firm wants to produce three flights and serve 300 passengers at the same time, it has to have $K=3$ and $L=6$, no matter the ratio of cost of capital to labor.

Although this fixed-proportions production function seems realistic, it may not be a good representation of the production process in the long-run (we will define the concept of long-run later in this chapter).[12] For instance, consider a scenario where the cost of pilots to the company increases tenfold, then it may become too costly to offer flights. In the short-run, the company is stuck with the fleet of planes it has, and so it takes two pilots to transport 100 passengers. This higher cost of labor may induce the company to substitute away from labor in the long-run by investing into planes with a greater seating capacity. For instance, in the long-run, the firm might respond by shifting to planes with a sitting capacity of 150 passengers and thereby spreading the higher labor costs over a larger level of output. Note, at the end of the substitution process, the firm will continue to have a fixed proportions function just with different coefficients; during the process of fleet substitution, the firm actually undergoes a substitution between the inputs and hence does not exhibit the fixed proportions behavior. This means that we should consider other production functions for this type of behavior.

PERFECT SUBSTITUTES IN PRODUCTION

Substitutability of inputs means that the same level of output can be produced with different combinations of inputs. An extreme case of this is perfect

---

[12] We will argue that in the short-run, a firm cam vary labor but not capital, whereas in the long-run, both inputs are variable.

substitutability where the rate of substitution is always the same, no matter the ratio of inputs:

6) $Q = aL + bK$

Note that a and b still represent the productivity coefficients of the inputs. In fact, they represent the marginal products of the inputs. The marginal product of an input is defined as the contribution to the output of the marginal unit of the input. For instance, the marginal product of labor is defined as:

7) $MPL = \dfrac{\Delta Q}{\Delta L}$

If we allow the change to approach zero, then we obtain the derivative, or the slope of the production function with respect to the input (in this case, labor). Note that in Equation 6, the slope of the production function with respect to labor is a. Thus, a serves as the marginal product of labor. Similarly, we can show that the marginal product of capital is represented by b in Equation 6.[13]

What makes the inputs perfect substitutes is that the marginal products remain constant no matter how many units of L and K are employed or the ratio of L to K.

Consider the following illustration, a supermarket can employ workers as cashiers or install automated cashier stations. Let's assume that each cashier serves 30 clients per hour (one unit of labor is defined here as a worker hour), while each automated station serves 15 clients per hour. Let's also assume that these levels of productivity remain the same no matter how many cashiers or automated stations are simultaneously employed or open. In this case, the production function would look like:

8) $Q = 30L + 15K$

The entire analysis, we are about to start developing in this chapter and the next, can be reduced to a simple comparison between the ratio of the costs of inputs to the ratio of their marginal products. For example, assume that the wage rate of a cashier is w, while the hourly rental cost of an automated station is r. Since each cashier produces twice as much output, it makes sense to hire only cashiers and

---

[13] This assumes long-run because marginal product of capital (a fixed input) cannot be constructed in the short-run.

have no automated stations as long as w is less than $2r$. If w exceeds $2r$, it makes sense to only have automated stations, and if $w=2r$, then the firm becomes indifferent between these two inputs. This is a great and simple case, which makes the rest of our discussion unnecessary, except that this case is highly unlikely as the assumptions employed here are way too unrealistic to fit any real world production process.

The main problem with our assumptions is that the marginal products are assumed to be constant no matter the level of input or the ratio of inputs. Should we expect the second or third cashier station to be just as productive as the first one? If our answer is no, then we need to define an alternative formulation.

IMPERFECT SUBSTITUTES IN PRODUCTION

Between the previous two cases, lies the case of imperfect substitutes. In fact, we already touched on it when we discussed what happens when a firm starts to substitute between planes of various capacity. The term imperfect substitutes implies that there is a possibility of substituting between the two inputs but the rate of substitution is not constant (recall that in the case of perfect complements the substitution is constant). The most commonly used function for this purpose, is called the Cobb-Douglas function:

9) $Q = A\left(L^{\alpha} K^{\beta}\right)$

A represents the overall productivity coefficient, while α and β represent the productivity coefficients of labor and capital. This function can be further amended in a variety of ways, but for our simple discussion here the form listed in Equation 9 is sufficient. In our discussion, we will even further simplify it by first dropping A and then by restricting $\alpha+\beta=1$. This last step will be a necessary assumption for the perfectly competitive model, and so we will start operating with it at this time. In economics, this assumption implies Constant Returns to Scale:

10) $Q = L^{\alpha} K^{(1-\alpha)}$

Despite its appearance, this function is also easily estimatable using a regression analysis. To estimate it empirically, one can simplify the function by simply taking the natural log of both sides:

11) $\ln Q = \alpha \ln L + \beta \ln K$

Here, computing the marginal products of the inputs is not as simple as it was in the previous function. We will come back to the Cobb-Douglas function later in our discussion, but first we need to create a simple example of a production process, so we can introduce the various measures of productivity and cost in an intuitive way.

TIME FRAMEWORK

In economics, we separate production into two separate time frameworks: long-run and short-run. The long run is the time needed for a firm to overcome all constraints and become fully flexible in its production decisions. The short-run is a time period in which a firm faces a constraint and therefore is not fully flexible in its production decisions.

The long-run versus short-run framework is not just limited to firms; as an individual worker, you are also subject to the same framework of analysis. For instance, why are you taking this managerial economics course? One reason might be that you want to obtain the necessary skills to complete your MBA and get a better position at work. Note that your current level of education/skills may not allow you to have this advancement, and as a result you want to obtain an MBA. This means that presently you are in the short-run where you are constrained by your level of education and skills. Your long-run horizon is the amount of time needed to complete your MBA and change your skill. Ironically, once you complete your degree, you will once again be in the short-run just with a different level of human capital.

The long-run serves as the planning horizon, while the short-run is your operational framework. We are always in the short-run, but we plan for the long-run. This is true for individuals, businesses, and entire economies.

In our framework, we have only two inputs in the production process: labor and capital. Since it seems to be easier for businesses to vary the level of employment rather than the level of capital stock, we will assume that in the short-run a firm is constrained by its inability to change the capital stock, while in the long-run a firm is fully flexible and can change all of its inputs. The logic behind this assumption is simple, just consider your university as an illustration. I would guess that your university can rather easily change the level of faculty it employs.

For instance, if we assume that the level of enrollment on your campus increases by 30%, the school can easily hire more faculty, and if it proves to be difficult to fill the full-time positions, the school can temporarily hire part-time faculty. Regardless of the hiring structure, expanding the faculty can be done relatively quickly, while adding an additional classroom building may take a few years. The amount of time it takes the school to change its classroom space to accommodate the change in the enrollment level is the long-run horizon for the school.

The duration of the short-run is different for different firms. For instance, a small consulting firm that only has some basic office equipment, like a computer and a printer, may have its short-run defined in days, while a large industrial firm may have its short-run span in years.

MEASURING OUTPUT

To illustrate the use of various measures of output, we need to construct a simple example. Consider a scenario where a university wishes to establish an economics department by hiring additional faculty and expanding the course offerings. We will also assume that the university is in the short-run and the classroom space is fixed.

Imagine that the university begins with just a single faculty member who teaches three economics courses per semester with an enrollment in each course of 40 students. At this point, let's assume that the university wishes to expand the economics department and hire one more faculty member to teach another three courses. Should it be expected that the second instructor will generate the same total enrollment of 120 students as the first instructor? The answer is that it most likely won't happen. One key reason is that the university may have to assign rooms with smaller capacity to handle the additional courses, implying that a rise in labor leads to overutilization of capital. Although this is unrelated to production, there may also be demand factors emerging that would lead to a reduced output contribution from a rise in labor. In our example, the classroom space is fixed making it difficult to schedule additional courses during convenient hours for the students. And if the university continues to expand the number of faculty members (labor units), it should expect to continue to see reduced productivity of each additional unit of labor. In economics, the observation of a rise in one input, while holding the other inputs constant, leads to a decreasing marginal product of the rising input known as the law of diminishing marginal product.

Initially, it is possible to see gains in the marginal productivity of labor as hiring the second faculty member may allow for increased specialization of labor (for instance, the first faculty member may specialize in teaching only micro courses, while the second may specialize in teaching only macro courses). In this case, the marginal product of labor will rise at first, but the law of diminishing marginal productivity will inevitably materialize as the level of labor increases further. In the example developed in Table 6.1, we will assume that the diminishing marginal productivity is observed with the addition of the third faculty member. We do this in order to demonstrate the relationship between the average and the marginal productivity measures.

Table 6.1 presents the course enrollment data for the first four faculty members.

Faculty Member	Class 1	Class 2	Class 3
First faculty member	40	40	40
Second faculty member	40	43	45
Third faculty member	40	39	36
Fourth faculty member	35	35	35

Table 6.1

This information is sufficient to construct the total product, average product of labor, and the marginal product of labor for your department. We already defined the first of these measures, the total product (or total output, Q), earlier in our discussion. The remaining two measures require an additional formulation. The average product of an input is a rather simple measure of the productivity of the input, where the total output is simply divided by the level of the input. For instance, to obtain the average product of labor, we can divide the output by the number of workers, or the number of worker-hours:

$$12) \ APL = \frac{Q}{L}$$

The average product is an interesting illustrative measure of productivity, but it is not one that enters the decision making process in terms of whether labor needs to be expanded or reduced. Every decision in economics is effectively a marginal decision. We always decide on the next unit or next several units of an input. Thus, we need a marginal measure of productivity. The marginal product represents the change in the output that results from increasing or decreasing (depending on whether our decision is to expand or contract the level of the input) the input by one unit. Sometimes varying the input level in individual units is not feasible, in which case the "average" marginal product is computed over a multi-unit change in the input. Formally, the marginal product of labor would be defined as:

13) $MPL = \dfrac{\Delta Q}{\Delta L} \quad \dfrac{Q_2 - Q_1}{L_2 - L_1}$

Note that by its definition the marginal product of an input is the slope of the total product with respect to that input.

With these equations, we compute the productivity measures for our example, see Table 6.2.

L	Q	APL	MPL
0	0		
1	120	120	120
2	248	124	128
3	363	121	115
4	468	117	105

$APL = \dfrac{Q}{L}$

Table 6.2

Note the relationship between the average product and the marginal product. If the marginal product exceeds the average product, then the average product is rising and vice versa. Just think about your grade in this class versus your overall GPA. Your GPA represents your average grade in the program so far, while your grade in the class represents the marginal contribution. If you earn a grade in this class that is higher than your GPA, your GPA will rise, while if you earn a grade that is lower than your GPA, your GPA will fall.

At this point, we are only one step away from determining the profit maximizing level of hiring. Let's introduce prices into our example. Let's assume that each student who takes the classes pays $1,000 in tuition. This enables us to compute the benefit of each additional unit of labor to the firm not in terms of output, but in terms of revenue dollars. The marginal product of labor represents the benefit of each additional unit of labor to the firm in terms of output. The first faculty member produces 120 units of output or credit hours to the school, while the second faculty member generates 128 units of output and so on. Since we measure the cost of an additional unit of labor, the wage, in dollars, we need to convert the benefit of an additional unit of labor from output (marginal product of labor) to dollars. This allows us to make a comparison between the benefit and cost of an additional unit of labor, which is essential for optimization. This is accomplished by computing the Value of Marginal Product, and in the case of labor, would be the value of the marginal product of labor:

14) $VMPL = MR \times MPL$

MR represents the marginal revenue. To simplify our discussion, we will assume that the marginal revenue and the price are the same thing. This assumption is a direct consequence of the perfectly competitive model, which will be discussed in a later chapter. This assumption implies that the demand faced by the firm is perfectly elastic (i.e. perfectly horizontal), which implies that to sell one more unit of output the firm does not need to lower the price on the marginal unit or all the other units being sold. In this case the value of marginal product (labor) simplifies to:

15) $VMPL = P \times MPL$

P is the price of the output which in our example is tuition. Table 6.3 adds two additional columns to Table 6.2: Total Revenue (Price times Total Output) and the Value of the Marginal Product of Labor.

L	Q (Total output)	APL	MPL	TR	VMPL	$P = 1000$
0	0					
1	120	120	120	120000	120000	
2	248	124	128	248000	128000	
3	363	121	115	363000	115000	
4	468	117	105	468000	105000	

Table 6.3

We actually have almost all the information needed to determine how many faculty members are optimal to hire. The only information missing is the cost of capital, which is needed to answer the question of whether we should operate in the short-run or not. Assuming that we decide to operate in the short-run, then the optimal hiring decision can be determined from the last column in Table 6.3. For instance, let's assume that the cost of hiring a faculty member is $110,000 in salary and benefits. Should the first faculty member be hired? The answer is yes because their contribution to the cost is $110,000, while their contribution to the revenue is $120,000. Should the second unit of labor be hired? Again, the answer is yes because their contribution to the cost ($110,000) still falls below their contribution to the revenue ($128,000). Should the third unit be hired? Once again the answer is yes as their contribution to the revenue ($115,000) continues to exceed their contribution to the cost ($110,000). Should the fourth unit of labor be hired? The answer is no as their contribution to the revenue ($105,000) is less than their cost ($110,000). The hiring rule is simple: hire as long as the value of the marginal product exceeds the cost of labor (from now on we will abbreviate it with w for wage), reduce the labor as long as the value of the marginal product of labor falls short of the cost of labor, and optimization is achieved when the two are roughly equal to each other. This is summarized in Figure 6.1.

Benefit of hiring a unit of labor		Cost of hiring a unit of labor	
Change in TR: VMPL		Wage	
If	VMPL	>	Wage	Expand Labor
If	VMPL	<	Wage	Reduce Labor
If	**VMPL**	**=**	**Wage**	**no adjustment in Labor is needed**

Figure 6.1

PROPERTIES OF MARGINAL PRODUCT

As seen from the preceding discussion, by far the most important measure of output when considering input, is marginal product. By its definition, the marginal product of an input is the slope of the production function with respect to that input. While it is possible to have the marginal product rising initially, eventually the law of diminishing marginal product materializes.

The initial gains in marginal productivity are often driven by increased specialization. Eventually, as we continue to increase an input, the ratio of other inputs to this input decreases. This leads to a decline in the marginal product of the rising input. It is possible to get to a point where the marginal product becomes negative and additional units of the input actually lead to a reduced level of output. Figure 6.2 captures graphically the relationship between the marginal product and the other two measures of output.

VALUE OF MARGINAL PRODUCT AND DEMAND FOR LABOR

Like any demand, the demand for labor is a derived demand that is derived from the output market. Firms hire labor in order to meet the demand for the output they produce. Our optimal hiring decision is expressed by the cost of labor being equal to the value of the marginal product of labor (see Figure 6.1). This condition also tells us how wages in a market economy are being determined. Since the wage equals the value of the marginal product of labor, anything that can increase the marginal product of labor will drive up the wage.

In practice, there are different types of labor, i.e. different occupations. Each occupation has its own wage, which is determined by the occupation's value of the marginal product of labor. Since the value of the marginal product of labor depends on the price of output produced by the type of labor, and on the marginal productivity of the labor, a rise in the output price of the marginal product would cause the wage to increase. The marginal product of labor can be increased by a rise in the ratio of other inputs such as capital (and in practice, human capital) to labor because this would effectively increase the relative scarcity of this type of labor. Some of the highest paid professionals restrict the supply of labor into their occupations. In most instances, this is achieved by creating professional standards such as requiring professional memberships, certifications, education, etc. Because the production process exhibits diminishing marginal productivity, another way to increase the marginal product of labor is to reduce the level of employment.

The process of wage (labor cost) determination takes place at the economy level. For the most part, individual firms adjust their hiring decisions to the market wage. In the process, these adjustments impact the marginal product of labor and the price of output, thereby impacting the market wage.

Since each firm adjusts its hiring decision to the market wage, we can construct the demand for labor by a firm. In the example of our economics department, the demand for labor can be seen in columns L and $VMPL$ of Table 6.3. Since the university reaches the optimal hiring level when the per unit cost of labor equals the value of the marginal product of labor, the $VMPL$ column represents the per unit labor cost, while the L column represents the desired level of employment.

For example, at a wage below $105,000, the university would hire four economists. At a wage between $105,000 and $115,000, three faculty members would be hired.

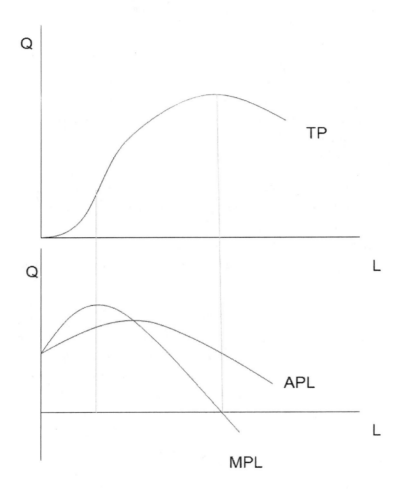

Figure 6.2

SHIFTING TO OUTPUT AS THE DECISION MAKING UNIT AND DERIVING THE COST FUNCTIONS

So far in our example, we focused on the optimal faculty hiring decision; however, most of the time the analysis focuses on the level of output rather than that of an input. Usually the profit function is structured as a function of output.

Indeed, in our earlier discussion, we structured the total revenues as a function of output. It makes sense to structure the cost of production as a function of output, and then combine it with the total revenue function to obtain profits. In this process, we will structure the profit function as a function of output.

In our production process, we have two inputs: labor and capital. This implies that there are two distinct cost components: those that are associated with labor and those that are associated with capital. In the short-run, these two cost components exhibit significant differences. Recall that the short-run is defined as a time period within which the firm is only capable of varying labor and the capital stock remains constant. This implies that the cost of labor can be viewed as a variable cost, a cost that varies depending on the level of output the firm chooses to produce. The cost of capital is fixed. It is fixed because it does not vary with the level of output.

Let's return to our economics department example one more time, but this time focus on the costs. Let's set the cost of each faculty member to the school, the wage (w) at \$110,000. This creates the cost of labor, sometimes referred to in labor economics as the wage bill, L times w. Table 6.4 produces all of the following computations for our example. Since labor is the only variable input in our production process, the wage bill will also become the Total Variable Cost of production in our equation:

16) $TVC = L \times w \Leftrightarrow TVC(Q) = L(Q) \times w = f(Q)$

Because the level of labor hired determines the level of output, the TVC is a function of output.

We can also introduce the cost of capital at this point. We will designate the rental cost of capital equipment with r, and K, will represent the number of units of capital.[14] Since the firm is assumed to be unable to change the level of capital in the short-run, the cost of capital becomes the Fixed Cost (or in our case, where capital is the only fixed input, the Total Fixed Cost). Fixed costs are not a function of output:

17) $TFC = K \times r \neq f(Q)$

In our example, the fixed cost is the cost of the classroom space. Let's assume that the cost of the classroom building to the school is \$30,000/semester. Note

---

[14] Recall the computation of rental cost from Chapter 1.

that this cost is not a function of the number of classes offered in the building or their enrollment. We incur this cost regardless of whether we have only one student attending the classes or they are filled beyond their capacity. The Total Cost is simply the sum of these two individual cost components:

18) $TC(Q) = TVC(Q) + TFC = L(Q)w + Kr$

If we divide Expression 18 by output (Q), we will obtain the average cost functions: Average Total Cost (ATC), Average Variable Cost (AVC), and Average Fixed Cost (AFC). Their relationship is represented algebraically as:

19) $ATC = \dfrac{TC}{Q} = \dfrac{TVC}{Q} + \dfrac{TFC}{Q} = AVC + AFC$

However, just as in the case of the optimal hiring decision where we needed a marginal measure of output, we will also require a marginal measure of cost. Marginal cost (MC) is defined as the cost of the marginal (decision) unit of output. That marginal unit is the next unit (or the last unit) produced. Marginal cost is defined by Expression 20:

20) $MC = \dfrac{\Delta TC}{\Delta Q}$

Ideally, we would prefer the change in the output in Equation 20 to be just one, but that may not always be possible. For instance, in a classroom setting the marginal cost of an additional student is not well defined. If we already have a class and that class still has some seating capacity left, then the cost of an additional student is zero. However, if we are at capacity and adding one more student implies offering one more class, then the cost of the additional student becomes equal to the cost of the class. As a result, we can only identify the "average" marginal cost based on the number of students in the class. For example, if the cost of offering one more class is \$20,000, and the class has the enrollment of 40 students, then the marginal cost is \$20,000/40 = \$500.

Algebraically, we can further expand Expression 20 and establish two important relationships. First, we can recognize that since the Total Fixed Cost does not change with a change in output (they are fixed regardless of the level of output), we can simplify Expression 20 to being a function of the Total Variable Cost only:

21) $MC = \dfrac{\Delta TC}{\Delta Q} = \dfrac{\Delta(TVC + TFC)}{\Delta Q} = \dfrac{\Delta TVC + \Delta TFC}{\Delta Q} = \dfrac{\Delta TVC + 0}{\Delta Q} = \dfrac{\Delta TVC}{\Delta Q}$

However, we can proceed one step further and define the marginal cost as a function of the marginal product of the variable input (in our case labor) by simply substituting the equation for the total variable cost:

22) $MC = \dfrac{\Delta(Lw)}{\Delta Q} = \dfrac{\Delta Lw + \Delta wL}{\Delta Q} == \dfrac{\Delta L}{\Delta Q} w = \dfrac{w}{MPL}$

Note that the above simplification employs two steps. First, we use the rule of the differentiation of a product. Second, we assume that a change in the output by the firm does not change the price of the variable input, which in this case is the wage (w). Expression 22 is actually very interesting as it helps define the shape of the marginal cost. If the marginal product of labor is rising (as it may initially), the marginal cost is decreasing. When diminishing marginal productivity is observed, the marginal cost becomes a rising function. We also see that the marginal cost is a function of the price of the variable input.

PROFIT MAXIMIZATION AND MARGINAL COST

The profit function can be defined as simply the difference between the total revenue function and the total cost function. Since both the revenues and the costs are functions of the firm's output, so is the profit function:

23) $\pi(Q) = TR(Q) - TC(Q)$

We actually know quite a bit about the shape of the profit function. Recall from our earlier discussion that the total revenue has a single maximum (see Figure 6.3).

The total cost function is also likely to have a simple appearance. If the law of diminishing marginal product applies, then the Total Variable Cost is rising at an increasing rate. Recall that the marginal cost serves as the slope of both the Total Variable Cost and Total Cost. The law of diminishing marginal productivity implies that as output increases the marginal product of labor decreases, resulting in a higher level of marginal cost. Thus, the shape of the Total Cost function can be represented by Figure 6.4. Putting these two diagrams together enables us to plot the profit function theoretically.

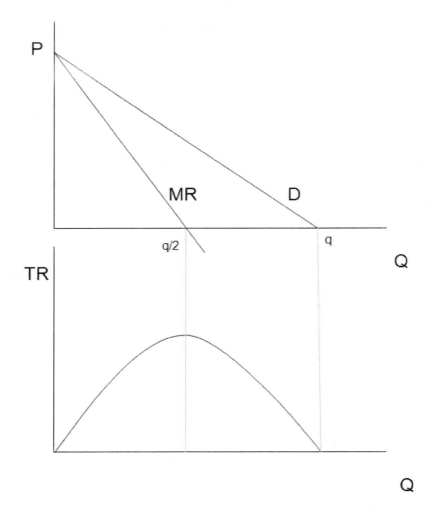

Figure 6.3

You may ask yourself, why we went through all these diagrams. The reason is simple, these diagrams demonstrate that if the law of diminishing marginal product holds and there is no price discrimination, then the profit function has a single maximum and is concave. This conclusion sounds more algebraic than economic, but it does have some importance as it basically allows us to use calculus to find the maximum of the profit function; most importantly it ensures that the maximum is unique and therefore is the profit maximizing point.

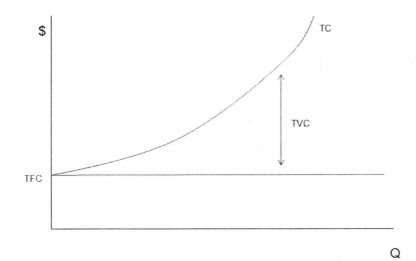

Figure 6.4

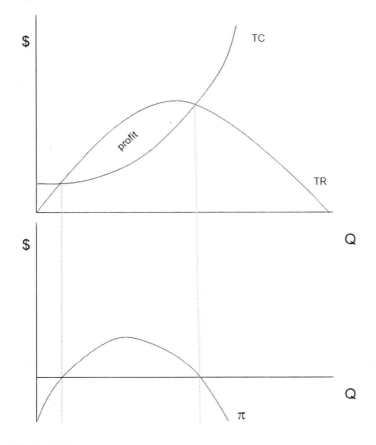

Figure 6.5

If we obtain the slope of the profit function with respect to output (differentiate the profit function with respect to output), then we will get the following expression:

$$24) \quad \frac{\Delta \pi}{\Delta Q} = \frac{\Delta TR}{\Delta Q} - \frac{\Delta TC}{\Delta Q} = MR - MC$$

At the profit maximizing level of output, the slope of the profit function must be zero as the function is parallel to the Q-axis. This provides us with what probably is the most important condition in the theory of the firm, the profit maximization condition:

$$25) \quad MR = MC$$

In fact, the above condition is intuitive. As long as marginal revenue exceeds marginal cost, it makes sense to expand production. However, expanding output causes marginal cost to increase (due to the law of diminishing marginal product), while marginal revenue to decline (due to the law of demand). This reduces the difference between marginal revenue and marginal cost. Eventually, the difference decreases to zero as the firm approaches the profit maximizing level of output.

The opposite is also true. If the firm finds itself in a situation where marginal revenue is less than marginal cost, then the firm should reduce output. As the level of output decreases, marginal cost decreases due to the law of diminishing marginal product, while marginal revenue increases due to the law of demand.

L	Q	TR	TVC wL	TFC rK	TC TVC+TFC	AVC TVC/Q	AFC TFC/Q	ATC TC/Q	MC ΔTVC/ΔQ	Profit
0	0		0	30000	30000					-30000
1	120	120000	110000	30000	140000	916.67	250	1166.67	916.67	-20000
2	248	248000	220000	30000	250000	887.10	120.97	1008.06	859.38	-2000
3	363	363000	330000	30000	360000	909.09	82.64	991.74	956.52	3000
4	468	468000	440000	30000	470000	940.17	64.10	1004.27	1047.62	-2000

Table 6.4

If we used the profit maximization condition from Equation 25 in our example of the economics department, we would obtain the same result as the one we obtained using the value of the marginal product of labor and wage comparison. Recall that our economics department charged $1000 in tuition and faced a perfectly elastic demand (marginal revenue equals the price). It would make sense to hire the first unit of labor as it results in a marginal cost of $916.67, while the marginal revenue is $1000. The profitability is improved by hiring the second unit of labor as the marginal revenue continues to exceed the marginal cost ($859.38). The university should hire the third unit of labor as well, however, that is where the hiring should end. The fourth unit of labor should not be employed as that would result in a situation where marginal cost would exceed marginal revenue.

Note that this same level of hiring was obtained when we examined the optimal hiring decision by comparing the value of the marginal product of labor to the marginal cost of labor, the wage (w = $110,000).

DETERMINANTS OF MARGINAL COST

From Expression 22, we know that marginal cost is affected only by the variable costs. Furthermore, we know that a rise in the price of the variable input increases marginal cost, while a rise in the marginal product of the variable input decreases marginal cost. For instance, if a labor union negotiates a higher wage for its workforce, then that causes the marginal cost to the employer to increase. A rise in the marginal cost would cause a reduction in the level of employment, all else held constant. To understand this, we need to start with a situation where the firm maximizes profits. A rise in the wage increases the firm's marginal cost, while its marginal revenue remains unchanged. The firm starts to experience losses on the marginal unit of output. This situation can be corrected in two ways. One, the firm may increase the price of output, and that will increase the marginal revenue, bringing the firm back to profit maximization where marginal revenue equals marginal cost. Two, the firm can lower its marginal cost by reducing the level of labor it hires. As the payroll is reduced, the marginal productivity of labor increases due to the law of diminishing marginal product.

A reduction in marginal cost can be accomplished by lowering the price of labor, but alternatively it can be accomplished by increasing the marginal productivity of labor. In the previous paragraph, a reduction in marginal cost was accomplished by reducing labor, but this is not a requirement. The marginal productivity of labor can be adjusted in two ways.

One, a rise in the ratio of other inputs to labor will increase the marginal and average products of labor. In our simple setup, this can be accomplished by increased investment into the capital stock of the firm. As we increase the ratio of the fixed inputs to the variable input, we increase the productivity of the variable input and thereby reduce the marginal cost. Appendix A presents an illustrated case of the Cobb-Douglas production function that demonstrates this effect algebraically. Two, increased marginal productivity can be achieved through technological improvements in the firm's production process.

ROLE OF FIXED COSTS AND THE SHUT-DOWN DECISION

Our economics department is actually profitable when three faculty members are hired, but what if the labor market for economists were to change? What if the costs of hiring a faculty member were to increase from the current $110,000 to $117,000? This can happen for a variety of reasons. We may have a rise in salary due to increased demand for economists outside of academia. Recall that firms and sectors compete for workers. For instance, it is a well-known fact that on average an economics professor earns less than a finance professor even though the two disciplines are closely related. The explanation for this pay differential is rather simple, the demand for finance professionals outside of academia is much greater than the demand for economists, and as a result schools face an increased competition for finance faculty. At the same time, the supply difference between these two markets is relatively small, resulting in a higher scarcity of finance Ph.Ds.

An even larger pay gap exists between mathematics and accounting faculty. In many schools, accounting faculty may be paid more than double what their mathematics counterparts receive. Again, the argument is the same as before, the private sector demand for accounting Ph.Ds. is much greater than for mathematics Ph.Ds. (relative to their corresponding supplies).

Government policies can also change input prices. For instance, changes in taxes, government transfer payments, regulations, and etc. can also alter the cost of labor. The U.S. government reports a number of employment cost indexes. These can be found on the Bureau of Labor Statistics website (www.bls.gov). One of the most general indexes for the economy as a whole is the Employment Cost Index (see BLS ECI News Releases at http://www.bls.gov/news.release/eci.toc.htm). The index is differentiated between the benefits and salary and across the public and private sectors. For instance, during the course of 2011 and 2012, inflation in the cost of employee benefits outpaced the rate of inflation of the actual wages and salaries, according to the BLS.

How would the rise in the employment cost of labor from $110,000 to $117,000 affect our economics department? Table 6.5 presents the new computations.

L	Q	TR	TVC wL	TFC rK	TC TVC+TFC	AVC TVC/Q	AFC TFC/Q	ATC TC/Q	MC ΔTVC/ΔQ	Profit
0	0		0	30000	30000					-30000
1	120	120000	117000	30000	147000	975.00	250	1225.00	975.00	-27000
2	248	248000	234000	30000	264000	943.55	120.97	1064.52	914.06	-16000
3	363	363000	351000	30000	381000	966.94	82.64	1049.59	1017.39	-18000
4	468	468000	468000	30000	498000	1000.00	64.10	1064.10	1114.29	-30000

Table 6.5

At this point, our economics department is no longer profitable. We need to examine the adjustment mechanism that the university has to go through to return to profit maximization. The first step would be to, as quickly as possible, reduce the faculty payroll from three to two. The marginal cost when we have three faculty members is now in excess of the marginal revenue (the tuition is still $1000). This will reduce the loss from 18,000 to 16,000. Note that labor is our variable input, and therefore it is all we can adjust (in the short-run). In the long-run, we will be able to attempt to reduce other costs, such as the cost of capital equipment. Although reducing labor from three to two does get us to the profit maximizing level of labor, we are not making any positive profits. Ultimately, we are in trouble and should close our economics department and terminate our economics program in the long-run because we are not in the business of losing money. Note that we should close our economics department in the long-run, not shut it down immediately. The department should be closed down when the lease on the classroom space expires and the capital stock can be reduced. Until then (in the short-run, while the capital stock is fixed), we should continue to operate because losing $16,000 is better than shutting down and just paying the rent for the remainder of the lease agreement, i.e. losing $30,000.

In summary, operating in the long-run with losses is not a proper course of action for a profit maximizing firm and as a result in the long-run the firm should exit. However, in the short-run, it may make sense to operate with losses even though there might be no clear foreseeable turn around for the situation because as long as the losses are less than the Total Fixed Cost (the alternative loss that would exist should the firm shut down in the short-run) continuing to operate becomes a loss-minimizing strategy. The same statement can be rephrased as folows: as long as all of the variable costs are covered by the total revenues, short-run operations are justified even when losses are incurred.

RELATIONSHIP BETWEEN AVERAGE COSTS AND MARGINAL COST

From our previous discussion, we can conclude several things about the relationships that exist between the average costs and marginal cost. We know that the average total cost is merely the sum of the average variable and the average fixed costs. In the diagram, this is simply represented by the vertical summation. Since the average fixed costs decrease with output, the average fixed cost asymptotically approaches the Q-axis, which means that as the output increases the average variable cost converges to the average total cost.

We also know that the marginal cost intercepts the average total and the average variable ~~fixed~~ costs at their minimum points. This discussion is usually summarized in what is often called the short-run cost-diagram of the firm (Figure 6.6).

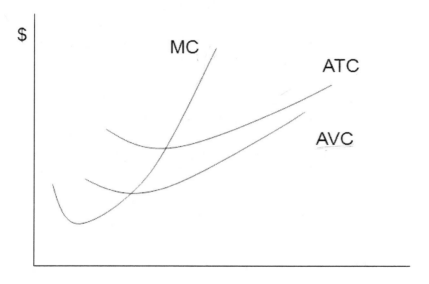

Figure 6.6

ECONOMIC PROFIT VERSUS ACCOUNTING PROFIT

In Chapter 1, we introduced the concept of opportunity cost. Recall that economic costs include explicit and implicit costs, while accounting costs tend to focus on explicit costs. This implies that the economic cost of an activity is likely

114

to exceed the accounting cost. The two will be equal, if there are no implicit costs, but that is an unusual scenario. Since the economic cost tends to exceed the accounting cost, the economic profits will tend to be less than the accounting profits. Consider the following simple example: an economics professor earning $100,000/year from her job at a college decides to open her own consulting business. Let's assume that to start the business she has to open an office with a rental cost of $12,000/year. We will also assume that the rent is her only business related expense and her revenues during the first year constitute $120,000. In the first year her business earns $108,000 in accounting profits (revenues minus her only business cost: $120,000 - $12,000), however, her economic profits are considerably lower. To start her business, she had to sacrifice her job at the college, and as a result she lost $100,000 in income that she would otherwise have earned. These implied costs need to be accounted for, and thus her economic profits are considerably lower, only $8,000.

The same argument applies to any business entity. You may ask what income does a company like CNN or Microsoft sacrifice when they produce their services or products. However, there are still owner supplied inputs in those production processes that have an alternative use. For instance, both companies have sizable real-estate and other forms of capital stock that they use in their own production processes, and they don't have to pay outside parties for their use. But these assets can be leased to generate a stream of income, so the sacrifice nonetheless takes place (for an example see Vieira, 2012).

References

U.S. Bureau of Labor Statistics, *Employment Cost Index News Release*, 2012, available online at: http://www.bls.gov/news.release/eci.toc.htm

Vieira, Gustavo. 2012. *"CBC renting out space at Toronto headquarters,"* Macleans.ca, available online at: http://www2.macleans.ca/2012/05/07/cbc-renting-out-space-at-toronto-headquarters/

APPENDIX A

THE ALGEBRA OF THE COBB-DOUGLAS FUNCTION

The Cobb-Douglas function, as introduced in our discussion, has the following form:

1A) $Q = L^\alpha K^{(1-\alpha)}$ with $\alpha \in (0,1)$

Recall that we simplified the function by requiring that it met the constant returns to scale assumption. Returns to scale refers to what happens to the output when all inputs are increased by a given percentage. If the output increases by the same percentage, then we have constant returns to scale. If the output expands at a lower percentage, then we have decreasing returns to scale and if it expands at a higher percentage, then there are increasing returns to scale. Algebraically, the Cobb-Douglas function presented in 1A will have this property. To illustrate it, we need to magnify each of the inputs by a given proportion, t, so that $L_2 = tL_1$ and the same for capital:

2A) $Q(L_2, K_2) = (tL_1)^\alpha (tK)^\beta = t^{\alpha+\beta} Q(L_1, K_1)$

If $\alpha + \beta = 1$, then the output is magnified by the same proportion as the inputs. If the sum of the coefficients exceeds 1, then we would have increasing returns to scale, and if it is less than 1, then we would have decreasing returns to scale.

The marginal product of an input is simply the derivative of the production function with respect to this input. For instance, the marginal product of labor is:

3A) $MPL = \alpha \left(\dfrac{K}{L} \right)^{1-\alpha}$

The above expression is actually rather informative as it shows that the marginal product of an input is a function of the ratio of the other inputs to that input. As the ratio of capital to labor increases, the marginal product of labor also increases. Since the cost of labor is simply the marginal product of labor times the price of the output, we can argue that the cost of labor, or any input (we can construct the marginal product of capital and it will be proportional to L/K) is a function of its scarcity relative to the other inputs. This offers an explanation to the wage differential between skilled and unskilled labor, between developed and developing economies, and so on.

cost of labor = MPL × P

Chapter 7

116

PRODUCTION AND COSTS IN THE LONG-RUN: SUBSTITUTABLE INPUTS

LONG-RUN

The long-run framework in economics is characterized by full flexibility. In the context of production, the implication is that there are no fixed inputs. The long-run time framework is defined as the amount of time required to adjust all inputs to their desired levels. In our two-input example, labor is assumed to be adjustable at any point in time making the fixed capital stock act as the constraint in the short-run. The amount of time it takes a firm to adjust its capital stock to a new desired level is the amount it takes to move into the long-run.

Obviously, this amount of time is different from industry to industry and from one firm to another. In some cases, the span of the short-run is very quick. This is true for many service firms where the needed time to fully adjust the capital stock might be defined in weeks or even days. However, for many industrial firms, the framework of time might be measured in months and even years. One example of this is the development of the new Kia Motors America plant in Georgia. The plans to build the new plant were formally announced in the press on March 13, 2006 after "… a Site Acquisition and Development Agreement had [already] been signed between the State of Georgia and Kia Motors America…" (Kia Motors Manufacturing Georgia, 2012). It took more than three and a half years to bring the plant online on November 16, 2009 although the official opening ceremony took place even later on February 26 of 2010 (Kia Motors Manufacturing Georgia, 2012). This example illustrates that for Kia Motors of America the long-run is defined as about four years (from the time the decision was made regarding a change in its capital stock to its full implementation).

It is important to note that once the plant became fully operational, Kia Motors America was once again in the short-run just with a different, but still fixed level of capital stock. The short-run is the operational framework while the long-run is the planning horizon.

This flexibility of all inputs has significant implications for the analysis developed in the previous chapter. We no longer have any fixed costs as all costs

117

are flexible. In the long-run, it is possible to substitute between inputs. Our framework of analysis needs to adjust to capture these characteristics. We will proceed in a simplified manner. We will begin with defining the long-run average cost structure and then proceed with constructing the condition for substitutability of inputs. We will conclude with a discussion of the characteristics of the optimal combination of inputs.

LONG-RUN AVERAGE COST STRUCTURE

Recall that in the short-run framework, there are three average cost functions: average variable cost, average fixed cost, and average total cost. In the long run, all costs are variable, and therefore there is only one average cost function.

Consider a simple example where we operate a small restaurant. The size of our dining hall is specifically catered towards a given number of clients being served at the same time. For instance, a 400 square foot dining hall might be appropriate to simultaneously serve around ten people. It is still possible to serve one-two people or to even serve twenty people at the same time, but that increases the cost per customer. If we fit twenty people, it will make it difficult for us to serve them, and some customers will have to wait for service. As the dining hall gets more and more crowded, we are likely to start turning customers away, providing poor service and experiencing accidents. All of this is what causes the average variable cost to be U-shaped, which in turn causes the average cost to also be U-shaped in the short-run and creates the short-run diagram depicted in Figure 7.1. Let's assume that facility 1 in Figure 7.1 is the 400 square foot dining room designed to ideally serve ten people at a time, while facility 2 is a 600 square foot dining area that is ideally suited to serve twenty customers.

Note that our dining hall and equipment constitute the physical capital stock. In the short-run, we are confined to a particular facility. We might have a lease agreement, and until it expires we are restricted to use it. Recall that the long run is defined as the amount of time needed to fully adjust the capital stock. If we initially have facility 1, then in the short-run we are stuck with it, but from the long run perspective, we do not need to remain with it. If our restaurant becomes popular, we may decide to expand the size of the dining area and move into facility 2. This flexibility exists in the long-run, which means that in the long-run we would not voluntarily choose to operate an inefficiently sized dining area.

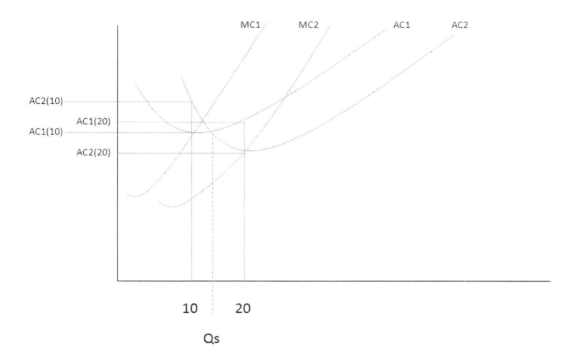

Figure 7.1

If the number of customers is less than Qs (Figure 7.1), then we should remain with facility 1 as its average cost lies below the average cost of facility 2. This makes facility 1 more efficient than facility 2 for output levels under $Q2$. For output levels above Qs, the average cost of facility 2 is below the average cost of facility 1, making facility 2 more efficient. Thus, in the long-run our average cost would follow the average cost of facility 1 between zero and Qs, and then follows the average cost of facility 2 for output levels above Qs. The long-run average cost (LRAC) effectively envelopes the short-run average costs as shown in Figure 7.2.

In the long-run, the firm would always select the level of capital that would minimize the cost of production on a per unit of output basis (i.e. be on the lowest possible short-run average cost). Since the long-run average cost curve envelopes all of the individual short-run average costs, it shows the lowest technologically possible cost of production for every output level when all inputs are variable.

Obviously, we can select other dining areas; in fact, if we can vary the size of the facility by individual feet, the LRAC will appear as a smooth curve that would be tangent to the individual short-run average cost curves as illustrated in Figure 7.3.

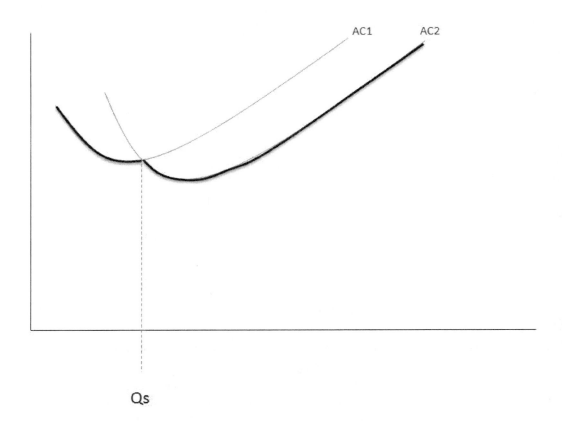

Figure 7.2

ECONOMIES OF SCALE VERSUS DISECONOMIES OF SCALE

The curve depicted in Figure 7.3 shows the three ranges of a possible long-run average cost structure: economies of scale, constant returns to scale, and diseconomies of scale. It is not necessary for every firm to experience all three ranges of the LRAC, and individual LRAC curves do not need to look like the one in Figure 7.3. A firm's LRAC may end up exhibiting only one or two of these ranges. However, Figure 7.3 presents a good way to illustrate the concepts of economies and diseconomies of scale, which are long-run characteristics of a production process and are seen in the structure of the LRAC.

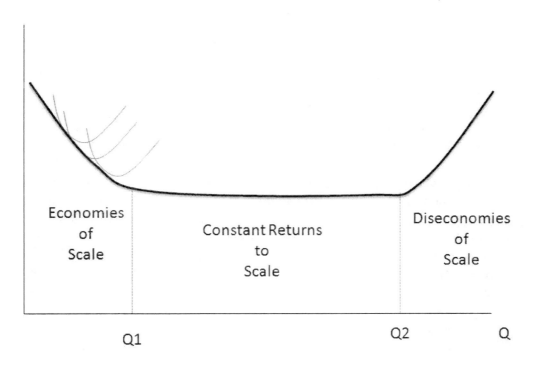

Figure 7.3

ECONOMIES OF SCALE

Economies of scale are characterized by decreasing average costs of production in the long-run, i.e. it pays to be bigger. Graphically, this is seen in a downward slopped LRAC. There are many explanations for economies of scale and the proceeding discussion provides some illustrations.

Bargaining Power and Quantity Discounts   Perhaps one of the most well-known examples of economies of scale is Wal-Mart. In the case of Wal-Mart, the economies of scale don't just come from gains due to sharing the existing logistics network over a larger number of stores, but most importantly from the fact that, in many markets (defined by products), Wal-Mart is one of the largest retailers, giving it significant bargaining power with suppliers. The result is that manufacturers have to place their products on Wal-Mart shelves in order to have a meaningful access to the market. Wal-Mart recognizes this and is able to negotiate better terms with the suppliers than smaller retail chains. As a result, Wal-Mart is capable of lowering the average cost of production.

Spreading Advertising and Other Costs   The 1999 sale by AB Volvo of its auto division to Ford Corporation was in part justified by the argument of economies of scale. In the news announcement as cited by Cisionwire, the AB Volvo management argued: "However, over the longer term and within the context of its current position as a relatively small niche player, Volvo Cars would benefit from the economies of scale inherent in being part of a very large automotive company" (Cisionwire, 1999). Several factors were expected to contribute to the economies of scale as a result of the acquisition by Ford. Given Volvo's relatively low output level compared to the other leading auto manufacturers, Volvo ended up spending more on a per unit of output basis in their advertising costs, dealership costs and so on. Ford, with its much larger output level, offered an access to a larger dealer network, reduced per car basis advertising and development costs, etc. The management of Volvo realized that economies of scale worked against them, and they had an uphill battle trying to catch up with those firms that were ahead of them on the long-run average cost curve and so decided to proceed with the sale to Ford.

Other Sources   There are many other sources of economies of scale. As the size of an enterprise expands, a firm may gain access to better production technology. For instance, larger enterprises can invest into more costly capital equipment that may enable them to lower the costs of production on a per unit basis. A larger size firm is capable of achieving further specialization of labor and gain productivity in this manner. Increased specialization of labor can also lead to learning by doing as workers tend to focus on repeating fewer tasks over time. An illustration of learning by doing can be seen in your classroom. In smaller schools, faculty tend to teach several different courses, while in larger schools, faculty tend to specialize in very few courses. This repetitive teaching of the same course can increase the productivity of faculty over time. Furthermore,

122

specialization of resources may also enhance their complementarity. For instance, as a school employs more faculty members, research skills of different faculty members may complement each other enhancing the ability of faculty to produce research and consulting. Thus, it can be argued that faculty productivity may be affected by the size of the school.

MINIMUM EFFICIENCY SCALE AND CONSTANT RETURNS TO SCALE

The lowest level of output at which a firm reaches the minimum level on its long-run average cost is defined as the minimum efficient scale. In the case of Figure 7.3, the minimum efficient scale is reached at Q1 when the firm enters the constant returns to scale range. In this range, an increase in the level of output in the long-run does not impact the per unit basis cost. This can be seen in a small retailer attempting to enter a different geographical market using their existing production technology in new stores. In this case, the expansion is too small to influence the bargaining power of the store with their suppliers. The expansion being undertaken in a different geographical area may not help spread the costs of their existing logistics network as that may have to be expanded in order to include the new area. Under these assumptions we're likely to observe constant returns to scale. Not every firm needs to experience constant returns to scale. In fact, the LRAC may be U-shaped and never really become flat over a meaningful range of output.

DISECONOMIES OF SCALE

Diseconomies of scale occur when expansion causes the average cost in the long-run to increase. This is a situation where being bigger actually hurts. At some point, an enterprise may become too big for its own good. One of the key symptoms of overexpansion is a rise in management costs on a per unit of output. Since management serves as the central nervous system of a company, the system has to be extremely efficient at communicating ideas not only from the top-down but also from the bottom up. In addition, it must be able to reduce the principal-agent problem and maintain efficiency. These abilities tend to decrease with an increase in the size of the enterprise requiring an emplacement of additional layers of management, thus further increasing costs of production. In essence, a large enterprise becomes a big dinosaur, and at some point its tail starts moving independently of its head, which marks the beginning of its end.

123

Recall that average costs, including the LRAC, can increase when additional cost factors are introduced (e.g. an additional layer of management); when costs increase on a per unit of input basis; or also because the productivity of inputs declines. The inefficiency that arises from the principal-agent problem manifests itself in lower productivity of inputs and therefore higher costs on a per unit of output basis. As the size of the enterprise increases, so does the magnitude of the principal-agent problem.

Enterprise Size and X-inefficiency   Ironically, being big may invite inefficiency. Large enterprises may be subject to lower competitive pressure, and as a result they may be able to "afford" to make a mistake. This ability, to be able to afford inefficiency, increases the likelihood of inefficiency. In economics, this is referred to as X-inefficiency, inefficiency arising from a reduced competitive pressure. A small enterprise is likely to be more competitive, to have fewer resources, and as a result have a more efficient management team. This higher efficiency in using resources occurs because the market penalty for inefficiency is more serious. The less competitive pressure a firm experiences, the greater is the potential effect of X-inefficiency.

OPTIMIZATION IN THE LONG-RUN

Theoretically, determining optimization in the long-run is rather simple, but practically it is a very challenging task. Let us continue with the assumption that our hypothetical firm employs two inputs (labor and capital). Optimization requires a good understanding of the marginal productivity measures of all the resources employed by the firm (in our case: labor and capital). Understanding the marginal productivity of capital can be a challenge as it requires identifying changes in output due to changes in capital equipment. This is rather difficult to do in the vacuum of an all else held constant assumption. Empirically, this can be achieved by collecting enough data over time or across different size facilities to capture enough variability in capital and other inputs used in the production process. When comparing observations from different time periods, one possible challenge arises from the fact that the state of production technology does not stay constant. Observations acquired in the previous 3-4 years may not be coming from the same distribution as new observations. Of course, there are ways around it, such as collecting observations from various facilities using similar production processes but different combinations of inputs. In our

124

proceeding discussion, we will assume that the marginal product of capital is known and not focus on the difficult task of obtaining it.

Ultimately, to understand optimization in the long-run, we need to follow the allocation of the marginal dollar. Just like the marginal unit of an input, the marginal dollar is simply the decision dollar. It can be the last dollar spent on an input or the next dollar to be spent. The firm has a choice to allocate that next dollar to capital investment or to labor hiring. Furthermore, in the long-run, the firm can relocate the marginal dollar from one input to another. In other words, the firm can reduce its capital stock, release the marginal dollar and then direct it to labor, or vice versa. To understand where the dollar needs to be allocated, we need to construct the per-dollar measures of benefit to the firm for each of the inputs.

When the firm hires an extra unit of labor, it obtains a revenue benefit in the form of the value of the marginal product of labor (see the short-run discussion).

1) $VMPL = MR \times MPL$

The benefit to the firm is perceived as the revenue contribution. When an additional (marginal) unit of labor is hired, the revenue increases by the value of the marginal product of labor. Recall that if the marginal revenue equals the price, then the revenue change is simply the market value of the output produced by the marginal unit of labor. The assumption of a price taking behavior was used previously in the short-run discussion to simplify things, but this simplification is completely unnecessary here as you will see from the following discussion.

Since the cost of hiring one more unit of labor is w (wage inclusive of all other costs associated with that unit of labor such as the cost of the benefits to the firm), the benefit on per dollar basis would be the value of the marginal product of labor divided by the wage (see expression 2).

2) Benefit of allocating the marginal dollar to labor $= \dfrac{VMPL}{w} = \dfrac{MR \times MPL}{w}$

Labor

For instance, consider that the value of the marginal product of labor is estimated to be $30, while the cost of the marginal unit of labor is $20, then the benefit per dollar for those $20 marginal dollars allocated to hire the marginal unit of labor is 1.5 ($30/$20).

125

Similarly, we can construct the benefit to the firm from allocating an extra dollar to capital investment. Since capital stock is variable in the long-run, we can construct the marginal product of capital from which we can obtain the value of the marginal product of capital:

capital

$$3)\quad VMPK = MR \times MPK = MR \times \frac{\Delta Q}{\Delta K}$$

From the $VMPK$, we can compute the benefit to the firm of investing an extra dollar into its capital stock by dividing the value of the output of the marginal unit of capital by the marginal cost of capital to the firm, r (see chapter 1 for computation of r, rental cost of capital):

$$4)\quad \text{Benefit of allocating the marginal dollar to capital} = \frac{VMPK}{r} = \frac{MR \times MPK}{r}$$

Now we are ready to discuss the optimal combination of labor and capital in the long-run.

If the benefit of the marginal dollar allocated to labor is greater than the benefit of the marginal dollar allocated to capital, then the firm needs to reduce its capital investment, and spend the released dollar on labor instead:

optimal combination

$$5)\quad \frac{MR \times MPL}{w} > \frac{MR \times MPK}{r} \Rightarrow \text{reduce K and increase L}$$

If we assume that the law of diminishing marginal product applies, then an increase in the level of labor leads to a lower marginal product of labor and therefore a lower benefit from the last dollar invested into labor. At the same time, a decline in spending on capital causes the marginal product of capital to increase, which increases the benefit of the last dollar invested into capital. This results in the difference between the two sides in Expression 5 to get smaller. The process continues until Expression 5 becomes an equality.

Similarly, if we were to start with a situation where the benefit of the last dollar spent on capital exceeded the benefit of the last dollar spent on labor, then the firm would start relocating its spending away from labor and into capital stock. Given the law of diminishing product, the relocation of spending would reduce the difference between the two benefits. The process would continue until there

126

is no longer any incentive to relocate the spending, i.e. the two benefits are equal.

The conclusion is that the last dollar spent on capital should produce the same return as the last dollar spent on labor. Since marginal revenue is present on both sides of Expression 5, we can further simplify the optimization condition to:

6) $$\frac{MPL}{w} = \frac{MPK}{r}$$

Since *MPL* and *MPK* are measured in terms of the output, we can argue that the last dollar spent on each input produces the same marginal output.

Often the optimization condition from Expression 6 is rearranged and stated as:

7) $$\frac{MPL}{MPK} = \frac{W}{r}$$

W — wage

r — cost of capital

The ratio of marginal products is referred to as the marginal rate of technical substitution. The ratio of the input prices represents the market given rate of transformation of one input into another. For instance, if the wage rate is $20, while the rental cost of capital is $10, then the market allows the firm to substitute one unit of labor for two units of capital.

Note that at the macro level, the ratio of the input costs is determined by the ratio of the marginal products, but at the micro level, each firm adjusts its production process to meet the ratio of the input costs. In other words, collectively firms help determine the ratio of the input costs, but individually each firm tends to be a price taker. If the ratio of *w/r* decreases, then the firm will gradually employ more labor and less capital and vice-versa. This is why the same industry might be relatively labor intensive in a country with low wages and high cost of capital, while in a country with high wages and low cost of capital it might be relatively capital intensive. An excellent example is observed in agriculture. While in many developing countries agriculture remains a labor intensive industry to this day, in most developed countries it is a capital intensive industry.

References

Cisionwire, 1999. "Volvo enters into agreement with Ford to sell Volvo Cars for SEK 50 billion." Available online at: http://news.cision.com/volvo/r/volvo-enters-into-agreement-with-ford-to-sell-volvo-cars-for-sek-50-billion,c6053 (accessed on 2/18/13).

Kia Motors Manufacturing Georgia, 2012. "Our Company." Available online at http://www.kmmgusa.com/about-kmmg/our-company/ (accessed on 2/18/13)

Chapter 8

INDUSTRIAL ORGANIZATION – PERFECT COMPETITION

So far, our discussion has been centered on a single firm. However, market supply is rarely ever determined by an individual firm. At this point, we need to examine how firms interact with one another and how that interaction produces a market supply. We are about to expand the scope of our discussion to the level of an industry, hence the title of this section – Industrial Organization.

In our analysis of a firm, we had a standard approach and developed tools that would apply for virtually every firm no matter its size or its product. However, now that approach is about to change as our analysis is complicated by the fact that every industry is a bit unique. This makes it impossible to create a standardized model that works across all industries and provides us with the full understanding of the supply side. For instance, can we argue that PC manufacturing and commercial-aircraft manufacturing are similar industries and thus can be analyzed using the same model? Both of these are manufacturing industries, but that is pretty much where the similarities stop. In one market, we have many producers that manufacture very similar products, and in the other, we have a very limited number of producers.

Ironically, we should not conclude that the number of firms is the key factor in determining the level of competition in an industry. Although more than one firm is needed to have competition, we should not rush to the conclusion that the number of firms is a measure of competitive pressure in an industry. For instance, an industry with ten firms, each accounting for about 10% of the total level of industry sales, may be more competitive than an industry with twenty firms but with one of these accounting for 80% of the market and the other nineteen sharing the remaining 20%.

Industries differ not only in terms of the number of firms, but also in terms of products they sell. For instance, a multi-billion dollar gold mining company may be a highly competitive firm, while a small family-owned restaurant may have significant market power. This is because the gold mining giant produces a product that is identical to that of its competitors, while the restaurant may use unique recipes.

To simplify things, we will classify industries into four separate categories and then develop a framework of analysis or a model for each of these. Each model will utilize its own assumptions about an industry. These assumptions define the conditions under which one can apply that particular model. Clearly, the more assumptions a model deploys, then the more restrictive the model is and as a result tends to apply to fewer cases.

The four models we will discuss are: Perfect Competition, Monopolistic Competition, Oligopoly, and Monopoly. If we were to ignore the issues associated with the differences in market shares of individual firms, then we could loosely differentiate between these models in terms of the number of firms in an industry. A monopoly is defined as a single producer of a product for which there are no close substitutes. In this case, the number of firms in an industry is just one. Oligopoly is a term used to describe an industry with a limited number of competitors. When the number of firms is limited, a strategic interaction between these firms becomes possible. We can immediately see that these two actualities are very different. In a monopoly setting, there is no interaction between firms as there is only one firm. While in the case of oligopoly, we have a strategic interdependence; actions of one company impact the other firms and as a result can initiate a response from the other firms. As the number of firms increases, the impact of actions of one firm on the market outcome and hence on the other firms diminishes. As each firm loses the ability to significantly impact the market outcome, we move into a more competitive environment and a different model is needed.

We will begin our discussion with Perfect Competition. This is the most restrictive of the models which makes it less frequently applicable. However, the model of perfect competition provides us with something incredibly valuable – the characteristics of perfection in the market place.

PERFECT COMPETITION

We need to start by defining the assumptions under which the perfectly competitive model applies. Then we can develop the actual model and discuss its outcome.

ASSUMPTIONS:

<u>Large Number of Firms</u>. Competition requires that there be a large number of firms. Perfect competition requires that each firm be small enough relative to the market such that it is incapable of influencing the market price. This assumption may seem like a restrictive one, but actually many industries meet it. For instance, it is easy to argue that the number of restaurants serving similar quality and type of food in any city is large enough so that no restaurant can influence the market price.

<u>Homogeneous Good or Service</u>. In a perfect world, we want our firms to compete not in terms of quality of a product but in terms of price. In fact, sufficiently large quality differentiation may split a market. For instance, do luxury cars compete against economy cars or do they operate in two different markets? Our own illustration of restaurants in the previous assumption may not be applicable here. Restaurants differ not only in terms of what food they serve but also in quality; as a result they compete not only in terms of price but also in terms of product characteristics. It might be true that there are many restaurants in any given city, but do restaurants that serve Italian food compete with those that serve French food? Does the reputation of a restaurant depend on the quality of its chef?

<u>No Barrier to Entry or Exit</u>. In a perfectly competitive world, we need firms to be able to freely enter and exit their market. Presence of entry barriers can over time turn a competitive industry into an oligopoly. However, the key point of this assumption is even simpler; we need to allow other firms to enter into an industry when that industry is profitable (economic profits), and allow their exit when they start to experience losses (note that entry and exit are long-run decisions). A rise in profits encourages entry by new firms, and no barriers to entry make that entry possible. This insures that an industry stays competitive over. However, is entry ever barrier free? High costs of initial investment may be just one form of a barrier to entry. For example, to compete successfully against a company like UPS or Intel would require billions of dollars of initial investment. Interestingly, this barrier is a function of the state of development of the financial system in an economy.

A poorly developed financial system will create a barrier to entry into any industry. In a way, the financial system is the heart of capitalism as it is the sector that channels financial capital into productive capital. A well developed and functional financial system helps reduce the entry barrier of an initial investment. In countries where the financial system is not well developed, industries tend to

developed countries
&
developing ^
barrier

be less competitive and business ownership is usually more concentrated. In economies with fully developed financial systems, industries tend to be less concentrated and business ownership tends to be spread over a larger population.

There are many other forms of barrier to entry. Some are legal, such as a patent that protects the intellectual rights of a product or service. As a result of the protection, the patent holder is protected from entry by another firm that might just replicate the product. Patents are necessary to encourage investment into research and development. Professional associations and licenses can also serve to restrict competition. The possible justification here is the facilitation of quality control.

Barriers to exit are just as important as they can also deter entry. If exit barriers are high, they may discourage investors from setting up firms even though the industry is profitable; in the event that the business does not succeed there may be serious losses encountered at the time of exit. Exit barriers may include things like a highly specialized nature of the capital stock needed to start a firm. In the event the firm decides to exit it may find it very difficult to liquidate its capital equipment, and as a result it may incur high losses on its assets.

Note that entry/exit is a long-run decision as it implies a change in the firm's capital level, i.e. a firm that exits reduces its capital stock to zero.

Complete Information. Competition between firms can only take place if consumers are well informed about the prices charged by each firm. Have you ever purchased something just to discover a few days later that you could have purchased it at a lower price from another seller? If yes, then the complete information was not available to you at the time of purchase. As a result the seller with the lowest price ended up with no sale, while the seller with a higher price had a sale. In this setting, the sellers no longer compete just in terms of price but also in terms of delivering information to the perspective consumers. This redefines competition away from the perfect world where firms compete on price.

Complete information requires that all market participants (buyers and sellers) have complete information about the market. In the absence of this, market participants have to incur search costs to obtain information.

Zero Transaction Costs. We want to have zero transaction costs in a perfectly competitive market. We don't want to have a situation where buying from one seller, leads to higher transaction costs than buying from another. For example, would you drive a distance of 100 miles to purchase a $20 item? The chances are that the commuting costs (transaction costs in this case) would not justify doing so. This effectively means that a local seller does not compete with a distant seller. However, this simply requires that there are identical transaction costs. Why require zero transaction costs? The zero transaction cost requirement is a simplification that in part has to do with one of the most important conclusions of the model, the equality of marginal cost of production to marginal benefit from consumption. Although this point is an important one in economics, it is not all that relevant in the context of managerial economics.

Some additional assumptions are also frequently listed as they are as well employed by the model. These typically include rationality in the behavior of buyers and property rights. The model also assumes that there are no economies of scale over a large range of output as that would lead to expansion of individual firms and possible horizontal mergers, which in the long run would result in a reduced number of firms. However, economies of scale can be viewed as an example of the no barriers to entry and exit assumption. Economies of scale may require an entry on a large scale, thereby creating a barrier to entry.

CAN THESE ASSUMPTIONS EVER BE MET?

The assumption of product homogeneity is a very restrictive one as firms tend to desire to differentiate their product. One of the reasons why firms differentiate their products/services is to avoid being in a perfectly competitive setting and compete solely on the basis of price. If all firms sell an identical product, then no firm would be able to charge a price above market price. On the other hand, when the product is differentiated, then it is possible for a firm to increase its price if consumers value the product's specific characteristics.

Product differentiation is a very creative process. There are many excellent examples of product differentiation, and in fact practically everything apart from generic medication is differentiated in some way. For manufacturing firms, this may be a somewhat easy issue as additional features can be easily incorporated into a product. Even retail businesses that compete in a market where they resell the same products as their competitors also manage to differentiate their service. Retail stores differ in terms of extended warrantees, support they offer to their customers, and the shopping experience. By offering these services they effectively differentiate themselves from other stores. For instance, Best Buy introduced its own tech support called Geek Squad for its customers. In doing so,

133

Best Buy has differentiated itself from other firms that sell the exact same products but without a similar support service.

THE CONSEQUENCE OF THE ASSUMPTIONS: THE MODEL OF PERFECT COMPETITION

Our assumptions require that a market be comprised of a large number of buyers and sellers. This implies that each seller or firm constitutes a very small section of a market. In fact, the assumptions require that each firm be small enough to have no influence on market price, which means that each firm is a price taker. Each firm simply accepts the market price (the same also applies to each buyer) and sells its output at that price. If a firm attempts to charge a price that is above the market price it will have zero sales. Figure 8.1 provides an illustration of a price taking firm.

The market equilibrium price is determined by the interaction between the market demand and the market supply (see the market diagram of Figure 8.1). The market supply is simply the sum of the quantities supplied by all firms in the industry. Each individual firm then takes the market equilibrium price for granted, and thus its demand function is simply a horizontal line at the market equilibrium price. The demand in the firm diagram of figure 8.1 is perfectly elastic (horizontal). Recall from an earlier discussion that a perfectly elastic demand has the magnitude of its elasticity value equal to infinity at all positive output levels. Thus, any firm that faces a perfectly elastic demand has zero market power.

MARKET POWER

Market power is an ability on the part of a firm to change (raise) the price and not lose all of its sales. A perfectly competitive firm has no market power as any increase in price from the market price results in its sales dropping to zero units. Thus, any firm that faces a downward slopped demand has some degree of market power.

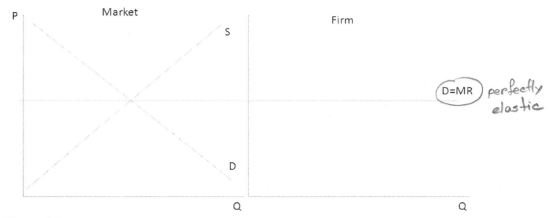

Figure 8.1

PERFECTLY ELASTIC DEMAND

A perfectly elastic demand has an important characteristic in that the marginal revenue (MR) function and the demand function are the same. In order to sell a higher level of output, a firm does not need to lower the price, and as a result the marginal revenue is simply the price. This is very different from what we observed earlier in our discussion when we had downward slopped demand. Recall that if a company with market power (e.g. a major car manufacturer) decides to expand its output by 10% in the next quarter, it would have to reduce the price in order for the market to absorb the extra output, all else held constant. Otherwise, the consumer quantity demanded will fall short of the level of output produced resulting in a surplus and an accumulation of business inventory. For a firm with no market power, this is not an issue. A perfectly competitive firm can expand the level of output without needing to lower the price.

Also recall that any firm that does not price discriminate or price differentiate would have its average revenue (AR) equal to the price of output:[15]

$$1) \quad AR = \frac{TR}{Q} = \frac{P \times Q}{Q} = P$$

---

[15] Price discrimination refers to charging different consumers different prices for the same product, even though the difference in the prices is not justified by differences in the costs. Price differentiation refers to charging different consumers different prices because the difference is justified by the differences in the costs of production.

135

Thus, for a perfectly elastic demand we have the following conclusion:

2) $P = AR = MR$

THE DIAGRAM OF THE FIRM

At this point, the cost curves can be inserted into the diagram depicted in Figure 8.1. We begin by examining the case of a firm that earns positive economic profits in the short run and derive the long-run equilibrium for the model. Figure 8.2 depicts such a firm in the short-run.

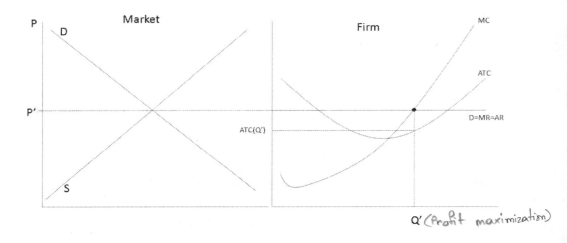

Figure 8.2

Recall that the market price is determined by the interaction between the market supply and the market demand in the market diagram of Figure 8.2. The market equilibrium price is the price taken by the firm. The firm's demand is simply the horizontal function at the market equilibrium price. The firm determines its profit maximizing level of output by comparing its marginal cost to its marginal revenue (the standard profit maximization condition from Chapter 6). Since the marginal revenue is the same as the price, the profit maximization occurs at Q' where the marginal cost function intercepts the marginal revenue function.

At Q' the firm earns positive economic profits as the average total cost falls short of the average revenue. In fact, the profits can simply be computed as the difference between the average revenue and average cost (both evaluated at Q') times the level of output:

3) $\pi(Q') = (AR(Q') - ATC(Q')) \times Q'$ ← Profit maximization

In the short-run, it is possible for a perfectly competitive firm to earn positive economic profits, but in the long-run it is not the case. Recall that there are no barriers to entry, so other firms can enter the market and mimic the production technology of a profitable firm. Positive economic profits effectively attract entry. As more firms enter the market, the supply starts to increase. This results in a decline of the equilibrium price. The process continues until the reason for entry, positive economic profits, simply disappears. Figure 8.3 demonstrates this process and its outcome.

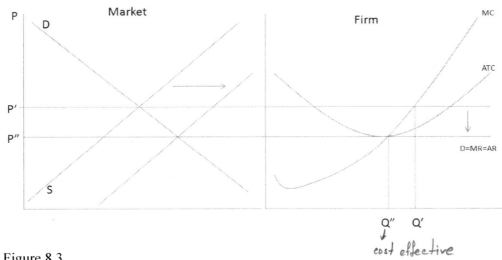

Long run)

Figure 8.3

cost effective

Once the economic profits of the firm decline to zero, there is no longer any reason for other firms to enter. As Figure 8.3 demonstrates, this happens when the price declines to the lowest level of the firm's average total cost. Any further reductions in the price will result in the firm experiencing losses, and no other firm would want to imitate a losing firm.

In fact, if we were to start with a firm that experienced economic losses, the process would simply be reversed. In the long-run, such a firm would exit, causing the market supply to decrease and the price to increase. The equilibrium price would continue to increase until there would be no desire for a firm to exit the industry, i.e. the price increased sufficiently to make the firm break even.

It is also interesting to note that in Figure 8.3, as the industry supply expanded due to the entry by new firms, the level of output produced by each firm in the industry actually decreased ($Q'>Q''$). This may seem like a paradox, but actually producing Q'' is more cost effective on per unit basis than producing Q' as seen from the comparison of the average total cost values for these two levels of output. The entry by other firms made the existing firms improve on their efficiency and in the process reduce their level of output. The long run adjustment shown in Figure 8.3 assumes constant returns to scale; this assumption is relaxed in Figure 8.5.

Recall that economic profits differ from accounting profits in the manner that costs are computed. Economic costs include implicit costs of resources, while accounting costs do not. Thus, zero economic profits imply that the resource owners (capitalists and workers) earn just enough to cover their implicit costs. Recall that implicit costs are equal to the return which would otherwise be obtained if resources were allocated to their next best alternative use. Thus, zero economic profits means that resources earn their normal rate of return.

CHARACTERISTICS OF THE SHORT-RUN

As seen from the preceding discussion, it is possible for a perfectly competitive firm to experience economic profits or economic losses in the short-run. The long-run adjustment of entry and exit brings the firm to the break-even level of output. However, in the short-run the firm still has two decisions to make: the level of output to produce and whether to stay in business or not. This second decision, referred to as the shutdown decision is based on a comparison of losses the firm experiences versus the level of its fixed costs (see the shutdown discussion in Chapter 6).

The shutdown is a decision to cease operations in the short-run. Since a firm cannot liquidate its capital stock in the short-run, ceasing all operations leads to experiencing only fixed costs until the firm can exit in the long-run by fully liquidating its capital stock. The firm should shut down if the losses it incurs from continuing its operations exceed the fixed costs of production. At this point, loss minimization will require it to select the better of the two losing propositions, the loss equal to its fixed costs. Diagram-wise, this occurs when the price declines below the minimum level of the average variable cost. As long as the price is above the average variable cost, the firm is capable of covering all of its variable costs and a portion of its fixed costs. When the price is equal to the minimum level of the average variable cost, the firm is only capable of covering all of its variable costs but none of its fixed costs. From the profit maximizing

138

point of view (or in this case loss minimizing), the firm is now indifferent between continuing to operate and shutting down. Thus, we refer to this point in our diagram as the shut-down point and the price that equals the minimum on the average variable cost as the shut-down price (see Figure 8.4).

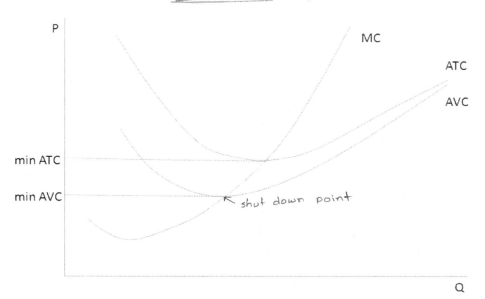

Figure 8.4

Q	TFC	TVC	TC TFC+TVC	AFC TFC/Q	AVC TVC/Q	ATC TC/Q	MC	
0	30							
1	30	3.1	33.1	30	3.1	33.1	3.1	
2	30	5.1	35.1	15	2.55	17.55	2	
3	30	7.3	37.3	10	2.43	12.43	2.2	
4	30	9.7	39.7	7.5	**2.425**	9.925	2.4	← shut down price
5	30	13.6	43.6	6	2.72	8.72	3.9	
6	30	18.5	48.5	5	3.08	8.08	4.9	
7	30	24.5	54.5	4.29	3.50	7.79	6	
8	30	32.3	62.3	3.75	4.038	**7.788**	7.8	← break even
9	30	42.3	72.3	3.33	4.70	8.03	10	
10	30	56.3	86.3	3	5.63	8.63	14	

Table 8.1

Table 8.1 presents an arithmetic illustration of the shutdown concept. Recall that profit maximization occurs when marginal cost equals marginal revenue. Also

139

$\dfrac{2.4}{9.6}$ 1

recall that for a perfectly competitive firm, the marginal revenue and the output price are equivalent, and thus profit maximization occurs when the marginal cost equals the market price. For example, if the market price was equal to $10, then the firm would produce 9 units of output because that is where the marginal cost would equal the price. If the price was to decline to $8, then the firm would reduce the output level to 8 units.

The breakeven price, the price at which the firm earns zero economic profits, is the minimum level of the average total cost. The firm can reduce its price down to the minimum average total cost without incurring any economic losses. This occurs when the firm in Table 8.1 produces 8 units of output. Thus, the breakeven price for this firm is about $7.8 because that is the level of marginal cost corresponding to 8 units of output. At the breakeven price, the firm's revenues (price times quantity) are $62.40, while the costs of production are (TC) $62.30. To be precise, in our example, the output should be slightly above 8 units as that is where the marginal cost and the average total cost intercept; if the output were only variable in whole unit increments, then 8 units would be the breakeven level of output.

In Table 8.1, the shutdown price is around $2.42 because that is where the marginal cost appears to intercept the average variable cost. This also appears to be near the minimum of the average variable cost. If the price equaled $2.42, then the output level would be 4 units. This would result in total revenues of $9.68, while the total average cost would be around $9.70. Again, technically the firm would choose to produce a little more than 4 units, but we round things here as we can only vary the output in whole units. At the price of $2.42, the firm barely covers the variable costs of production; none of the fixed costs are offset by the revenue. If all of the variable costs were completely covered ($9.70), then the firm would be indifferent between operating and losing $30, or shutting down and losing the fixed cost of $30. Any price below $2.42 is unacceptable to the firm as the operating losses would exceed the fixed costs. Therefore, at any price below $2.42, the firm in Table 8.1 would have to shut down.

Note how we determined the level of output produced by the firm. In Figure 8.2 (and also in Table 8.1), we determined the quantity of output that the firm would elect to produce (the quantity that maximizes its profits) by comparing the marginal revenue to the marginal cost. However, the marginal revenue is the same as the price, so we effectively compared the price to the marginal cost and determined the quantity from the marginal cost function. Effectively, the marginal cost connects the price the firm receives with the level of output the firm chooses to produce, and thus the marginal cost assumes the role of the firm's supply function. It is important to recall that the firm would shut down its operations if the price were to decline below the minimum level of the average variable cost. Thus, it is the portion of the marginal cost that is above the average variable cost which constitutes the short-run supply function of a perfectly competitive firm. This is often referred to as Marginal Cost Pricing, an important consequence of perfect competition. In fact, economists often measure market power by examining how far away from its marginal cost the firm is capable of pricing its product (one such measure is the Lerner's Index to be defined later).

The industry supply is simply the summation of all the individual supply functions, i.e. the summation of the marginal cost functions, and therefore is itself the marginal cost function of the industry in the short-run. In economics, this is yet another very important consequence of the model as it basically implies that economic welfare, defined by the sum of producer and consumer surpluses, is maximized under perfect competition.[16]

CHARACTERISTICS OF THE LONG-RUN EQUILIBRIUM

As seen in Figure 8.3, in the long-run a perfectly competitive firm breaks even, i.e. it earns zero economic profits. Note that it can have positive accounting profits. Our discussion so far focused on entry and exit as factors responsible for pushing the price to the minimum level of the average total cost, but there is one additional mechanism that also insures the same result. A perfectly competitive firm is unable to alter the market price, but it is capable of exploring the possibility of reducing its costs of production by changing the capital stock. If the firm finds itself not operating at the minimum of the average total cost in the short-run as is the case with Q' of Figure 8.3, it will adjust its capital stock in order to switch to a lower average total cost. The process will continue until no more improvements are possible, which is achieved when the short-run average total cost is just tangent at its minimum to the long-run average cost. Recall from our discussion of the long-run costs of production that a short-run average total cost is tangent at its minimum point to the long-run average cost when the long-

SRATC   LRAC
minimum   Lowest Level

---

[16] Consumer surplus represents the net marginal benefit to the consumer when purchasing a unit of the good and is defined as the difference between the willingness to pay and the price. Producer surplus is the net marginal benefit to the producer from a unit of the good and is defined as the difference between the price and the marginal cost of production of the unit. Market consumer and producer surpluses are aggregated across all units of output produced.

run average cost is at its lowest level. This implies that the firm reaches productive efficiency as it produces output with the least costs on a per unit basis in the long-run.

To better illustrate this process, we relax the constant returns to scale assumption used in Figure 8.3 and draw a long-run average cost function that exhibits increasing and decreasing returns to scale. It is important to note that economies of scale should be limited to low levels of output; otherwise, they may lead to consolidation and reduced competition. Figure 8.5 depicts the adjustment process with the firm initially starting at *Q1* where the firm is not minimizing its costs of production on a per unit basis. The firm explores ways to reduce its costs of production in the long-run by varying its capital stock. Given its *LRAC*, the most cost effective method is described by *ATC2*, which is tangent to the *LRAC* at the minimum of both functions. Ultimately all firms in the industry will get to this point and expand their level of output; as this happens, the price in the market will decrease to the level of the minimum on both the *ATC2* and the *LRAC*.

Although there are zero economic profits in the long-run, there is still the possibility of some perfectly competitive firms earning economic rents. An economic rent is a return on an input in excess of the normal rate of return. For instance, imagine that there is a farmer whose land is particularly productive due to its soil content, location, and so on. In this case, the farmer will earn a higher rate of return on this land; higher than what would the normal rate of return be for agricultural land of similar size.

THE COST STRUCTURE OF A COMPETITIVE INDUSTRY AND THE LONG-RUN

In our preceding discussion, we assumed that the firm's cost curves (*ATC* and *MC*) remained stationary while the industry expanded due to entry by other firms. However, form our discussion in Chapter 7, we know the long-run average cost function does not need to remain flat. Just as in our long-run cost discussion from Chapter 7, we have three possible cases: increasing cost, decreasing cost, and constant cost industry.

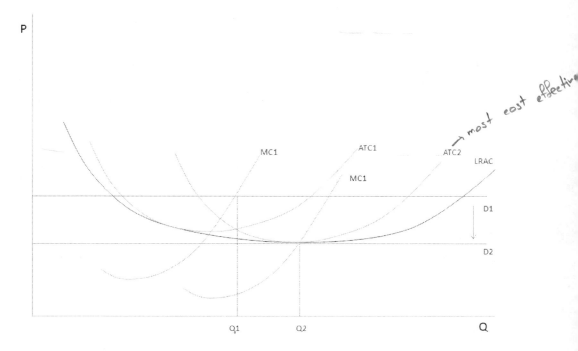

P

MC1   ATC1   ATC2   LRAC

→ most cost effective

MC1

D1

D2

Q1   Q2   Q

Figure 8.5

Increasing Cost Industry   An increasing cost industry is one where, as the industry expands, the cost of production on a per unit basis of output rises, causing the *ATC* and *MC* curves in the firm diagram of Figure 8.3 to shift upwards. One of the primary causes for an industry to experience increasing costs in the long run is a rise in the input prices. For instance, consider what would happen if the fast food industry were to rapidly expand in a given geographical area. One consequence would be a possible increase in the cost of commercial real estate zoned appropriately for the industry. Another consequence would be a rise in the wages of workers employed by the industry since firms would need to raise the wage rate in order to attract more workers. A rise in the cost of land or capital equipment would impact the fixed costs of the firm, causing the average total cost to shift upwards while keeping the position of the marginal cost the same. A rise in the wage rate would cause the variable costs to increase, resulting in an upward shift of both the average total cost and marginal cost curves in Figure 8.3.

Constant Cost Industry   A constant cost industry is one where a change in the industry supply does not impact the costs of production on a per unit basis in the long run. This is actually depicted in Figure 8.3 where we see no change in the firm's cost structure as the industry expands.

Decreasing Cost Industry   A decreasing cost industry is one where as the industry expands, then in the long run the cost of production on a per unit basis declines. One way this occurs is through a reduction in input prices. It can also occur because of increased productivity of inputs. One possible illustration of a decreasing cost industry resulting from declining input prices occurred in the software development industry. At the start of the 1990s, computer programmers were scarce and that was reflected in their relatively high salaries. During the 1990s and the early part of the XXI century, the educational sector responded to the high demand for computer programming skills with an expansion of IT programs. As a result, the relative salary of computer programmers actually decreased, helping reduce the cost of software development. In the U.S., the Bureau of Labor Statistics publishes the Occupational Employment Statistics survey which reports amongst other things the average salaries across occupations. The average salary for a computer programmer in 1997 was $50,490 (BLS, 1997). The average occupational salary (weighted by the number of occupations, not by the number of employees) in 1997 was $31,013 (BLS, 1997), resulting in a salary index of 1.63 ($50,490/$31,013) for computer programmers. A decade later, in 2007, the average salary of a computer programmer was $72,010, while the average occupational salary was $47,964 (BLS, 2007). Thus, the salary index for computer programmers in 2007 was 1.50, demonstrating a significant reduction in the relative salary of the occupation.

SUMMARY

In a perfectly competitive model, firms compete on the basis of price alone. As a result, this simple competition in price leads to a reduction in per unit production costs and achieves economic efficiency in production. In summary, the perfectly competitive model has several important implications:

- Zero economic profits in the long-run
- Marginal cost pricing
- Production with the least cost per unit basis in the long-run

- Marginal cost above the average variable cost serves as the short-run supply function of a firm
- Maximization of net benefit from the market

COMMODITY PRODUCERS AND PERFECT COMPETITION

Commodity producers, including giant multi-national mining companies, may very well resemble perfectly competitive firms. One industry that fits this description is the gold mining sector.

One of the most restrictive assumptions of the perfectly competitive model is that of a homogeneous good. However, this assumption is well met in most commodity markets. For instance, does it really matter if a bar of gold is manufactured by Gold Corporation or Newmont Mining Corporation? Gold is gold, regardless of what company puts its stamp on it. As a result, the assumption of product homogeneity is met. Interestingly, over the last couple of decades we saw some product differentiation even in commodity markets. One example of this can be found in organically grown agricultural commodities. Some agricultural producers differentiate their products by excluding certain chemicals or methods from their production process. This is a form of product differentiation that effectively splits the market and separates the output of these producers from that of the rest of the industry.

The assumption of a large number of firms is also met in most commodity markets, including the gold mining sector. Although it is appealing to think that gold mining companies are large, and as a result there are few of them, but that actually is not a fully adequate assessment as the number of firms is relatively large. According to 24hGold.com, as of March 1, 2013 there were 73 gold mining companies with a stock capitalization value of over one billion dollars (24hGold.com). That number increases to 229 firms when the stock market capitalization is set to be above $100 million (24hGold.com).

Commodity markets, including the market for gold, certainly exhibit perfect pricing information, meeting the requirement of the model. Gold as a commodity is traded on a number of various exchanges, and as a result its pricing information is available to all market participants.

Much like many other commodity-producing industries, gold mining requires a sizable initial investment, which seems to contradict the no barriers to entry and

145

exit assumption. Then again, well functional financial markets help reduce the effect of this barrier. Since the industry is global, firms in this industry and potential entrants can gain access to well-developed financial markets. Though, given the size of initial investment needed, this assumption is only weakly met.

Other commodity markets offer a closer resemblance of perfect competition at work. For instance, a better example is in agriculture where the number of individual farmers is large and barriers to entry and exit are considerably lower. Nevertheless, gold mining is selected as an illustration here for a slightly different purpose; gold mining is an illustration of an increasing cost industry. Between 2000 and 2012, the price of gold demonstrated a spectacular rise as it increased from about two hundred dollars per ounce to nearly seventeen hundred dollars. This rise in the price of gold caused gold mining companies to expand their production and seek out new mining properties, which in turn resulted in bidding wars and increased property values. Mining was also expanded to properties with lower grade ore, which further contributed to rising costs of production. Many of the mining companies as well faced higher labor costs. The resulting outcome was an increase in the cost of gold production.

References

24hGold.com, 2013. *List of gold producers*, available online at: http://www.24hgold.com/english/listcompanies.aspx?fundamental=datas&data=company&commodity=pl&commodityname=GOLD&sort=resources&iordre=7

U.S. Bureau of Labor Statistics, 1997, *1997 Occupational Employment and Wage Estimates*, available online at: http://www.bls.gov/oes/oes_dl.htm

U.S. Bureau of Labor Statistics, 2007, May *2007 Occupational Employment and Wage Estimates*, available online at: http://www.bls.gov/oes/oes_dl.htm

Chapter 9

INDUSTRIAL ORGANIZATION - MONOPOLY

The previous chapter focused on perfect competition, a world with a very large number of participants. At this point, we jump to the opposite extreme and visit the framework where there is only one single seller in the market.

A monopoly is defined as a single producer of a product or service for which there are no close substitutes, and thus a firm effectively faces the entire market demand. The above definition constitutes the only assumption of the model. A monopoly is a rather simple structure as there is no competition and therefore no interaction with other firms in the industry, but despite the lack of this interaction there is still some strategic interaction taking place between a monopoly and its consumers.

A perfectly competitive firm from Chapter 8 effectively had no choices and was completely guided by the market. The firm took the price as given and, depending on its state of production technology, adjusted its output level in response to the market price. The firm had no strategic decisions to make at all. A monopoly actually has a decision to make and that is how to interact with consumers. One way is to set the price, and have demand generate the equilibrium quantity. Another is to commit to a certain level of output, and then let demand come up with the market clearing price. In either case, a monopoly has a decision to make, and then the response is determined by the market demand. This implies that, for a monopoly, it is important to have an understanding of market demand and be able to predict consumer response. Before we discuss the outcome of the model it is important to understand why monopolies and market power exist.

BARRIERS TO ENTRY AS SHIELD FROM COMPETITION

Monopolies emerge due to barriers to entry. Barriers to entry enable the firm to earn positive economic profits over time and not be challenged by a potential competitor because a competitor is deterred by an entry barrier. In fact, this is true for not just monopolies but in general for firms with any market power. Barriers to entry can take a variety of different forms.

Legal Barriers. Pharmaceutical firms often enjoy marker power given to them legally through a patent that protects them from any other firm mimicking their product. This effectively creates a heterogeneous good, a product that is different from other products (this is a violation of one of the key assumptions of perfect competition – homogeneous product). Legal barriers can also take other forms such as licensing requirements, regulations, etc.

Corruption. Corruption can serve as a barrier to entry as well, as it can integrate the business sector with the government sector. As a result the integrated businesses will enjoy preferential treatment, while their competitors may receive a more adverse treatment.

Startup costs. Economies where the financial system is not well developed can have starting capital act as a serious barrier to entry since not many investors would be able to setup a business where a substantial initial investment is required. However, even in economies with a well-developed financial system a sizable investment may serve as a deterrent. For instance, UPS Corporation is a highly profitable enterprise, but to compete against UPS, a newcomer has to start with a large and well-developed network that would cover at a minimum the entire U.S. if not most of the world. Additionally, UPS parcel delivery service caters itself to its business clients. So, would a business client switch to a shipper who has a network in Georgia and Tennessee but not in Alabama and South Carolina? Or instead, would the business utilize a shipper who can deliver to any location in the U.S.? Generally, any business and especially any business engaged in business to consumer commerce would need to utilize a shipper with a fully developed national network. This implies that any potential competitor to UPS Corporation has to start with a fully developed or integrated network, which is a rather substantial startup requirement that serves as a barrier to entry. We should note that the cost of establishing such a costly and specific to the shipping industry network may also act as a barrier to exit. In the event, the new firm decides to exit, it would likely be forced to assume sizable losses on its capital investment. The highly specialized nature of its capital investment reduces the number of potential buyers.

Economies of scale. Economies of scale can also serve as a barrier to entry. In this case, the largest firm would simply enjoy a lower average cost of production in the long-run; therefore, it would be able to out-compete smaller firms and new entrants who start with a lower level of presence in the market and subsequently a higher average cost. An example of this is observed in the competition between Wal-Mart Corporation and smaller so called Mom and Pop stores.

Natural Monopoly. A natural monopoly is simply an extreme form of economies of scale. What makes it an extreme form is that the economies of scale are observed throughout the relevant range of the market demand (the market demand intercepts the *LRAC* of the firm, when the *LRAC* is decreasing). In this case, it naturally makes sense to have only one firm since the presence of another firm will simply cause the costs of production on a per unit basis to increase in the long-run. Natural monopolies usually occur when there are high fixed costs that are required to be dissipated over a large level of output. Historically, natural monopolies could be found in the utilities sector. For instance, it makes no sense to have two sets of pipes connected to each house so that homeowners would have a choice of which company would deliver the natural gas to their property. As a result, there is only one network of pipes and hence only one company delivering the natural gas.

Gas

It is interesting to note that due to technological progress what was a natural monopoly in the past may be losing that status with time. One example is the fixed-line telecommunication sector. Prior to wireless phones and wireless networks, fixed-line wiring was the only way to connect to a telecommunication network. But that changed in the last couple of decades, and now cell phone providers can serve as competitors to landline providers.

Phone line

Network Externalities. Network externalities increasingly become more widespread in part due to a rapid increase in online commerce. Network externalities occur when consumers benefit from a larger number of consumers purchasing a product or service. Network externalities can lead to monopolization because the consumer is better off purchasing a product from the firm with the greatest level of sales, thereby further increasing their level of sales. The externality is the external benefit to the consumer from the size of the network or consumer base. Note that the firm itself does not create a barrier but the consumer behavior causes one to emerge. A good example of network externalities comes outside of economics – language. Imagine you are interested in learning a new language for business purposes. Would the number of countries and individuals using the language enter into consideration? Would you consider learning a language that is used by one million people, or would you rather learn a language that is used by one hundred million people? When learning a foreign language you are joining a network, and the benefit of the network appears to increase with the number of users. Thus, as more users join the largest network, it becomes even larger and therefore increases the externality effect further. In this scenario the largest network continues to increase and eventually becomes the

language

only network. The same logic applies in economics, and the PC operating system software industry offers an example.

When one shops for PC application software, one is usually flooded with MS Windows based software, and yet there are other operating systems like Linux for instance. When entering the PC software section of an electronics store, we usually see just a tiny area dedicated to Linux based applications, while almost all of the remaining shelf space is dedicated to MS Windows based applications. This is an example of network externalities. A developer of PC application software has a choice of which operating system software to design their application for. Since the developer's objective is to increase their sales, they would design their software for the most commonly used operating system software. This would allow the developer to access the largest potential market. If we have three operating software platforms and one of these has the highest market share (let's assume that the first platform has 30% market share, the second has 30% market share, and the third has the remaining 40%), then the one with the highest market share (the third firm) is likely to grow its market share. Eventually, it would become if not a complete monopoly, then clearly a dominating firm in the industry.

A similar argument can be constructed for social network communities including websites like Facebook, Twitter, and so on. Some communication firms including AT&T have even introduced ways to encourage network formation. For instance, AT&T cell phone customers tend to enjoy free minutes when communicating with other AT&T cell phone users. Thus, as the network increases, the cost to the network consumers may decline.

Brand Loyalty. Brand loyalty can also serve as a barrier to entry and provide a firm with market power. If consumers tend to be loyal to a particular brand, then other firms would find it difficult to enter the market and attract consumers away from the established and recognized brand. Perhaps one recent example of this is the brand name of Apple Corporation. Apple Corporation was successful at establishing a positive brand image with consumers. Businesses that wish to compete against Apple have to be able to overcome this established brand image.

High Switch Costs. If consumers experience high costs associated with shifting their consumption from one firm to another, then that can give market power to the firm they currently purchase from and act as a barrier to entry for a potential competitor. Switch costs are present in many situations. However, not in all situations are these costs high enough to present a meaningful barrier. For

150

instance, as a college student you can transfer to a competing school; however, the further you are through your program the more costly this switch might be. The more credit hours you have, the greater might be the cost of switching to another school as you may lose some credit hours in the process and as a result would be required to spend extra time working on your degree. This effectively establishes a switching cost, but is this cost meaningful? To a current senior it is, but this is not the relevant market participant. Schools compete for new students and those students have no commitment yet, and therefore they face no switching costs.

switching college

Consider a different scenario. A small town has a couple of established apartment subdivisions. These subdivisions meet almost all of the market demand for rental housing in the area. Can another subdivision enter into this market and compete? The answer depends on whether there is a large turnover in renters at the existing subdivisions. In other words, do the same people tend to rent for a long time or is there significant mobility with new consumers continuously entering the market? If the answer is that the same people tend to rent over a prolonged period of time with limited turnover, then there are switching costs. In this case, the switching costs are in the form of moving costs that the renters would face if they were to move into the new subdivision. These costs can deter some people from moving and as a result provide the established subdivisions with an advantage over the newcomer.

Apartment rent

THE OUTCOME OF THE MONOPOLY MODEL

Figure 9.1 illustrates the case when there is only one firm, in which case the diagram of the firm and the diagram of the market are the same because the firm faces the entire market demand. Since the market demand is downward slopped, the marginal revenue function is positioned below the demand curve and has twice the slope (recall the earlier discussion on marginal revenue).

Profit maximization requires that marginal revenue equal marginal cost, which occurs at Q'. Since the price is determined by the market demand, P' is the price at which Q' is absorbed by the demand. The resulting economic profit equals to the difference between P' and $ATC(Q')$ multiplied by level of output (Q').

economic profit = $P' - ATC(Q') \times Q'$

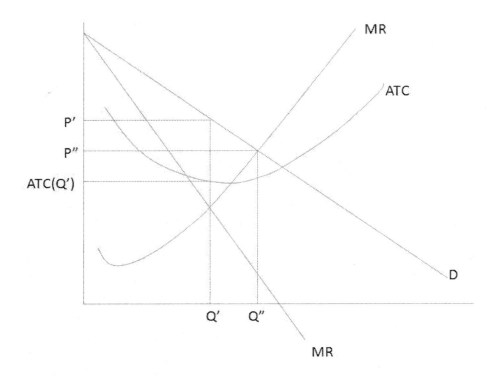

Figure 9.1

Note the differences between this case and that of perfect competition. The price still equals the average revenue, but it is no longer equal to the marginal revenue. As a result, we no longer have the marginal cost pricing, and the price exceeds the marginal cost at the profit maximizing level of output. Because there are barriers to entry, economic profits can be sustained in the long-run. Furthermore, there is no supply function. The firm determines the output level by setting the marginal cost equal to the marginal revenue, but the price is determined by a completely different function – the demand. Recall that in perfect competition, the demand (faced by a perfectly competitive firm) and the marginal revenue were the same function, and as a result it allowed the marginal cost to act as the supply function. We can even compare the outcome of perfect competition with that of a monopoly. A perfectly competitive industry would have the marginal cost act as the supply function which means that the perfectly competitive outcome in Figure 9.1 would be at Q''. The monopoly underproduces relative to the perfectly competitive outcome. This underproduction increases the scarcity of the product and therefore results in a higher market clearing price. Relative to

152

perfect competition, the monopoly restricts the output level, which causes the price to increase. This results in higher profits but also creates a deadweight loss to society. Figure 9.2 illustrates this impact of market power. Here, the area outlined by points *abc* represents the deadweight loss to society; it includes the unproduced units of output for which the marginal benefit, represented by the demand, exceeds the marginal cost.

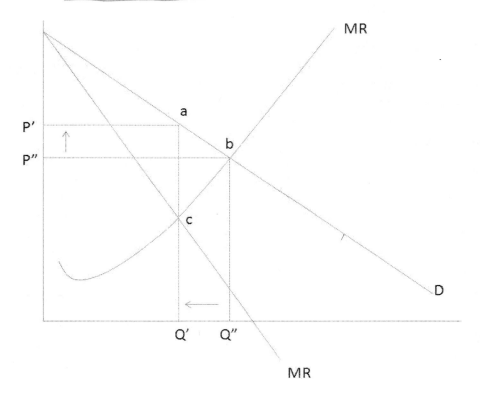

Figure 9.2

It is because of this negative effect on society that we have antitrust laws. It is interesting to point out that in the U.S., the antitrust laws predate most other economic regulations. For instance, the first major antitrust legislature in the U.S. was passed by Congress in 1890 (the Sherman Act). The Sherman Act consists of seven paragraphs (see U.S. Department of Justice, 2012). The first paragraph of the act makes trusts and other restraints of trade illegal, while the second paragraph makes monopolization illegal and classifies it as a felony (U.S. Department of Justice, 2012).

It is interesting to point out that the Sherman Act predates even such institutions as the Federal Reserve, which was established more than two decades later in 1913. This underscores the historical recognition of the implications of market power by the U.S. government.

PRICE DISCRIMINATION

Nowadays some people tend to confuse price discrimination with price differentiation, so we should first define these two practices. Price differentiation is a practice where different consumers or different consumer groups are being charged different prices because there are differences in the cost of the provision of goods or services. In other words, the price differences are being explained by the cost differences. There are numerous examples of price differentiation. For instance, male drivers tend to pay more for auto insurance than female drivers, and this is usually justified by a higher expected cost of insuring a male driver due to the differences in auto accident rates between the two groups. Another historical example would be the price difference of a life annuity for men and women. Historically, women were charged more for the same annuity (equal payout annuity) compared with men, and the explanation there seems to have been based on the expected differences between the average life expectancies of the two groups.

Price discrimination is slightly different because here different consumers or different consumer groups are being charged different prices for the same good or service, and there are no cost differences justifying the price differences. There are numerous examples of price discrimination. For instance, movie theaters offer discounts to students, and yet there is no cost differential for providing that seat to a student or a different consumer.

Sometimes it is complicated to determine if a case constitutes price discrimination or price differentiation. One example is the difference in airfares depending on how far in advance they are purchased. Technically, there is no cost difference for the company in terms of when that particular airfare is sold. The cost of delivering a passenger is the same whether they purchased their ticket one month in advance or one day in advance, and yet the price difference might be rather significant. So, one might be tempted to label this as price discrimination and perhaps one might be right, but there is another issue to consider. From the company's perspective, it is better to book as many tickets as early as possible. That way the company is more certain about the revenue from

154

the flight. Certainty may have value (if it did not, the insurance industry would be bankrupt).

Price discrimination comes in three main forms: first, second, and third degree. However, in all cases there are some essential conditions that have to be met. One, the firm must be able to split the market into individual consumers or consumer groups. Two, there has to be no ability by any consumers to resell the product to other consumers in the market. Three, the different consumer groups should have different valuations of the product or service, otherwise separating them makes no sense.

Third Degree Price Discrimination   Here, the firm splits consumers into groups based on some identifying characteristics like age, location and so on. For instance, senior discounts and student discounts offer examples of this type of price discrimination. Previously, we mentioned movie theater ticket discounts for students. Students generally have lower incomes and since going to the movies may constitute a normal service, the willingness to pay would be lower. However, other customer groups may have a higher level of willingness to pay as their incomes are higher. Movie theaters can increase attendance by offering a discount to consumers with a lower willingness to pay without reducing the price to the other consumer groups. This effectively allows the firm to split the market demand based on its willingness to pay and charge different groups prices that are closer to their corresponding willingness to pay levels. Of course any possibility of reselling the ticket would make this price discrimination impossible.

Second Degree Price Discrimination   Here, the firm offers volume discounts thereby differentiating between the various consumers based on their individual quantity demanded. This is widespread in wholesale and sometimes even present in retail sectors. This is also frequently present in the business-to-business commerce.

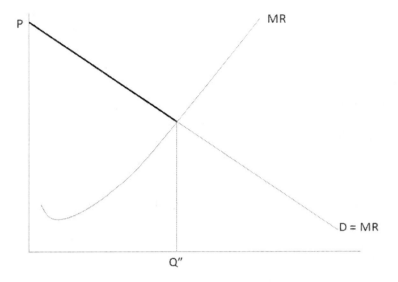

Figure 9.3

First Degree Price Discrimination   This can be the most profitable one of the three, but also the most difficult one to accomplish. Here the firm charges every individual consumer a different price that is equal to or near the consumer's willingness to pay (sometimes referred to as the reservation price). One example of attempting to achieve first degree price discrimination is a practice frequently used by auto dealers. Auto dealers often sell their cars through individual negotiations. In such settings, the customer typically negotiates on the price with a sales representative who then allows the manager to determine the sale's final price. In this case, two different buyers of the same make and model car at the same dealership may end up paying substantially different prices depending on their ability to negotiate in this setting. In such a scenario, the dealership effectively attempts to deduce something about the willingness to pay of each individual consumer and get the price as close as possible to that level. Ironically, if the dealership succeeds, then we reach the same quantity of output that we would under perfect competition.

All forms of price discrimination can result in a higher level of output sold relative to the single-price equilibrium. However, the first degree price discrimination scenario can lead us to the perfectly competitive outcome because in this case the demand once again becomes the marginal revenue curve. If every consumer pays their willingness to pay, then there is no need to change the price for other consumers when offering a discount to one particular consumer. Figure

9.3 illustrates this case. The highlighted part of the demand represents the part of the demand where each consumer is charged their own willingness to pay.

PROFITABILITY AND MONOPOLIES

Are monopolies sure investments as they can earn economic profits in the long-run? The answer is no. Monopolies can also experience economic losses and be forced to exit in the long-run. In figure 9.1 our firm is profitable, but we could have positioned the *ATC* at a higher level so that the *ATC* would exceed the price at *Q'*. In this case, our firm would be experiencing losses and would have to exit in the long run.

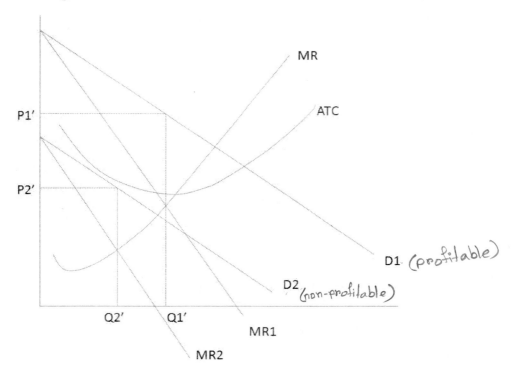

Figure 9.4

Figure 9.4 illustrates how a decline in the demand can make a profitable monopoly become a non-profitable one. Based on D1, the firm is profitable and would operate at *Q1'*. However, after the decline in demand to D2, the firm becomes unprofitable as its *ATC* never drops below the demand curve; thus, resulting in no output level where the price or the average revenue would exceed

157

the average total cost. There are many examples of such demand declines in monopoly markets.

The monopoly status may change over time as technological progress may erode the barriers to entry. For instance, for many decades the USPS had been unchallenged in the market for letter delivery. In fact, it still remains the leading player in the market, but the market is shrinking rapidly. With the evolution of the internet, an alternative emerged in the form of email. Recall that a monopoly is a producer of a product for which there are no close substitutes. For a long time, there was no close substitute to a letter delivered by the USPS, but this is no longer the case today.

Another historical example of technological progress and its impact on market power was experienced by Eastman Kodak Corporation. For many decades Eastman Kodak was the dominant player in the film industry and there was no substitute to film. However, the emergence of digital photography and video successfully challenged the market power of the firm.

MEASURING MARKET POWER – THE LERNER INDEX

The Lerner's index is an intuitive measure of market power that evaluates it relative to the perfectly competitive outcome. In perfect competition, the price equals marginal cost, so naturally one way to evaluate market power is to measure the firm's ability to deviate from the marginal cost pricing, which is what the Lerner Index accomplishes:

$$1) \quad L.I. = \frac{P - MC}{P}$$

Here, MC denotes marginal cost and P represents the price of the product. The index expresses the deviation as a fraction of the product price. For instance, if the firm charges \$20/unit, while the marginal cost of production is \$15, then the index would be 0.25. Note that for a perfectly competitive firm, the value of the index is zero as the price and the marginal cost equal each other.

SUBSTITUTABILITY AND MARKET POWER

Recall that a monopoly is a producer of a product for which there are no close substitutes. We can measure the degree of substitutability by computing the cross-price elasticities. Recall that a cross-price elasticity is a measure of responsiveness in the demand for one product to changes in the price of another product:

$$2) \quad \varepsilon_{X,Y} = \frac{\%\Delta Q_X^D}{\%\Delta P_Y}$$

If two products are substitutes, then the cross-price elasticity will have a positive sign. The demand for X will increase as the price of Y increases. For example, two passenger airline carriers that serve the same market can be viewed as substitutes for each other. As one of these carriers increases the price, the demand for the other carrier's services increases. The higher the value of the cross-price elasticity, the greater is the degree of substitutability between the products. For examples of advanced empirical studies into cross-price elasticities in markets with high degree of concentration see Robinson (2007) and Cigno et al (2013).

ADDITIONAL WAYS OF EVALUATING MARKET POWER

Concentration ratio   When an industry consists of more than one firm, but the number of firms is still low (Oligopoly), then concentration ratios can be used to evaluate market power. A concentration ratio examines the total percentage of the industry's sales generated by a number of the largest firms. Usually such ratios examine the percentage of sales generated by the largest four, five, or six firms.

Herfindahl-Hirschman Index   A more widely used measure of industry concentration is the Herfindahl-Hirschman Index, often abbreviated as *HHI*. The *HHI* is rather simple in construction, and it also allows us to account for the differences in the market shares:

$$3) \quad HHI = \sum_{i=1}^{N} S^2$$

Here, S is the market share of the firm. The *HHI* is simply the sum of squares of the market shares of all firms in the industry. Because each market share is

159

squared, the index increases rapidly as the market share of any firm increases. Table 9.1 presents some sample computations for the *HHI*.

Firm	Market Share (%)		
	Industry I	Industry II	Industry III
1	10	5	8
2	10	5	8
3	10	5	8
4	10	5	8
5	10	5	8
6	10	5	8
7	10	5	8
8	10	5	8
9	10	5	32
10	10	55	32
HHI	1000	3250	2560

Table 9.1

The level of the *HHI* increases as the industry becomes more concentrated. For a perfectly competitive industry where each firm is infinitely small compared to the market, the index would be at zero. In Table 9.1, the index is lowest when all ten firms are relatively small and highest when one firm is the dominant player in the industry. The *HHI* index is often used by the U.S. Department of Justice in horizontal merger cases. Generally, the U.S. Department of Justice appears to consider industries with an *HHI* less than 1500 as unconcentrated, and an *HHI* of 2500 and higher as highly concentrated (see U.S. Department of Justice and the Federal Trade Commission, 2010). A merger that results in a 100 point increase in the index appears to be considered as a minor change in the concentration (U.S. Department of Justice and the Federal Trade Commission, 2010). Thus, if in our industry I we had a merger of two firms, resulting in nine firms with one firm accounting for 20% of the market, and the remaining eight accounting for 10% each, then the *HHI* would be:

4) $HHI = 8 \times 10^2 + 20^2 = 1200$

As a result, our index increases by 200 points, which may raise questions regarding the level of market power.

References

Margaret M. Cigno, Elena S. Patel, and Edward S. Pearsalli (2013), *Estimates of U.S. Postal Price Elasticities of Demand Derived from a Random-Coefficients Discrete-Choice Normal Model.*" Published in "Reforming the Postal Sector in The Face of Electronic Competition" by Michael A. Crew and Paul R. Kleindorfer, Edward Elgar Publishing, MA, USA.

Robinson, A. (2007): "A Review of Price Elasticity Models for Postal Products," Pitney Bowes Background Paper 2007-01.

U.S. Department of Justice, 2012. Division Manual, Chapter II. Available online at: http://www.justice.gov/atr/public/divisionmanual/

U.S. Department of Justice and the Federal Trade Commission, 2010. Horizontal Merger Guidelines. Available online at: http://www.justice.gov/atr/public/guidelines/hmg-2010.html#5c

APPENDIX A

THE ALGEBRA OF THE MONOPOLY MODEL

A monopoly faces the entire market demand. Assume that the demand is governed by the following relationship:

1A) $Q = a - bP$

with the above formulation we assume $b > 0$. The marginal revenue that corresponds to this demand equation can be obtained using some basic calculus. Recall that marginal revenue is the slope or derivative of the total revenue function. Thus, first we need to obtain the revenue function. However, since we usually prefer to define functions like total revenue, marginal revenue, marginal cost, and profits in terms of quantity and not price, we need to obtain the inverse demand (the willingness to pay function) for the demand in 1A:

2A) $P = \dfrac{a}{b} - \dfrac{1}{b}Q$

From this we can obtain the total revenue function:

2A) $TR = P \times Q = \left(\dfrac{a}{b} - \dfrac{1}{b}Q \right)Q = \dfrac{a}{b}Q - \dfrac{1}{b}Q^2$

The derivative of the TR function with respect to Q will provide us with the marginal revenue:

3A) $MR = \dfrac{\partial TR}{\partial Q} = \dfrac{a}{b} - \dfrac{2}{b}Q$

Note that the marginal revenue has the same intercept as the inverse demand but twice the slope of the inverse demand. This observation holds true for all linear, downward-slopped demand functions.

If we estimate the marginal cost to be represented by the following equation:[17]

---

[17] The marginal cost depicted in equation 4A is a simple linear and rising function with respect to output. Its positive slope makes it consistent with the law of diminishing marginal product.

4A) $MC = c + dQ$,

then the profit maximizing level of output would be determined by finding the quantity at which the marginal cost and the marginal revenue are equal:

5A) $MC = MR \Rightarrow c + dQ = \dfrac{a}{b} - \dfrac{2}{b}Q \Rightarrow Q = \dfrac{\dfrac{a}{b} - c}{d + \dfrac{2}{b}}$

The price is simply determined by plugging the expression for Q into 2A.

Chapter 10

STRATEGIC INTERACTION

The two models we covered so far provided virtually no strategic interaction within an industry. Actions of a perfectly competitive firm produce no impact on the consumers or the other firms in an industry. A monopoly has no other firms in an industry with which to interact. At this point, we need to expand our discussion to those industries where strategic interdependence between firms exists.

OLIGOPOLY

In an oligopoly, a market is dominated by a limited number of firms. In fact, the meaning of the root "oli" is few. The number of firms has to be small enough in order for each firm to be able to influence the market outcome. Oligopolies are characterized by few firms with large market shares. Just as in the case of a monopoly, oligopolies need to be protected by sizable barriers to entry; otherwise, an oligopolistic industry may evolve into a perfectly competitive or a monopolistically competitive industry over time due to entry by other firms.

The requirement that there be only a few firms leads to mutual interdependence and potential strategic interaction between firms. Since each firm controls a sizable share of the market, actions by one firm have an impact on the market outcome and therefore on other firms in the industry. This mutual interdependence leads to strategic interaction. Since strategic interaction can assume different forms, an oligopoly does not have a single and concise model like the previous two cases. In our discussion, we will use different models to illustrate several important characteristics of oligopolies. Generally, firms may cooperate with each other or they can behave in a non-cooperative way.

Cooperation in oligopolies can also take a number of different forms. For one, firms can explicitly form a cartel, an organization where different producers coordinate their actions and attempt to mimic a monopoly outcome by maximizing the total profits to the cartel. Cartel formations are illegal in the U.S. under the Sherman Act, 15 U.S.C. § 1 which declares that it is a felony to restrain trade through any form of cooperation. However, outside of the U.S., we can still find cartels, with perhaps the most well-known being OPEC (the Organization of

cartel

the Petroleum Exporting Countries). A cartel restricts the level of output produced by its members in order to cause an increase in price and maximize the total profits for the cartel.

Cooperation between firms may also be a tacit one. A firm may just follow another firm's lead without any explicit agreement or arrangement. For example, one firm may announce its new pricing strategy for the year in January where it increases its prices by a certain percentage, while the other firm announces its pricing strategy in February and also announces a similar price increase.

However, oligopolistic industries do not need to be characterized by cooperation (explicit or implicit), and in fact uncooperative behavior is also common. As a result, economic theory includes models that allow for cooperation and models that don't. In fact, one of the oldest economic models of an oligopoly, the Cournot Duopoly model, allows us to contrast a cooperative outcome against a non-cooperative one. The model also enables us to examine the implications of the strategic interdependence between firms. For an example of a Cournot Duopoly computation see Appendix A.

The conclusions of the model are rather intuitive. In a non-cooperative setting, two firms respond to each other's actions. Each firm effectively subtracts the expected supply of the other firm from the market demand and treats the residual demand as available for its product. As a result of there being two firms, the output level increases relative to the monopoly level. Thus, a non-cooperative equilibrium represents an improvement over that of a monopoly.

The model can also be used to illustrate a cooperative setting. In a cooperative setting such as a two-firm cartel where the two firms work together and try to maximize their total profits, the model demonstrates that the output level decreases relative to the non-cooperative equilibrium. Appendix A also compares these two outcomes to that of perfect competition.

STRATEGIC INTERACTION AND THE USE OF GAMES

Oligopolies are characterized by strategic interaction. We saw an illustration of this in the Cournot model where each firm had its own best response function to the output decision by the other firm. Since the inception of the Cournot model, economic theory has evolved in its analysis of strategic behavior, and a new form of economic analysis, game theory, has emerged as a tool used in such a setting.

In fact, we can model the behavior of firms in a cartel using a simultaneous form game to illustrate the basics of game theory.

SIMULTANEOUS MOVE GAME: CARTEL

A simultaneous move game is one where the players commit to their strategies at the same time. If the number of players is limited to two, then such a game can be easily depicted by a matrix. Figure 10.1 illustrates an example of a two player, two strategy game in matrix form.

		Column Player	
		Strategy 1	Strategy 2
Row Player	Strategy 1	payoff to column player / payoff to row player	payoff to column player / payoff to row player
	Strategy 2	payoff to column player / payoff to row player	payoff to column player / payoff to row player

Figure 10.1

The matrix is simply a way to present the information on the payoffs from the cartel. Similarly, we could have presented the same information in tree form (see Figure 10.4 for an illustration of a tree form game), but the tree form is better suited for a sequential move game. Note that these are just ways of presenting information in a convenient and easy to interpret way. The matrix above has four cells, or four states of the world. The top left-hand cell is one where both players select Strategy 1. The bottom left-hand cell represents the state of the world where the column player selects strategy 1, while the row player selects strategy 2. The values inside each sell represent the payoffs or outcomes for each of the players. Usually, the top line in each cell represents the outcome for the column player, and the bottom line represents the outcome for the row player.

The game below provides a simple illustration of a cartel (see Figure 10.2). The game consists of two players (A and B), with each player having two available strategies or choices. The amounts in the cells represent the returns (profit) to the players. For instance, if player A restricts output while player B expands output, the return to player A is 25 while the return to player B is 75.

166

Player A

Restrict Output   Expand Output

	Restrict Output	Expand Output
Restrict Output	60 *profit maximise* 60	75 *cheater* 25
Expand Output	25 75	30 30

Player B

Figure 10.2

In a cartel, each member agrees to abide by the rules of the cartel. The cartel's objective is to maximize the total sum of the profits to all its members. To do so, the cartel needs to restrict the level of combined output to that of the monopoly level. Recall that a monopoly restricts the level of output in order to create scarcity and drive up the price. The same applies to a cartel as it is merely an attempt to organize several producers to act as one.

In Figure 10.2, the members of the cartel can follow the cartel's agreement and restrict output. If both members (player A and player B) restrict their output levels, the cartel will function as a monopoly and the return to the members as a group will be maximized. The total return to both members is 120, which is the highest compared to all other possible states of the world.

However, if one of the members of the cartel cheats on the agreement and expands output while the other remains loyal to the agreement, the return to the cheater substantially increases. This is because the non-cheating member restricts their output and therefore causes the output price to remain higher than it would be otherwise. This is depicted in the upper right hand and lower left hand cells. If player A expands the output while player B does not, then the return to player A increases to 75, the highest possible return in this game. However, player B suffers a decline in his return to a mere 25, the lowest in this game. Note that cheating by one of the players causes the combined return to decline to 100. If both players start cheating on the cartel agreement and expand output, the return to the group declines to 60 (30 to each).

What is the most likely outcome of this game if it were to be played only once? Let us construct the best response strategies for the players. A best response strategy is the best answer to a particular strategy of the other player. Since our game is perfectly symmetric (the outcomes for the two players are identical), we can examine just one player's behavior and then infer the other player's behavior.

Let us examine the game from player A's perspective. If player B were to restrict his output, what would be the most rewarding action for player A? If player A also were to restrict his output, he would get 60, but if he were to cheat and expand the output, he would receive 75. This means that expanding output is player A's best response to player B's restricting output. Now, if player B were to expand his output, what would be the most rewarding action on the part of player A? If player A were to restrict his output, he would get 25, but if he were to expand his output, he would receive 30. This makes expanding output the best response to player B's output expansion.

In this case, expanding output is always the best response no matter what player B does. A strategy that is always the best response is called a dominant strategy and is the most likely one to be selected.

Since the game is perfectly symmetric, player B also has output expansion as his dominant strategy. In this case, the most likely outcome of the game is that each player selects their dominant strategy which is to expand their output. In fact, if there is no possibility of future retaliation, then indeed cheating on a cartel becomes a dominant strategy. Ironically, this cheating results in the worst outcome for the cartel members as a group. Note that the combined return to the players is actually lowest in the dominant strategy equilibrium.

Our game provides a well-defined equilibrium outcome; nevertheless, it is important to understand the assumptions behind this game. The game is assumed to be played once, and thus there is no room for retaliation at a later time period.

SEQUENTIAL MOVE GAME: ENTRY DETERRENCE

An excellent illustration of a sequential move game is chess where two players take turns playing. However, chess is too complex in terms of the number of available strategies to the players to be a manageable illustration in this chapter.

A workable illustration of a sequential move game and also an important tool to demonstrate the concept of contestable markets is entry deterrence.

Consider a scenario where there is a single company operating in a particular market, but there is a possibility of another company entering this market. The game of entry deterrence primarily focuses on the behavior of the firm that is already in the market, and analyzes its best course of action by taking into consideration the possible behavior of the entering firm. This game is often constructed on the example of the U.S. passenger airline industry. Generally, the U.S. passenger airline industry is an excellent example of an oligopoly. In any given market (defined as a route between two destinations), the number of companies is usually low enough to allow for strategic interdependence.

An entry deterrence game consists of two players, one company that is already established in a given market and another player who considers entering the market. The established company has two available choices. One strategy is to simply act as a monopoly; after all, it is the only firm operating in the market. If the company decides to act as a monopoly, it will reduce the number of flights in this market and therefore create more scarcity, which would result in higher prices. As a monopoly, it would maximize its profits from this market. Alternatively, the company can overcommit to the market by offering more flights and therefore reduce prices. This will result in lower profits relative to the monopoly level of output commitment to the market but will make it more difficult for another company to enter into the market. Once the established firm makes its commitment to the market, the other firm will make its decision on whether to enter into the market or continue to stay out. Since each firm has two available strategies, there are four possible states of the world, or outcomes. As mentioned earlier, a sequential move game is usually illustrated using a tree form game (see Figure 10.3).

Here, company A is the one that is already in the market and company B is the potential entrant. The amounts listed in the outcomes represent the returns or profits from monthly operations in this market to the companies.

169

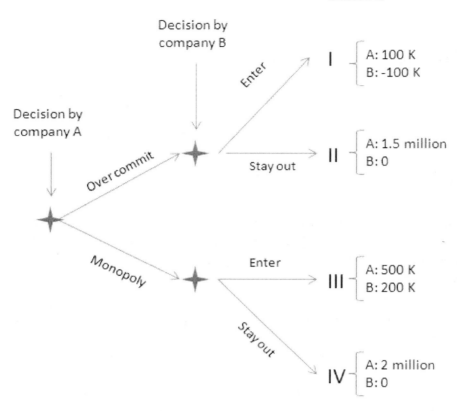

Figure 10.3

Clearly, from the perspective of company A, the best outcome is to act as a monopoly and have company B stay out. In this case, the profits to company A will be the highest at $2 million (outcome IV in Figure 10.3). The worst possible outcome for company A is to act as a monopoly but have company B enter into the market (outcome III in Figure 10.4). Note that if A acts as a monopoly and restricts the level of output in order to maximize its profits, then that leaves enough room for B to enter into the market and earn a profit ($200 K). Alternatively, if A overcommits to the market, then that leaves little room for B to enter, and if B does enter (outcome I), B will experience economic losses of $100 K. In this case, A will also suffer as the increased level of output, and the presence of the competitor results in a lower price and lower profits.

Which of the four outcomes of this strategic interaction has the highest probability of occurrence? Tree form games are usually solved backwards starting with the last decision making node and eliminating those choices that are not likely to be selected. Let's start with the state of the world where A overcommits. If A were to overcommit to this market what would B do? At this point, the game tree is reduced to only its upper branch (see Figure 10.4). In this setting, B has to choose between only two states of the world (I and II). Since outcome II produces zero profits while outcome I results in losses of $100K, outcome II is preferred and therefore is more likely to be selected. This allows us to eliminate outcome I from our decision tree as it is not likely to be chosen by the last decision maker.

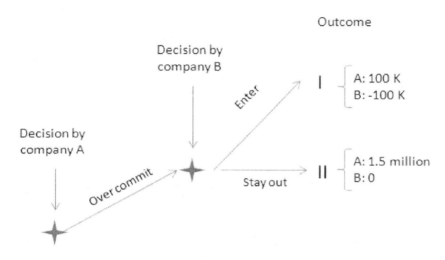

Figure 10.4

If we were to focus on the lower branch of the tree and restrict ourselves to the scenario where A selects to act as a monopoly (leaving us with only two possible outcomes: III and IV), then B would select outcome III and enter into this market. The reason B would enter is because it would be making $200K (outcome III), which is better than making nothing (outcome IV). This enables us to eliminate outcome IV as it would not be selected by the last decision maker. Now we are ready to analyze the decision of company A. Even though the game has four outcomes, only two of those are likely (II and III). So effectively, when company A decides on its strategy, it decides between these two outcomes. Since company A fares better under outcome II than under III, it is likely to overcommit to the market. Thus, the equilibrium outcome of this case is outcome II.

Although company A is a monopoly, it chooses not to act as one because it knows that acting as a monopoly will increase the odds of entry into the market by company B. Company A selects to overcommit in order to discourage the entry by B, hence the name of the scenario: entry deterrence. This is an illustration of contestability of markets. The fact that the market is contestable makes the monopoly produce a higher and therefore more competitive level of market output. If economies of scale or the level of startup capital is a barrier to entry, then a well-developed and fully functional capital markets become an important condition for contestability to work. This further underscores the importance of capital markets as they impact the level of competitiveness across virtually all markets.

One important premise of the entry deterrence game is that the threat of sustained overcommitment is real. Company A must be willing to remain committed to the higher level of output after the market entry by B even though reducing the commitment would lead to higher profits. It is this threat of sustained higher level of output that acts as the entry deterrent.

PRICE STABILITY AND KINKED DEMAND

Oligopolies are generally characterized by stable prices. Once again, the airline industry serves as an excellent example. Between 1999 and 2013, the price of jet fuel had experienced enormous volatility, and yet airfares had exhibited relative stability. In February of 1999, the spot price of U.S. Gulf Coast Kerosene-Type Jet Fuel touched $0.29 per gallon (U.S. Energy Information Administration, 2013). By the first week of October of 2005, the price reached $3.13 per gallon, just to fall to $1.657 in December of 2005 (U.S. Energy Information Administration, 2013). The volatility increased further during the financial crisis and the beginning of the monetary expansion in 2007 by the Federal Reserve System. On July 3rd of 2008 the price reached $4.207 per gallon, but pulled back to $1.111 on March 11th of 2009, and more recently the price has hovered around $3 per gallon (U.S. Energy Information Administration, 2013). Yet despite this volatility, airfares remained relatively stable.

The fact that prices tend to be relatively stable in oligopolistic industries may be a consequence of expected strategic responses on the part of each firm. The Kinked Demand model provides an explanation of this phenomenon where output prices remain stable even in the presence of volatility in variable costs.

Consider a market where several airline carriers operate, and let us examine the pricing decision of any one of these firms. Generally speaking, a firm has three options: to increase the price, to keep it constant, or to reduce it. However, the firm has to anticipate a likely response by its competitors.

What would the likely response be to a price increase? If any firm in the market were to increase its price, the other firms would not be expected to follow the price increase. And if they were to follow it, they would not match it but increase their prices by a smaller percentage. The logic here is simple: a firm that increases its price effectively surrenders its market share to the other firms. If the other firms don't match the price increase they will simply absorb some of the market share from the firm with the rising price. Thus, a price increase would cause the firm to rapidly lose its market share to the competitors because its output becomes more expensive relative to that of the competition.

What would be the likely response by the other firms to a price decrease? If one firm were to initiate a price decrease, it would effectively attempt to capture some of the market share of its competitors. The other firms would have to reduce their prices to keep their relative position in the market. This would reduce the ability of the initial firm to expand its sales through price decreases.

These responses on the part of the other firms create a kink in the demand faced by the instigating firm. When increasing its price the firm rapidly loses its market share, but when decreasing its price the firm's ability to increase its market share is restrained. This means that the demand faced by the firm when it increases its price is relatively more elastic than the demand it faces when it decreases its price. In fact, there are two different demands (see Figure 10.5). These two different demands are created by the differences in the responses of the other firms. Each of these two demands has its corresponding marginal revenue function. Recall that for a linear demand, the marginal revenue has the same P-axis intercept but twice the slope of the demand.

These two marginal revenue functions have a discontinuous range at the starting output level. Since profit maximization requires that the marginal cost be equal to the marginal revenue, any fluctuations of the marginal cost function within the discontinuous range of the marginal revenue result in no change in the profit maximizing quantity level. Therefore, the firm has no incentive to change its price as long as the marginal cost fluctuates within the discontinuous range of the marginal revenue.

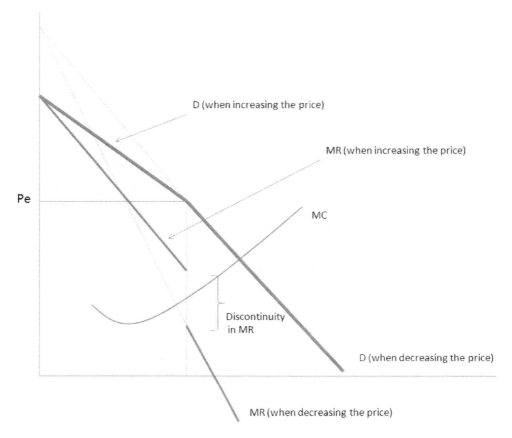

Figure 10.5

This observation is very different from perfectly competitive industries or monopolies. In each of those other cases, a change in the marginal cost resulted in a change in the output level of the firm.

PRICE DISCRIMINATION

Just as a monopoly, oligopolies can also practice price discrimination. Airlines present an illustration of a third-degree price discrimination. Airlines are capable of splitting the consumers into different groups based on their price sensitivity (elasticity) by making prices a function of how far in advance the airfare is purchased. The price tends to increase and become more volatile as time elapses. Consumers who decide to purchase their tickets in advance demonstrate that they are more flexible, and as a result their elasticity values are higher in absolute value than of those consumers who purchase their tickets just a few days before departure.

Thus, oligopolies exhibit a number of interesting characteristics. Oligopolistic industries tend to exhibit price stability and have the potential for sustaining economic profits in the long-run.

MONOPOLISTIC COMPETITION

Monopolistic competition is a model of competition between many tiny "monopolies." The emphasis, however, is on the word competition as the number of firms is rather large. The assumptions of the model are:

- Many firms
- Product differentiation
- Low barriers to entry/exit

The key characteristic of monopolistic competition is product differentiation. In monopolistic competition, each firm effectively has a monopoly status over its own brand, and as a result competition occurs not only in terms of price but also in terms of product characteristics. Many industries fit the criteria of monopolistic competition. Local restaurants are one example of businesses where each firm differentiates itself by the quality and type of food it serves, location, interior design, and so on. The apparel industry is another example of monopolistic competition.

The economics of the model are rather simple. Despite its small size relative to the market, each firm has some market power as its product is somewhat unique due to product heterogeneity. Presence of market power results in a downward slopped demand function (see Figure 10.6).

In the short-run, a monopolistically competitive firm can earn economic profits, but the long-run equilibrium is characterized by breaking even. Two factors cause the firm to lose the ability to sustain economic profits in the long run. One is the fact that economic profits attract imitation. Other firms will attempt to imitate the product characteristics that lead to economic profits. Successful imitation will result in a reduction of the demand for the output of the firm whose product is being imitated. For instance, if one restaurant is profitable because it located itself in a particularly busy area, then other restaurants will move into the same area, and this will result in a decline in the demand for the first restaurant over time.

Profits will also suffer from a cost increase in the long-run. If a firm is profitable, it will have to spend resources protecting those profits and in the process increase its average cost of production. Monopolistically competitive firms have to protect their market share and this means they have to continuously spend resources on advertising. Advertising helps deliver information to the consumers about the product. In a market with product differentiation, advertising is an essential tool. However, advertising increases the average cost of production.

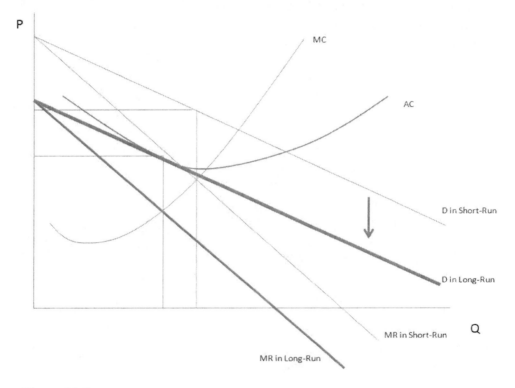

Figure 10.6

The battle for profits continues until those profits are driven to zero. Figure 10.6 illustrates a decrease in the demand for a profitable firm's output that occurs in the long-run due to mimicking of its product characteristics by other firms. For clarity, Figure 10.6 ignores the changes in the average cost of production that occur as the firm increases its spending on advertising. The effect of this would be an upward shift of the average cost.

The economic profits disappear when the average cost becomes just tangent to the demand function. At that level of output, the average cost and the average revenue (price) are the same. Profit maximization still occurs when the marginal revenue is equal to the marginal cost, but now that also coincides with the average cost being tangent to the demand curve.

$AC = AR$

$MR = MC$

$AC = D$

Since the demand curve is downward slopped, the tangency occurs when the average cost is also downward slopped, and this implies that the average cost of production is not minimized in the long-run (unlike in the case of a perfectly competitive firm).

References

U.S. Energy Information Administration, 2013. Petroleum & Other Liquids. Available online at http://www.eia.gov/petroleum/

APPENDIX A

COURNOT DUOPOLY

As the name suggests, the model includes two firms operating in an industry (although it can be expanded to any number of firms). For the purposes of our example, we need to assume a particular functional form for the market demand and make simplifying assumptions about the marginal costs of the two firms. For simplicity (this is not a requirement of the model), we will assume that the marginal cost functions are equal and constant. A constant marginal cost is a violation of the law of diminishing marginal product; however, it is not such a stretch of reality in some industries. For instance, software development may have a constant marginal cost if we define output as the number of units of software and not the size of its code. The marginal cost of an additional CD containing the software code is the same as that of the previous unit. This can be demonstrated algebraically. Let us assume that the marginal costs are:

1A) $\quad MC_1 = MC_2 = 10$

We also need to introduce the demand:

2A) $\quad Q = 1000 - 10P$

The inverse demand for the above function is:

3A) $\quad P = 100 - \dfrac{1}{10}Q$

The market output (Q) is met by the sum of the outputs of the two firms (q_1, q_2):

4A) $\quad P = 100 - \dfrac{1}{10}(q_1 + q_2)$

At this point we are ready to construct the revenue functions for each firm:

5A) $\quad TR_1 = P \times q_1 = [100 - \dfrac{1}{10}(q_1 + q_2)]q_1 = 100q_1 - \dfrac{1}{10}q_1^2 - \dfrac{1}{10}q_1q_2$

6A) $\quad TR_2 = P \times q_2 = [100 - \dfrac{1}{10}(q_1 + q_2)]q_2 = 100q_2 - \dfrac{1}{10}q_2^2 - \dfrac{1}{10}q_1q_2$

From the total revenue functions we can construct the marginal revenue functions:

7A) $\quad MR_1 = \dfrac{dTR_1}{dq_1} = 100 - \dfrac{2}{10}q_1 - \dfrac{1}{10}q_2$

8A) $MR_2 = \dfrac{dTR_2}{dq_2} = 100 - \dfrac{2}{10}q_2 - \dfrac{1}{10}q_1$

Each firm maximizes its profits by setting its marginal revenue to its marginal cost and obtaining the reaction (or best response) functions for each firm as a function of the other's output:

9A) $MR_1 = MC_1 \rightarrow 100 - \dfrac{2}{10}q_1 - \dfrac{1}{10}q_2 = 10 \rightarrow q_1 = 450 - \dfrac{1}{2}q_2$

10A) $MR_2 = MC_2 \rightarrow 100 - \dfrac{2}{10}q_2 - \dfrac{1}{10}q_1 = 10 \rightarrow q_2 = 450 - \dfrac{1}{2}q_1$

At this point, we have a system of two equations (9A and 10A) and two unknowns (q_1 and q_2). If we plug the expression for q_2 from 10A into 9A, we can solve for q_1. Economics-wise, we are solving for the most likely outcome, i.e. the equilibrium of the model:

11A) $q_1 = 450 - \dfrac{1}{2}\left(450 - \dfrac{1}{2}q_1\right) \rightarrow q_1 = 300$

This results in q_2 also being 300. The reason the two outputs are the same is because we simplified the model by assuming equal marginal costs (identical production processes). The assumption is not essential, and the only thing it accomplishes is that the output levels are equal.

Our equilibrium is characterized by the total output of 600 units being produced and sold at the price of 40 (just plug 600 into expression 3A). Then each firm's revenue is 12,000. If we assume that the average cost is the same as the marginal cost (effectively assuming that there are no fixed costs), then the profit for each firm is equal to 9,000. The industry as a whole earns 18,000.

Let us compare this equilibrium with two others, the perfectly competitive outcome and the monopoly outcome.

Monopoly (or Collaborative Equilibrium: Cartel)   What if our two firms were to get together and form a cartel? They would effectively act as a single firm and maximize their total profits. In this case, the total revenues to the cartel would be:

12A) $TR_{cartel} = P \times Q = \left(100 - \dfrac{1}{10}Q\right)Q = 100Q - \dfrac{1}{10}Q^2$

The corresponding marginal revenue would be:

13A) $MR_{cartel} = \dfrac{dTR_{cartel}}{dQ} = 100 - 0.2Q$

Given that the two marginal costs are the same and equal to a constant, then the marginal cost of the cartel is just that constant. If the two marginal costs were different, then we would have to horizontally sum them up to determine the cartel's marginal cost. Setting the marginal cost equal to the marginal revenue gives us the equilibrium level of output for the cartel:

14A) $MR_{cartel} = MC_{cartel} \rightarrow 100 - 0.2Q = 10 \rightarrow Q = 450$

The cartel outcome (or the monopoly outcome) results in the level of production of 450 units and the sales price of 55 for the total revenue to the cartel of 24,750. If we continue to assume that there are no fixed costs, then the profits of the cartel are 20,250. This represents a 2,250 increase in the industry profits relative to the non-cooperative outcome.

Perfect Competition (for comparison purposes)

Under perfect competition the price would equal marginal cost:

15A) $Q = 1000 - 10P = 1000 - 10MC = 1000 - 10 \times 10 = 900$

CONCLUSION

The uncooperative outcome results in a higher level of output and lower industry profits compared to the cooperative outcome of a cartel. However, even the uncooperative outcome falls short of the competitive outcome of perfect competition.

Chapter 11

SPECIAL CASE: THE ECONOMICS OF EBAY

eBay is a relatively young firm that was started by Pierre Omidyar on Labor Day in 1995. In the span of just a few years, eBay not only became one of the most recognizable brands in the world, but its name practically became synonymous with online auctions. In the first quarter of 2013, eBay reported that the volume of merchandise traded on its websites across the world (excluding the motor vehicles) exceeded 18.3 billion dollars, of which 40.2% was attributed to the U.S. market (eBay 2013). The eBay success story is made particularly interesting by the fact that the company faced several serious challenges and yet was able to meet them with simple but creative solutions.

eBay is merely a platform for its users to engage in online consumer-to-consumer commerce. It sells its services to those users who wish to sell on the eBay website. Thus, eBay can be defined as a market mechanism that facilitates the exchange between buyers and sellers. Although some eBay sellers are large and established businesses including large national retailers like BestBuy Outlet Store (see Alm and Melnik, 2010), the majority of eBay sellers tend to be small businesses and even "occasional" sellers. For these individuals, eBay offers a convenient, nearly planet-wide "flea" market.

Today, eBay is a fully developed and integrated online business that allows its users to buy, sell, and make payments from the comfort of their own home. The PayPal payment platform allows any eBay seller, no matter how small their business, to accept credit card payments. Under certain restrictions, eBay provides its own buyer protection that covers the buyer in the event of a misspecification or no delivery (see eBay Buyer Protection policy explanation at: http://ebay.com/coverage). Other payment mechanisms, such as credit cards, offer their own warrantees to their clients. All of these mechanisms are designed to reduce the risk in an online transaction and to make it easier experience for consumers. Therefore, these provisions are aimed at encouraging consumers to participate in online commerce. Given the trend of the data it seems to be working. In 1998, online retail commerce constituted a mere 0.19% (just under 5 billion dollars) of the overall retail commerce in the U.S. (U.S. Census, 2013). In

2011, this number reached 4.69% or almost 194 billion dollars (U.S. Census, 2013).

However, during the first couple of years of its existence, when eBay was becoming a success story, PayPal was probably an idea and buyer protection in consumer-to-consumer online commerce was something to be desired.[18] When making a payment for an eBay transaction a buyer was typically first asked to mail in their payment in the form of a money order or a personal check. Only after the clearing of the payment would the seller proceed with shipping the purchased item to the buyer. In such a setting, the buyer had to trust the seller, and hope that the seller would comply with the terms of the transaction and indeed ship the purchased item. In the absence of buyer protection, this was indeed the nature of online consumer-to-consumer commerce. This does not present a challenge for a reputable retail chain like Walmart or BestBuy. However, when dealing with a private individual on an online website and being asked to first submit the payment, the problem of trust naturally arises. Economists refer to this issue of trust as the asymmetry of information problem (see Akerlof, 1970). The asymmetry of information problem threatened to not only make things difficult for eBay but outright destroy the entire business model, and yet not only did eBay survive but managed to turn this serious weakness of its business model into a powerful strength against its competitors.

eBay also masterfully applied another important lesson of economics, one that states that economics is all about incentives. Just as eBay was starting to develop its brand recognition, a powerful competitor at the time decided to enter the online consumer-to-consumer auction market and a competitive battle between eBay and Yahoo began. The battle spanned for several years but eBay emerged victorious.

The discussion below examines these two issues: the use of incentives in the competition with Yahoo and the solution to the asymmetry of information problem.

ASYMMETRY OF INFORMATION

In online consumer-to-consumer commerce the problem of asymmetry of information potentially can be rather severe, and eBay is not immune to it. This

---

[18] PayPal was founded in June of 1998.

issue was particularly important early on in the history of eBay when buyer protection simply did not exist. Yet, the problem of asymmetry of information did not derail eBay's growth.

eBay's solution to the problem was the eBay rating. Through the rating, eBay allows its members to rate their experience with other members on their website. The mechanism has two important characteristics. One, it is very simple and therefore easy to interpret. Two, it is transaction based and limited to unique users, thus reducing the potential for a bias.

After completing a transaction the participants have an opportunity to rate each other. Note that this opportunity is available only after completing a transaction. Even more important is the condition that no matter how many transactions two users have between themselves, the contribution to the rating is limited to only one. For example, any two eBay users may have ten transactions between themselves and leave ten positive comments about each other. Although all ten comments will be visible, the rating of each user will increase by only one point. This makes it impossible for two user IDs to conduct multiple transactions between themselves and build up their ratings.

Perhaps the key advantage of the rating mechanism is its simplicity. Originally, the rating system allowed the users to leave a brief comment and select between just three options for the rating purpose: positive, negative, and neutral. The system evolved over time, and currently it allows the rating to be more specific in terms of the various characteristics of the transaction. For instance, today buyers may be given an option to rate the speediness of the shipment, the accuracy of the description, the quality of communications, and so on. Despite these changes, the rating value itself remains simply the difference between the number of positive and negative responses.

Obviously, the rating mechanism is much more important in the case of sellers rather than buyers since the asymmetry of information problem favors sellers in this case. For the most part the buyer's rating is not important as sellers ship their products upon clearing the payment. On the other hand, the seller's rating is an important mechanism aimed at conveying the reliability of the seller to the perspective buyer. Several econometric studies have examined the effects of the seller's eBay rating on the realized auction price and the probability of sale (see Dellarocas and Resnick, 2003; Reiley et al, 2007; Melnik and Alm, 2002). The findings of these were supported by controlled experiments (see Resnick et al, 2006; Katkar and Reiley, 2006). These studies demonstrated that the difference between an established rating and a low rating could account for as much as several percent of the item's price. Furthermore, this difference rose with the item's value (see Melnik and Alm, 2005). This meant that the seller's eBay rating was perceived by buyers on eBay as a valuable mechanism of representing the reliability of the seller on eBay.

This simple rating mechanism enabled eBay to solve a potentially serious problem of asymmetry of information. Interestingly, the rating mechanism had a side effect of making it costly for established sellers to switch from eBay to an alternative consumer-to-consumer platform. Since rating comments posted on eBay belonged to eBay, an individual user would not be able to move their rating to another website (a point that was discovered later when Yahoo entered the online auction market in the U.S.). This meant that an established seller would have to start from scratch should they decide to leave eBay for a competing platform, and the seller would forgo the price benefit generated by their established rating. Thus, the rating mechanism created a barrier to entry for a potential competitor and therefore established a degree of market power for eBay. eBay managed to turn a weakness into a strength with a simple and intuitive mechanism – the eBay rating.

YAHOO COMPETITION

On September 14 of 1998, just after eBay had celebrated its third anniversary, Yahoo launched its own competitor to eBay, Yahoo Auctions. At the time, Yahoo had already been established as a well-known search engine. This entry by a popular search engine into the online auction business was potentially a serious threat to eBay. However, Yahoo Auctions ultimately failed in the U.S. market, and in the summer of 2007 Yahoo closed its U.S. Yahoo Auctions website.

The reason for Yahoo's failure and eBay's success in the auction business includes, but is not limited to the barrier to entry role of rating mechanism, but they don't stop there. Another key reason is the difference in the emphasis of the two business models. eBay focused on making its website appealing to buyers, while Yahoo focused on attracting sellers. This difference in approaches proved to be disastrous for Yahoo Auctions in the U.S. It is true that eBay's consumer is not a buyer on eBay, but a seller. It is that seller who pays the fees for the use of the eBay website. But it is important to understand that the only reason the seller comes to eBay in the first place is because the seller expects the transaction to end in a sale. Without a buyer there can be no sale, and as a result there is no incentive for a seller to list on a website where little buying activity takes place.

eBay recognized the importance of luring potential buyers to its site and created a fee system that encouraged sellers to lower the starting (or asking) prices of their eBay auctions (later this applied to fixed price listings as well). The eBay fee structure consists of three categories of fees: closing fees, insertion fees, and promotional fees. Promotional fees are applied if special promotional services are used. For instance, a seller can select to have their listing title in bold, add another line of information below the title, and so on. Closing fees are fees applied at the completion time of a listing and are subject to the output of the listing. Closing fees tend to be a function of the closing price and are charged only in the event the listing results in a sale, otherwise these are not charged. However, the most interesting category of the fees is what eBay refers to as the insertion fee. The insertion fee is a rising function of the opening price of the item and is charged no matter what the outcome of the auction is. Table 11.1 shows the insertion fee structure used throughout 2001, during the height of the competition with Yahoo.

Opening Price Range	Insertion Fee
0.01 - 9.99	0.30
10.00 - 24.99	0.55
25.00 - 49.99	1.10
50.00 - 199.99	2.20
200.00 and higher	3.30

Table 11.1

The seller selects the opening price for their listing and is charged an insertion fee based on the opening price no matter the outcome of the listing. Because this fee increases with the opening price, it creates an incentive to lower the opening price. Note that as the opening price increases, the risk of the listing resulting in no sale also increases. If the listing results in no sale, then the seller simply incurs the cost of the insertion fee and no benefit (for more on the impact of a rising listing fee structure see Melnik et al, 2009).

Yahoo's approach was rather different. Yahoo made listing on its website completely free. As a result, the number of listing on the Yahoo site increased rather quickly. Just within the first year, the average number of available listing on Yahoo Auctions increased from 20,000 to 725,000. However, the opening prices on Yahoo website were also significantly higher than those on eBay. This discouraged buyer participation and lead to a much lower sales rate.

Yahoo started to introduce insertion based fees only in November of 1999. Even then, the fee was applied to optional promotional tools. In January of 2001, some two end a half years after establishing the auction business, Yahoo introduced an opening price based insertion fee. However, the fee was a small fraction of the eBay structure and ranged between $0.2 to $2.25 per auction with many sellers receiving various free listing credits and paying only $0.05. In 2001, this policy was too little too late. In June of 2005, Yahoo made its auctions free once again and in the summer of 2007 Yahoo abandoned the U.S. auction market for good. For more on the role of insertion fees in the Yahoo/eBay competition, see Melnik (2011).

The insertion fee structure not only created a stream of revenue for eBay, but much more importantly it created an incentive mechanism aimed at encouraging sellers to list their items with lower starting prices. This made the website more attractive to buyers and resulted in more transactions, which in turn attracted more sellers. Effectively, eBay applied a very important principle that without a buyer there is no sale even though eBay buyers are not the customers of eBay as they directly pay no eBay fees.

The insertion fee continues to play its role as an incentives mechanism, although more recently eBay started to deviate from its use in this manner. Such deviations, along with the potential for development of online mechanisms rivaling PayPal may create an opportunity for successful competition against eBay. It is also interesting to point out that online payment mechanisms such as PayPal, and buyer protection in online commerce minimize the role the seller's rating plays, thereby reducing the barrier to entry it produces. eBay may have recognized this early on and took steps in both of these directions. In 2002, eBay purchased one of the leading firms in processing of online consumer-to-consumer payments, PayPal. And eBay also introduced its own buyer protection program.

eBay represents an excellent business case study as the firm has made a number of very creative decisions that helped shape the online consumer-to-consumer commerce at the turn of the century.

References

eBay Inc., 2013. *eBay Inc. Reports Strong First Quarter 2013 Results*, available online at: http://investor.ebayinc.com/financial_releases.cfm

Alm, J. and M. I. Melnik, 2010. "Do eBay sellers comply with state sales taxes?" National Tax Journal, 63 (2), 215–236.

Akerlof, G. A. (1970). "The Market for "Lemons": Quality Uncertainty and the Market Mechanism." The Quarterly Journal of Economics 84 (3): 488-500.

Dellarocas, C., and P. Resnick. 2003. Online reputation mechanisms: A roadmap for future research. Summary Report of the First Interdisciplinary Symposium on Online Reputation Mechanisms. http://www2.sims.berkeley.edu/research/conferences/p2pecon/papers/s8-dellarocas.pdf

Katkar, R., and D. Reiley. 2006. "Public versus secret reserve prices in eBay auctions: Results from a Poke´mon field experiment." Advances in Economic Analysis & Policy 6 (2): Article 7.

Melnik, M. 2011. "Listing fees and their role on eBay: evidence from a natural experiment." Journal of Internet Commerce Volume 10, Issue 4, pp 270 – 290.

Melnik, M., and J. Alm. 2002. "Does a seller's ecommerce reputation matter? Evidence from eBay auctions." Journal of Industrial Economics L (3): 337–349.

Melnik, M., and J. Alm. 2005. "Seller reputation, information signals, and prices for heterogeneous coins on eBay." Southern Economic Journal 72 (2): 305–327.

Melnik, M., J. Alm, and Y. Xu. 2009. "The choice of opening prices on eBay." The Manchester School 77 (4): 411-429.

Reiley, D., D. Bryan, N. Prasad, and D. Reeves. 2007. "Pennies from eBay: The determinants of price in online auctions." Journal of Industrial Economics 55 655 (2): 223–233.

Resnick, P., R. Zeckhauser, J. Swanson, and K. Lockwood. 2006. "The value of reputation on eBay: A controlled experiment." Experimental Economics 9 (2): 79–101.

U.S. Census (Department of), 2013. *E-Stats*. Available online at: http://www.census.gov/econ/estats/2011reportfinal.pdf

Chapter 12

EVALUATING ECONOMIC ACTIVITY

"Supply Creates Its Own Demand"

Say (1803)

OUTPUT, EMPLOYMENT, PRICE STABILITY

In the most recent downturn of the U.S. business cycle, the aggregate output as measured by GDP contracted for five out of six quarters between the first quarter of 2008 and the second quarter of 2009. During this period, the U.S. Central Bank (the Federal Reserve) and the U.S. Federal government focused on economic expansion. Their primary issue of concern was the contraction in the level of aggregate output as measured by GDP. The Federal Reserve reduced the interest rate (the federal funds rate) from 4.25%, where it stood at the end of 2007, to between 0 and 0.25% where it ended 2008.

In the third quarter of 2009, the U.S. GDP returned to positive growth and yet the accommodating monetary and fiscal expansionary policies continued. Although the U.S. economy has been continuously expanding since the third quarter of 2009 (at the time of writing this discussion, the data were available to 2012:QIV), both the balance sheet of the Federal Reserve and the national debt of the U.S. Federal government continued to expand, indicating an expansionary nature of the monetary and fiscal policies. The GDP recovery that began in 2009:QIII was not accompanied by a meaningful recovery in the level of employment. As a result, the focus of the policy makers shifted to the labor market (Bloomberg News, 2012). The Fed (Federal Reserve) formalized this view when Chairman Dr. Ben Bernanke tied the monetary policy to the unemployment rate in late 2012 (The New York Times, 2012).

In the second half of 2012 and into 2013, the Fed made numerous references to inflation being under control to justify an ongoing monetary expansion. Historically, though, there were periods when the Fed was willing to raise interest rates to combat inflation. Perhaps the most well-known example of this was the stance the Fed took under the leadership of Paul Volcker between 1979 and 1981. In more recent history, we can also find two cases of contractionary monetary policy which occurred in the 1999-2000 and 2004-2006 periods.

The above discussion illustrates that there are at least three important criteria for evaluating the health of an economy: output, employment, and price stability. Most often, the general order of importance is the one in which they are listed here. Perhaps output is the most important of these three as it represents the size of the overall economic pie that we all share. Traditionally, recessions in economics represent contractions in real output. Some economists would define a recession as negative growth in output as measured by real GDP (Gross Domestic Product) when it exceeds a period of two or more consecutive quarters (see Slavin, 2014). However, this is not the definition used by the NBER (National Bureau of Economic Research) in its evaluation of the health of the U.S. economy. The NBER considers not only the U.S. real GDP but also a number of other criteria including the labor market and income changes (NBER, 2013a). The NBER also allows for brief periods of expansion within a recession (NBER, 2013a). For instance, the NBER determined that the last recession spanned between December of 2007 and June of 2009 even though the U.S. economy posted positive output growth in the second quarter of 2008 (NBER, 2013b).

The discussion below focuses on measuring the three important criteria of economic performance.

OUTPUT

As mentioned earlier, output may very well be the most important single measure of economic activity. Output measures the level of production activity and production creates economic wealth. Since output represents production, the value of output generates the incomes to the factors of production. In a way, the value of the aggregate output serves as the "income" to the economy. We must first recognize that output (and income) is a flow variable as it takes time to produce. In the U.S., most output measures including GDP are reported quarterly but at annualized rates.[19]

---

[19] For instance, when the Bureau of Economic Analysis reports that the US real GDP grew at 4% during a given quarter, the real GDP did not increase by 4% during that quarter but rather increased by about 1%, which constitutes the reported 4% annual rate.

Circular Flow Figure 12.1 presents a simple look at the circular flow concept in an economy. In this simple view, we have two sectors (households and businesses) and two markets (output and input). These two sectors interact with each other through these two markets. Households supply businesses with factors of production (labor, capital, land…) and in return receive payments for supplied factors of production (wages, profits, rents…). Businesses then combine these factors (inputs) in a production process and produce output that is then sold to households in the output market. In return, households pay market value for output to businesses. There are several important observations coming from this simple model.

The value of output sold to the household sector is exactly equal to payments made to it by the business sector and these payments represent the income to factors of production supplied by the household sector. This in itself has two implications. The first is that the sum of income payments generated from production is equal to the value of output. This chapter started with a quote from Say, "Supply creates its own demand." In economics, this quote is referred to as Say's Law. It is difficult to envision this law in the context of every single market, but for the economy as a whole it seems to fit well.[20] The value of output produced (supply) is equal to the value of payments or income it generates, which in turn finances demand.

The second implication is that there are two ways to evaluate the level of economic activity: summing up consumption, investment, government, imports, and export expenditures or adding up the earnings of all factors of production. In practice this leads to two ways of measuring the level of economic activity: the expenditure approach and income approach.

Another implication of the circular flow diagram is that businesses are simply a way to combine the inputs in a production process. An often overlooked fact is that businesses are owned by households. Businesses employ individuals, are owned by individuals, and produce their output for individuals. The reason this is an important observation is because we often think of business taxation separately from taxation of individuals and yet economically they are not. Since only people pay taxes, if a tax is imposed on a business, it is shared between the business owners, its workers, and consumers of its product. The economic incidence of business taxation is on households.

---

[20] Say indeed argued at the level of the individual producer. He argued that individuals produce output in order to generate the means to pay for their consumption, and the two are exactly equal as there is no incentive to store monetary wealth over time.

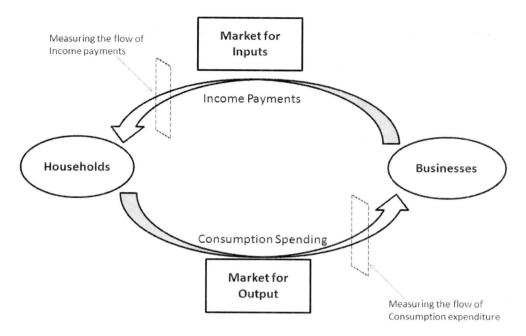

Figure 12.1: Circular Flow Diagram.

Since we have already mentioned the term GDP a few times in our discussion, it is important that we understand what it is and what it actually measures.

Gross Domestic Product represents the sum of the market value of all final goods and services produced within the boundaries of a country during a given period of time, usually defined as one year.

This definition effectively computes the total sum of the value added of all production located within the boundaries of the country. The definition of GDP includes several important points. First, it is important to understand that GDP tracks production, as it is production that best represents economic activity. Production serves as a process of wealth creation. Second, the value of output is measured using market prices. Market prices represent the true valuation of output. However, not everything that is produced has a market value. For instance, what is the market value of government services such as law enforcement? In such instances, the evaluation is done using the cost of production method. Generally, this is not an issue as public sector purchases of goods and services are done at their market values (law enforcement personnel are paid wages that reflect market values), but if there is a difference in government payments and market value, then an issue might arise.

Third, only prices of final goods and services are used in the computation of GDP as the value of intermediate products is included in the value of final goods. For instance, the price of your textbook includes the value of the paper it is printed on. Note that the same product may be intermediate in one setting and final in another. For instance, when you purchase a new set of tires, being a consumer, you make those tires a final good. On the other hand, if those tires are purchased by a car manufacturer just to be put on their newly manufactured cars, the tires become an intermediate good.

However, one of the most interesting aspects of the GDP definition has to do with the fact that it is a measure of output produced domestically. The relevant question here is, what is an economy? Is it comprised of the people who live in that country, or is it simply restricted by the country's geographical boundaries?

We have two measures of output that address this issue: GDP, which focuses on the production that takes place within the borders of a country, and GNP (Gross National Product), which captures the production produced by the factors of production owned by the residents of a country.[21] Consider a simple scenario where a Japanese auto manufacturer has an assembly plant in the U.S. Assume that the retail price of a car assembled by the plant is $19,000, and the car is sold to a consumer in the U.S. Also assume that the car includes $3,000 worth of Canadian made parts, $10,000 of U.S. made parts, $4,000 worth of U.S. labor, and the remaining $2,000 is the return on the capital stock (the facility is owned by a holding company located in Japan). The return on the capital is credited to the holding company in Japan. This scenario is summarized in Table 12.1.

The U.S. GDP consists of the value added to the car in the U.S. (geographically). Since the Japanese assembly factory is located in the U.S., the contribution to the value added by the Japanese owned capital stock is actually included in the U.S. GDP. Note that the combined GDP across all three countries is equal to the price of the car. The car is a final good as it is sold to a consumer. In the GDP computation, the U.S. GDP will include $19,000 in the Consumption (durable goods) account and -$3,000 in the Imports account (imported from Canada parts). Thus, the total contribution of the car to the U.S. GDP will be $16,000 ($19,000 - $3,000). Canada will record $3,000 in the Exports account of its GDP, and Japan will record nothing in its GDP, as none of the production took place within the borders of Japan.

---

[21] GNP is defined as the sum of the market value of all final goods and services produced by the factors of production owned by the residents of a country during a given period of time.

	per car	GDP			GNP		
		Canada	Japan	USA	Canada	Japan	USA
Price	19000	3000	0	16000	3000	2000	14000
US Parts	10000						
US Labor	4000						
Canadian Parts and Labor	3000						
Return on Japanese Capital	2000						

Table 12.1

The GNP computation will differ for the U.S. and Japan. The U.S. GNP will still include $19,000 in the Consumption account and -$3,000 in the Imports account, but it will also have a debit of $2,000 in the Income Payments to The Rest of the World account, resulting in the net contribution of $14,000. The GNP of Japan will include the $2,000 payment coming from its production that took place in the U.S (Income Payments from The Rest of the World).

From this, we can conclude that if a country has been a net recipient of foreign investment in the past, it is more likely to have its GDP exceed its GNP, and vice versa for an economy that has been a net lender internationally. *[handwritten: GDP>GNP]* *[handwritten: → GDP<GNP]*

Conversion from GDP to GNP is an essential step in computing National Income (NI). As stated earlier, GDP is an "income" to a country (geographically defined); however, if we were to focus on the population of a country, we would need to examine the income earned by the factors of production owned by its population. Table 12.2 presents a basic look at the relationship between the U.S. GDP, GNP, and NI (the source of the data is the U.S. Bureau of Economic Analysis).

	2012
Gross domestic product	15684.8
Plus: Income receipts from the rest of the world	782.3
Less: Income payments to the rest of the world	539.3
Equals: Gross national product	15927.8
Less: Consumption of fixed capital	2011.7
Equals: Net national product	13916.1
Less: Statistical discrepancy	67.2
Equals: National income	13848.8

Table 12.2 All values are in billions of U.S. dollars (Source: BEA, March 2013).

Note that the difference between GDP and GNP is net income receipts from the rest of the world. Examples of these income receipts include: profits, dividends, interest payments, salaries, and so on. For instance, if a U.S. corporation receives income from its foreign subsidiaries, then this income will be included in the income receipts from the rest of the world. Dividend payments made by a U.S. firm to a resident of Canada will be included in the income payments to the rest of the world.

Note that GNP is not equal to National Income because the BEA subtracts consumption (depreciation) of fixed capital from GNP to compute National Income. The logic for this is simple; income is an increase in wealth. Not all economic activity creates new wealth; some production occurs to compensate for "loss of wealth" or depreciation of capital. Two scenarios can help illustrate this concept. In scenario 1, a developer installs a new roof on a new residential property. The value of the roof enters into the value of the residential property. Therefore, the GDP increases by the value of the house (including the value of the roof). Indeed, in this case a brand new house and a brand new roof are being added to the country's capital stock. In scenario 2, a storm causes damage to an existing roof, and as a result the roof is replaced. The GDP still increases by the value of the roof as a new roof is being produced and installed. However, does this new roof add to the wealth of the country? Does it represent an addition to the country's capital stock? In the latter scenario, the wealth of the nation did not increase as we simply produced a roof to compensate for the damaged one.

ACCOUNTS OF GDP

In a recession, it is not just sufficient to know that the level of output is declining, but rather it is important to understand why it is declining. It is important to know which sectors drive the decline. Knowing the source of the problem can help in the development of a corrective policy mix. Table 12.3 presents a summary of the main accounts of the U.S. GDP (source: BEA).

Computing GDP data is a complex task, and the BEA conducts multiple revisions of the data. The first release, an advance estimate, is typically released one month after the end of each quarter. A month later, the advanced estimate is replaced by a preliminary estimate and later by a final estimate. The final estimate is still subject to annual revisions. Chances are that by the time you read this material, the numbers in Table 12.3 will be very different. However our discussion focuses not on the numbers but rather on the accounts and their roles.

We have highlighted in bold font the main accounts of GDP: Consumption (C), Investment (I), Net Exports (x-m), and Government Spending (G).[22] It is the sum of these accounts that constitutes GDP:

1) $$GDP = C + I + G + x - m$$

		2012 current dollars (in billions)	%
1	**Gross domestic product**	**15684.8**	**100**
2	**Personal consumption expenditures**	**11119.6**	**70.89**
3	Goods	3783.2	24.12
4	Durable goods	1218.9	7.77
5	Motor vehicles and parts	407	2.59
6	Furnishings and durable household equipment	265.8	1.69
7	Recreational goods and vehicles	354	2.26
8	Other durable goods	192.1	1.22
9	Nondurable goods	2564.2	16.35
10	Food and beverages purchased for off-premises consumption	829.1	5.29
11	Clothing and footwear	365.9	2.33
12	Gasoline and other energy goods	440.3	2.81
13	Other nondurable goods	929.1	5.92
14	Services	7336.5	46.77
15	Household consumption expenditures (for services)	7035.1	44.85
16	Housing and utilities	1965.9	12.53
17	Health care	1818.1	11.59
18	Transportation services	312.8	1.99
19	Recreation services	410.2	2.62
20	Food services and accommodations	713.6	4.55
21	Financial services and insurance	829.1	5.29
22	Other services	985.5	6.28
23	Final consumption expenditures of nonprofit institutions serving households	301.4	1.92
24	Gross output of nonprofit institutions	1215.5	7.75
25	Less: Receipts from sales of goods and services by nonprofit institutions	914.1	5.83

Table 12.3 (Source: U.S. Bureau of Economic Analysis, 2013). Reprinted with permission.

---

[22] Net Exports are defined as the difference between exports and imports. The usual notation is to use the lower case letters from the second letters of the terms (e.g. x and m). The reason the second letters are used is because the first letters of these terms are already assigned (e.g. E – expenditures, I – Investment). Also, capital M typically represents money supply.

		2012 current dollars (in billions)	%
26	**Gross private domestic investment**	**2062.3**	**13.15**
27	Fixed investment	2004.2	12.78
28	Nonresidential	1621.3	10.34
29	Structures	463.4	2.95
30	Equipment and software	1157.9	7.38
31	Information processing equipment and software	555.4	3.54
32	Computers and peripheral equipment	79.3	0.51
33	Software 4	293.4	1.87
34	Other	182.7	1.16
35	Industrial equipment	197.5	1.26
36	Transportation equipment	196.9	1.26
37	Other equipment	208.1	1.33
38	Residential	382.9	2.44
39	Change in private inventories	58.1	0.37
40	Farm	-16.1	-0.1
41	Nonfarm	74.1	0.47
42	**Net exports of goods and services**	**-559.9**	**-3.57**
43	Exports	2184	13.92
44	Goods	1542.8	9.84
45	Services	641.2	4.09
46	Imports	2744	17.49
47	Goods	2291.9	14.61
48	Services	452.1	2.88
49	**Government consumption expenditures and gross investment**	**3062.8**	**19.53**
50	Federal	1214.3	7.74
51	National defense	809.1	5.16
52	Consumption expenditures	703.6	4.49
53	Gross investment	105.6	0.67
54	Nondefense	405.1	2.58
55	Consumption expenditures	356	2.27
56	Gross investment	49.1	0.31
57	State and local	1848.5	11.79
58	Consumption expenditures	1530.8	9.76
59	Gross investment	317.7	2.03

Table 12.3 Continued (Source: U.S. Bureau of Economic Analysis, 2013). Reprinted with permission.

Note that in the U.S. economy, the single largest component is spending by households (Consumption). Consumption spending is split into goods and services. Goods are further classified as either durable or nondurable. According to the BEA, a nondurable good is one that is expected on average to last less than three years (U.S. Bureau of Economic Analysis, 2012).

The next important component is Investment ②(Gross private domestic investment). Investment may not be such a large component of the U.S. GDP as it only accounts for about 13%, but it plays an important role in job creation. Before new jobs are added, new office space, retail space, and factories need to be built.

Note that investment contains fixed investment and changes in private inventories. Changes in private inventories represent accumulation or depletion of inventory stock, while fixed investment represents the formation of capital stock. Within fixed investment, a distinction is made between residential and nonresidential investment. Residential investment represents the formation of housing stock. When a new residential housing unit is built, its value is entered on line 38.

It is important to understand that residential housing is a form of capital stock (capital input) as it produces a service – shelter. As a result, residential housing is treated as capital stock. When built, it is counted under Investment, and when it is being used, it is counted under Consumption (line 16). Consider a simple example, a $200,000 house is built in 2012 and is sold to a household in 2012. The entire value of the house will enter into the GDP of 2012 on line 38 since that is when the production of the house took place. However, after the house is sold, it starts to create a housing service (shelter). This service will be produced over a number of years, and it needs to be accounted for in the GDP during those years. The BEA will impute the rental value of the house, and use it in the computation of housing services on line 16. Note that the imputed value does not come from the mortgage value. Two identical homes standing next to each other might have very different mortgage payments depending on the type of financing that was used at the time of their purchase, and yet if these homes are identical in terms of their sizes, structures, locations, etc., then they should generate equal rental values.

Nonresidential investment is a form of investment that contributes to both productivity growth and job creation. Line 29 represents spending on business structures, a form of investment needed for future job creation. Line 30 represents spending on productive equipment, an investment component that helps increase the productivity of existing labor. Recall that average and marginal measures of labor productivity depend on the ratio of capital to labor.

The GDP statistics reported in Table 12.3 also provide a breakdown of government spending between the Federal and State - Local level governments.

In the US, the Bureau of Economic Analysis provides a vast amount of detailed level data to the general public for free. All these data are available for public access through their website at www.bea.gov.

	Contribution to Real GDP Growth	2012
	GDP	**2.2**
1	**Consumption**	**1.32**
1.1	Goods	0.74
1.11	Durable	0.58
1.12	nondurable	0.15
1.2	Services	0.58
2	**Investment**	**1.19**
2.1	Fixed Investment	1.05
2.11	Nonresidential	0.78
2.111	Structures	0.29
2.112	Equipment and Software	0.49
2.12	Residential	0.27
2.2	Change in private inventories	0.14
2.21	Farm	-0.06
2.22	Nonfarm	0.20
3	**Net Exports**	**0.04**
3.1	Exports	0.47
3.2	Imports	-0.43
4	**Government**	**-0.34**
4.1	Federal	-0.18
4.11	Defense	-0.17
4.12	Nondefense	-0.01
4.2	State and Local	-0.17

Table 12.4 (Source: U.S. Bureau of Economic Analysis, 2013)

In each GDP news release, the BEA also provides measures of contribution to the GDP growth by each of the GDP components (see Table 2 of U.S. Bureau of Economic Analysis, 2013). These are very useful instruments in understanding the driving engines of growth (or causes of recessions). Table 12.4 presents an illustration of the contribution factors for 2012. If you add up the contributions by each of the major accounts (Consumption, Investment, Net Exports, and Government), you will obtain the GDP growth rate, which in this case is 2.2%.

The usefulness of this contribution method over the growth rates method is that it helps identify the impact of each sector on the GDP growth rate. For instance, if we take out the contribution by the public sector (-0.34%), we would obtain the growth created by the private sector (households [Consumption], businesses [Investment]) and the foreign sector (Net Exports). In the case of 2012, the private sector and the foreign sector contributed 2.54% in growth. The implied interpretation is that the government spending was not one of the drivers of growth in 2012.

From Table 12.4, we can also see that of the 2.2% annual expansion experienced by the U.S. economy in 2012, more than half (1.19%) was caused by investment growth. Residential investment accounted for 0.27% or one eighth of the overall growth (0.27/2.2). We also see that the U.S. export growth slightly outpaced the import growth.

Table 12.4 introduced a new term, *real* GDP. By its setup, GDP is simply the sum of price times quantity across all final goods and services produced domestically during a given time period. However, the prices used in this computation are nominal prices and nominal prices have a serious problem. Nominal prices are measured in a monetary unit, like the USD (U.S. Dollar), and monetary units are not a perfect yardstick as they tend to change in value over time due to inflation or deflation. An ideal measure of production would be a measure of output only, but the problem is that we need prices to underscore the relative importance of the various products. For instance, how would we know that an apple is less important than a car without considering the prices of the two goods?

One solution is to fix prices and measure the value of output across all years using prices from a given year. In fact, this is how the U.S. used to compute real GDP. However, that method changed in the late 1990s when a chain-weighted method replaced it. Table 12.5 works out an example of a real GDP computation using both methods (for more information, see Steindel, 1995).

The example in Table 12.5 describes a hypothetical economy with only two products (both final goods): apples and pears. Between these two years, the production of pears increases while the production of apples declines. Also, apples become relatively more expensive in year 2. First, we compute the nominal GDP for each year. The nominal GDP shows significant growth; however, some of that growth may be due to inflation in the price of apples. Next, we compute the real GDP using the fixed price method. At first, we compute it using the prices of year 1 and then using the prices of year 2 (80 for the first year and 110 for the second year). These results allow us to compute the index of real GDP with year 1 being the base year, see Equation 2.

	Year 1				Year 2			
	Apple		Pear		Apple		Pear	
	Price	Quantity	Price	Quantity	Price	Quantity	Price	Quantity
	0.2	200	0.4	100	0.5	150	0.3	200
Nominal GDP	0.2 x 200 + 0.4 x 100 = 80				0.5 x 150 + 0.3 x 200 = 135			
Nominal GDP Index	80 / 80 = 1.000				135 / 80 = 1.688			
	Real GDP at constant prices							
At year 1 prices	0.2 x 200 + 0.4 x 100 = 80				0.2 x 150 + 0.4 x 200 = 110			
At year 2 prices	0.5 x 200 + 0.3 x 100 = 130				0.5 x 150 + 0.3 x 200 = 135			
	Real GDP Index (year 1 is 1.000)							
At year 1 prices	80 / 80 = 1.000				110 / 80 = 1.375			
At year 2 prices	130 / 130 = 1.000				135 / 130 = 1.039			
Chain-weighted	1				(1.375 x 1.039)^0.5 = 1.195			

Table 12.5

$$\text{2)} \quad \text{Real GDP Index for year}_t = \frac{\text{Real GDP in year}_t}{\text{Real GDP in base year}}$$

Note that, in both cases (using year 1 or year 2 prices), the growth in the real GDP is less than the growth in the nominal GDP. This is because the economy experiences inflation between these two years. Interestingly, our computations of growth in real GDP differ significantly depending on which year's prices are being used. Which prices are the correct ones for this computation? We simply don't know, as both prices are valid for the computation. One solution is to simply use some sort of average of the two computations, which is exactly what the chain-weighted method does. A chain-weighted computation simply takes the geometric average of the two computations:

$$\text{3)} \quad \begin{aligned} &\text{Chain - weighted Real GDP Index for year 2} = \\ &= \sqrt{\text{Real GDP Index (year 1 prices)} \times \text{real GDP Index (year 2 prices)}} \end{aligned}$$

The chain-weighted method can also be used for the computation of inflation. Although we have not yet defined inflation, we can already examine it in the context of our example in Table 12.5. We need to start with computing the GDP deflator, an instrument used to deflate nominal GDP (convert nominal GDP into real GDP):

$$\text{GDP deflator index} = \frac{\text{Nominal GDP index}}{\text{Real GDP index}}$$

4)

In our example, the GDP deflator index for year 2 is 1.688/1.195 = 1.413. This implies that our economy experienced about 41.3% inflation as measured by the GDP deflator.

EMPLOYMENT

The next criterion of economic performance is employment. In the U.S., labor statistics are gathered and reported by the U.S. Department of Labor and its agency, the Bureau of Labor Statistics. It is important that we understand the process of labor data collection, the main measures of labor market activity and their implications.

The U.S. Bureau of Labor Statistics releases employment situation reports each month. Typically, the previous month's report is released to the public on the Friday of the first full week of the following month. The reports contain the results of two separate monthly surveys.[23] Each month, the U.S. Bureau of Labor Statistics conducts two separate surveys designed to capture the state of the labor market. One of these surveys, the Current Population Survey, is conducted jointly with the U.S. Department of the Census and is used to obtain the household level data (see U.S. Department of the Census, 2013). The CPS is used to construct unemployment and labor force statistics. The other survey, the Establishment Survey is a survey of businesses used to tabulate employment growth.

Since the CPS survey cannot be revised (it is a survey of households and taking it more than once for the same month makes no sense), the labor force statistics obtained from the survey, including the monthly unemployment rate, are not revised. The same cannot be said about the payroll data obtained from the establishment survey (see U.S. BLS, 2013b).

HOUSEHOLD SURVEY (CPS)

---

[23] The most recent report can be accessed online at http://www.bls.gov/news.release/empsit.toc.htm.

To understand why the household survey is an essential part of the labor situation review, we need to understand the definitions of unemployment and labor force. The civilian labor force is comprised of a non-institutionalized adult population. In the US, the adult population is defined as those who are 16 years of age and older. Note that there is no upper age cut-off for the purpose of the labor force computation of and the reason for this is in the way we define unemployment. The civilian labor force consists of those individuals who are employed and those who are unemployed. An individual is considered as employed if they have a job (any job, including a part-time job). Furthermore, that job does not need to match their labor market skills either. An individual is considered as unemployed if they meet two conditions. First, and this is rather straight forward, they have to have no job. Second (and this is the reason for the survey and why there is no upper age cut-off in the labor force), they must be actively seeking work. If an individual stops seeking employment, they simply exit the labor force. Retired individuals are not included in the labor force because they are no longer seeking employment. In essence, the labor force represents the economy's active or participating labor supply.

Since the labor force serves as the economy's active supply of labor, we can compute the rate of participation in the labor market, referred to as the labor force participation rate. The rate measures the percentage of the total non-institutionalized civilian adult population that chooses to participate in the labor market:

$$5) \quad LFPR = \frac{LavorForce}{TotalCivilianNoninstitutionalizedAdultPopulation} \times 100\%$$

Table 12.6 presents a summary of the U.S. labor market statistics for February of 2013 from the BLS news release of March 8, 2013.

The labor force includes those employed (143,492 thousand) and those unemployed (12,032 thousand). The labor force participation rate is the ratio of the civilian labor force to the civilian population (155,524/244,828). The total civilian non-institutionalized population represents the potential labor supply, while the labor force represents the active labor supply. The ratio suggests that over a third of the adult population chose not to participate in the labor market. Mainly, these are retired individuals, those attending schools, and so on. However, this group also includes those individuals who are discouraged to participate in the labor market by economic conditions. A discouraged worker is a worker who has no job and stops looking for work because they perceive the probability of finding a job to be too low to justify the search costs.

Civilian noninstitutional population	244828	
Civilian labor force	155524	employed + unemployed
Participation rate	63.5	labor force / noninstitutional population
Employed	143492	
Unemployed	12032	
Unemployment rate	7.7%	unemployed/labor force
Not in labor force	89304	Noninstitutional population - labor force

Table 12.6 Employment figures are in thousands (US Labor Market Summary for February 2013). Source: U.S. Bureau of Labor Statistics, March 8, 2013 release.

According to the BLS, there were 2.6 million workers marginally attached to the labor force in February of 2013.

"These individuals were not in the labor force, wanted and were available for work, and had looked for a job sometime in the prior 12 months. They were not counted as unemployed because they had not searched for work in the 4 weeks preceding the survey." U.S. Bureau of Labor Statistics, March 8, 2013 (US Bureau of Labor Statistics, 2013).

Out of these 2.6 million individuals, 885,000 were identified as discouraged workers. The presence of discouraged workers not only reduces the labor force (and the labor force participation rate), but also reduces the unemployment rate. Discouraged workers represent an outflow of unemployed workers from the labor force. If the discouraged workers were included in the computation of unemployment, we would have the number of the unemployed at 12,917 thousand, resulting in an unemployment rate of 8.3%.

Weak labor market conditions cause a rise in the number of discouraged workers and reduce the labor force participation rate. The recession that began in late 2007 and the subsequent, nearly jobless recovery are a further illustration of this condition (see Figure 12.2).

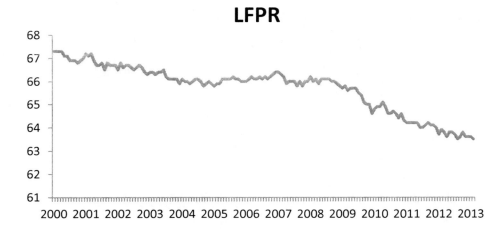

LFPR

Figure 12.2. U.S. Labor Force Participation Rate (01.2000 – 02.2013), source: U.S. Bureau of Labor Statistics.

Of course, there are other factors that can alter the labor force participation rate. For instance, a rise in welfare provisions, an extension in the period of coverage by unemployment insurance, and etc., can raise the reservation wage at which the workers would want to reenter the labor market. The reservation wage is the lowest wage at which an individual would want to supply their labor.

The unemployment rate itself is simply the percentage of the labor force that is unemployed:

$$UR = \frac{Unemployed}{Labor\ Force} = \frac{Unemployed}{Employed + Unemployed}$$

6)

In the context of Table 12.6, the unemployment rate is the unemployed (12,032 thousand) divided by the total labor force (155,524 thousand).

ESTABLISHMENT SURVEY

The establishment survey (Current Employment Statistics) is used to obtain payroll numbers. Unlike the household survey results, the establishment survey results are subject to two monthly revisions as more survey participants (businesses) report their numbers.[24] The U.S. Bureau of Labor Statistics reports detailed numbers on payroll changes by industry and sector. The data are also available by geographical location. Given the size of the U.S. population and its recent dynamics, the U.S. economy should produce about 150 thousand new jobs a month just to keep up with the growing population.

It is important to note that the two surveys do not have to match each other. For instance, in February of 2013, the household survey numbers indicated that the employment went up by 170 thousand, but the establishment survey reported the creation of 246 thousand new jobs. In fact, the two surveys can potentially move in opposite directions to one another. It is possible to see a negative employment growth being reported by the establishment survey at the same time as the household survey reports a reduction in the unemployment rate. There are several plausible explanations that can account for such a scenario. A pessimistic explanation would be that the establishment survey is correct and a drop in unemployment occurs due to a rise in the number of workers who are marginally attached to the labor force. An optimistic explanation would be that new firms are being started and more workers become employed by small businesses or workers become self-employed. These jobs would not be observed by the establishment survey right away.

INFLATION

Inflation is a disease of money. Money is not a resource in economics, and so it is not immediately obvious why its affliction should be perceived as a danger to an economy but unfortunately it is. Perhaps the biggest issue with inflation is its uncertainty. If inflation were correctly anticipated by everyone, then it would not produce much of an impact, but the problem with inflation is that it is unlikely to be predictable. We should start our discussion by defining what inflation actually is and how it is measured. After that, we can examine its causes and effects.

The definition of inflation can be stated in two synonymous ways:

- Inflation is the rate of growth in the average of all prices

- Inflation is the rate of loss in the purchasing power of money

---

[24] The survey is also rebalanced annually to calibrate it to the unemployment insurance tax records.

The two formulations are identical in their meaning. Measuring inflation requires measuring the average price. The problem with the average price is that it is different for everyone depending on their consumption behavior; as a result, we have a number of different measures of inflation.

CONSTRUCTING A SIMPLE MEASURE OF INFLATION

Consider a scenario where a typical consumer purchases three goods: food, gasoline, and housing. To understand what the average price is for this consumer, we need the quantities of each good purchased (the market or consumption basket). The quantities allow us to construct the shares of spending on each of the goods (the weights) which will allow us to compute a weighted average price. Let's consider that each month the consumer purchases 30 units of food (frozen dinners), 20 gallons of gasoline, and one unit of housing (rental for an apartment). Let us also assume the following prices of the three goods: the price of food is $3, the price of gasoline is $4, and the price of housing is $800. Table 12.7 summarizes all this information, reports the value of the market basket, and the weight of each of the goods.

	Food		Gasoline		Housing		Value of Market Basket
	Price	Quantity	Price	Quantity	Price	Quantity	
	3	30	4	20	800	1	970
Weight	9.278		8.247		82.474		

Table 12.7

The weight is simply the percentage share of the value in the market basket that is allocated to the good. For instance, the weight of food in the market basket would be the spending on food expressed as a percentage of the total spending (the value of the market basket):

$$
7) \quad W_f = \frac{P_f Q_f}{P_f Q_f + P_g Q_g + P_h Q_h} \times 100\% =
$$

$$
= \frac{3 \times 30}{3 \times 30 + 4 \times 20 + 800 \times 1} \times 100\% = 9.278\%
$$

More generally, the weight of product i is:

$$8) \quad W_i = \frac{P_i Q_i}{\sum_j P_j Q_j} \times 100\%$$

From these weights we can compute the average price in our example as:

$$9) \quad P_{average} = \sum_{i=,f,g,h} W_i P_i = 9.278 \times P_f + 8.247 \times P_g + 82.474 \times P_h$$

Recall that inflation is the rate of growth in the average price. Expression 9 constructs the average price for our consumer, so the way our consumer feels inflation can simply be seen in the growth rate of the average price:

$$10) \quad \begin{aligned} Inflation &= \%\Delta P_{average} = \\ &= 9.278 \times \%\Delta P_f + 8.247 \times \%\Delta P_g + 82.474 \times \%\Delta P_h \end{aligned}$$

Note that we could have computed inflation alternatively by simply computing the rate of increase in the value of the market basket. As inflation represents a rate of change, its computation requires more than one time period. Table 12.8 expands the example by introducing two additional time periods and computing their rate of inflation.

Period	Food		Gasoline		Housing		Value of Market Basket
	Price		Price		Price		
	nominal	% change	nominal	% change	nominal	% change	
I	3		4		800		970
II	3.12	0.04	4	0	824	0.03	997.6
III	3.12	0	4.1	0.025	820	-0.00485	995.6

Period	Inflation	
	MB method	Average Price
I		
II	2.845361	2.845361
III	-0.200481	-0.194175

Table 12.8

The market basket method is simply the computation of the rate of change in the value of the market basket, while the average-price inflation computation is based on Equation 10. This is an intuitive illustration of the inflation computation, but it is a bit simplified. Note that the two methods seem to differ slightly for the third time period. The reason for this is that as prices change, the weights need to change as well. And we did not allow for this since we kept things simple in our formula. To make the two computations identical, we would need to compute the new weights for period II and use them in the average price computation (for food and gasoline the new weights will be 0.09382518 and 0.080192462, respectively).

Allowing the weights to change over time is an important requirement of a measure of inflation. Consumer behavior changes over time and that makes the experience of inflation differ. One example of this is the emergence of new products. Once a new product emerges, it tends to enter the market with a high price, and then over time, as competition increases, the price tends to decline. There are numerous examples of this which include: cellphones, computers, LCD and LED monitors, and etc. When a new product emerges, its weight in the market basket naturally increases from zero to a value greater than zero. Over time, as the price of this product declines, its weight in the market basket of the consumer might continue to change. The previously mentioned chain-weighted method of computation can be used to compute inflation. The chain-weighted method allows for weight adjustments and in this sense is a more accurate measure of inflation.

It is worth mentioning that allowing the weights to be dynamic can also hide the effects of inflation on the standard of living. For instance, consider that you purchase two gallons of milk each week. The price of one gallon of milk is $3, and your total spending each week is $300. This means that milk has a weight of 2% in your market basket (2 gallons at the price of $3 out of the total spending of $300). Now, let's assume that the price of milk increases to $4.50, and as a result you reduce your purchase of milk from two gallons to one gallon a week. To compensate, you purchase a gallon of iced tea priced at $1.50 (also assume that the price of iced tea did not increase). In this scenario, milk inflated by 50%, from $3 to $4.50, but at the same time the weight of milk in your market basket declined from 2% to 1.5%, thus reducing the effect of the price change of milk on the rate of inflation. So, it would appear that inflation was not as high because the consumer switched from a product with an inflating price to one that had no inflation. However, the standard of living of the consumer declined as the consumer substituted away from a more valuable product to a cheaper one, a result of the change in the relative price.

In the preceding discussion, we focused on the computation of the average price. The average price, like any price is measured in a monetary unit, such as the U.S. dollar. We can abandon the monetary unit by converting our measure of the average price into a percentage. This is accomplished by indexing the average price, or computing a price index. A price index is simply an indexation of the average price (or the value of the market basket) by expressing each time period's average price as a multiple (or percentage) of the average price from the base period:

$$11) \quad PI_t = \frac{P_{average(t)}}{P_{average(base)}} \times 100\%$$

Period II, $PI = \frac{997.6}{970} \times 100$
$= 102.845\%$

Period III, $PI = \frac{995.6}{970} \times 100$
$= 102.639\%$

Here, t represents the time period for which the index is computed. We can also use the value of the market basket instead of the average price in Equation 11. Using the market basket and assuming that period I is the base period, we can show that the price index for period II would be 102.845%, while the price index for period III would be 102.639%. Inflation can be computed from the price index by simply examining the rate of growth in the price index. Note that the price index is simply another way of describing the average price (or in our computation, the value of the market basket). The average price is measured in dollars, while the price index is measured as percentage of the average price (or the value of the market basket) in the base time period. Regardless of the selected base period, the resulting computation of inflation remains the same.

Our computation of inflation required identifying the average price or the market basket. Since individuals differ in terms of their consumption behavior, every consumer experiences inflation a little bit differently. For instance, as a college student, you would have experienced a higher rate of inflation in the last few years given the behavior of college tuition and textbook prices. Obviously, we would not want to compute an inflation index for every consumer, but we do wish to differentiate between how inflation is experienced by a typical business versus a typical consumer. Because price fluctuations may be influenced by factors external to the economy (such as is the case in food and energy prices), we may also want to differentiate between inflation in these more volatile goods and inflation in the rest of the goods and services. As a result we have multiple measures of inflation:

measures of inflation:

- Consumer Price Index (measures the average price for a typical urban consumer)

- Producer Price Index (measures the average price for a typical business)

- Employer Cost Index (measures the average cost of labor)

- Core indexes, such as Core CPI and Core PPI (exclude food and energy from their corresponding market basket)

	Relative importance January, 2013	Unadjusted indexes		Unadjusted percent change		Seasonally adjusted percent change
		Jan. 2013	Feb. 2013	Feb. 2012- Feb. 2013	Jan. 2013- Feb. 2013	Jan. 2013- Feb. 2013
All items	100	230.28	232.17	2	0.8	0.7
Food	14.33	236.34	236.3	1.6	0	0.1
Food at home	8.62	234.24	234.03	1.2	-0.1	0.1
Food away from home	5.71	240.71	240.93	2.3	0.1	0.1
Energy	9.58	234.62	248.15	2.3	5.8	5.4
Gasoline (all types)	5.27	286.42	315.24	3.3	10.1	9.1
All items less food and energy	76.09	231.61	232.43	2	0.4	0.2
Commodities less food and energy	19.53	146.49	147.09	0.3	0.4	0
Apparel	3.53	124.69	126.3	2.4	1.3	-0.1
New vehicles	3.2	145.87	145.93	1.1	0	-0.3
Services less energy services	56.56	283.28	284.23	2.6	0.3	0.2
Shelter	31.68	260.04	260.72	2.3	0.3	0.2
Owners' equivalent rent of residences	24.02	268	268.45	2.1	0.2	0.2
Medical care services	5.46	448.23	451.63	3.9	0.8	0.3
Transportation services	5.84	277.41	277.96	3.1	0.2	0.1
Motor vehicle maintenance and repair	1.15	259.75	260.23	1.3	0.2	0.2
Motor vehicle insurance	2.49	415.51	416.15	5.2	0.2	0.2
Airline fare	0.77	306.6	309.28	3.6	0.9	-0.3

Table 12.9 Source: U.S. Bureau of Labor Statistics. Reprinted with permission.

In the U.S., the inflationary data is reported by the U.S. Bureau of Labor Statistics. Table 12.9 is a partial reprint of the CPI release of March 15, 2013 from the U.S. Bureau of Labor Statistics.

The Relative Importance column represents the weight of the spending category. For all categories of goods and services, the weights must add up to 100%. The Unadjusted Indexes columns represent the actual CPI (with 1982-84 being the base period). For example, the index was 232.17 for February of 2013, which represents 132.17% inflation relative to the base period's prices. Note that inflation was not uniform as gasoline, housing, medical services, motor vehicle maintenance, and insurance all went up above the average rate, while apparel and new cars inflated at lower rates.

There was an interesting pattern to U.S. inflation during this period. Goods and services that are domestically produced inflated at higher rates than imported goods and services. The process of globalization helped keep the overall inflation lower during the 1990s and the early part of the XXI century. Those areas of the economy that did not see foreign competition experienced considerably higher inflation.

The last four columns present the monthly rates of inflation. The first two are not seasonally adjusted, while the last two are. Since the index is not seasonally adjusted, the unadjusted inflation rates are simply the rates of growth in the index. For instance, the change in the CPI index from January into February of 2013 is 0.8% and computed as follows: $(232.17-230.28)/230.28 = 0.008$.

The process of collecting the price data is also a survey. Each month, the BLS collects prices on 80,000 items. The BLS has a number of workers (economic assistants) who either call or visit various retail locations (stores, business to consumer businesses, etc.) and scan price labels to collect the data each month (for more information on this process see BLS, 2004).

MONEY

Before we discuss the implications of inflation, we need to understand what inflation does to money. To understand the impact inflation has on money, we first have to define the properties of money.

While not the definition of legal tender, practically anything can serve as money as long as it meets the following three fundamental properties:

- Medium of Exchange
- Unit of Account
- Store of Value

The first two properties are unrelated to inflation. The first property simply implies that money has to be easily exchangeable and acceptable for exchange purposes. The second states that money should be easily measurable, so that the value of goods and services could be specified by money. The last property is the most interesting to us. Money has to store value over time, otherwise it makes no sense to hold it as a form of savings. Historically, the three properties were nicely served by precious metals such as gold and silver. Small, easily exchangeable coins could be made out of these metals. The price of any product can be valued in weight of gold or silver. And since the supply of precious metals has historically grown at relatively low rates (relative to the population and economy), these metals remained precious over time.

Inflation undermines the store of value property of money. A very high inflation, or hyperinflation, can cause money to stop functioning. In a world of fiat currencies (not backed up by any commodity), hyperinflation can lead to barter or a replacement of the domestic currency with a foreign one. This last situation refers to dollarization. Dollarization is a term used to indicate the percentage of the value of domestic transactions being conducted in foreign money. The term dollarization originated with the U.S. dollar. Given the size of the U.S. economy and the widespread use of the U.S. dollar as a reserve currency, it is only natural to have residents of countries with high inflation start shifting towards the U.S. dollar. However, in modern context, the term dollarization does not just refer to the use of the U.S. dollar. For instance, at the start of the XXI century, real estate prices in Russia have frequently been quoted in roubles, dollars, and euros. In this case, dollarization would refer to the volume of transactions in Russia that are conducted in all foreign currencies.

Hyperinflation is just a very high inflation. There is no real cutoff point at which we would label inflation as hyperinflation as that would depend on the history of an economy. However, inflation in excess of 50% a year is generally labeled as hyperinflation. In a hyperinflationary environment, holding money is similar to holding a piece of ice in the palm of your hand. The longer you hold it, the smaller it becomes. The value of money literally melts away. Naturally, you would want to get rid of it as quickly as possible by converting it into something that tends to maintain its value better and is generally liquid.[25] Inflation is not only a problem in itself (as the discussion below will illustrate), but it is also a

---

[25] Liquidity is the property of an asset that represents how quickly (with little loss in value) the asset can be turned into cash. By definition, the liquidity property of cash is 100%.

symptom of some underlying economic problem. In this sense, inflation is similar to a fever. A human body will run a fever when there is some underlying problem, such as an infection. However, when the fever becomes too high, it itself needs to be addressed. The same is true about inflation. Inflation signifies that something is going wrong and needs to be addressed. If inflation becomes too high, it itself needs to be addressed. The discussion below does not look at the causes of inflation but merely presents some of the implications of inflation on the economy.

ECONOMIC IMPACT OF INFLATION

With the prior two criteria of economic activity, the implications of their changes were intuitive. A decline in output would inevitably hurt the standard of living of the population, all else held constant, as it would mean that less output becomes available to the population. A rise in the unemployment also has somewhat clear economic, social, and even political implications. However, in order to fully understand the implications of changes in unemployment, we need to define the concept of full employment or natural unemployment, which is accomplished in Chapter 13.

With inflation, the situation is a bit more confusing. We started the discussion on inflation by defining it as a disease of money. Unlike labor, money is not an economic resource, and so it is not immediately clear why inflation can be perceived as a problem. Yet, inflation is perceived as an economic woe, and central banks sometimes go as far as to induce an economic slowdown to combat this enemy.

Before we discuss the implications of inflation, we need to differentiate between anticipated and unanticipated inflation. If inflation is fully anticipated, then it produces relatively few negative effects on an economy. However, the key problem with inflation is its uncertainty. If inflation is unanticipated, then it can create significant distortions in an economy. To understand the difference between anticipated and unanticipated inflation, consider a simple scenario of investing into a corporate bond. A bond is nothing but an IOU where the issuer borrows from the holder. Imagine that this is a one year bond. The nominal interest on the bond will be determined by market forces and the creditworthiness of the borrower. Indeed, the nominal rate is a function of a number of variables including: the stability and creditworthiness of the country where the business is based, the interest rate on the currency in which the bond is denominated, the outlook for the firm and the industry, and most importantly for the purpose of our discussion, the market expectations of future inflation.

Let's assume that the nominal rate is 4%, while the market expects inflation to be about 3% during the next year. This implies that the real rate of return is 1%. There are several ways of defining real rate of return and they are all identical. One simple way would be to view real rate of return as simply compensation to the lender for postponing their consumption. From the perspective of the borrower, real rate of return is simply the cost of forwarding their consumption (or income) from a future period of time into the present.[26] In economics, real rate of return is computed using the Fisher equation:

12) Real Rate = Nominal Rate – Rate of Inflation

Depending on whether the computation is forward looking or backward looking, the rate of inflation can be the expected future inflation or the already realized inflation during the existence of a past financial arrangement.

It is the expected rate of inflation that is of interest to us. Let's assume that the market's expectation of inflation was correct and inflation indeed materialized at 3%. In this case, there is no negative impact of this inflation on the borrower or the lender as both parties had agreed to a real rate of return of 1%, and that is exactly what they got. This is the case of anticipated inflation.

expected inflation

Let us now assume that inflation surprised the market and materialized to be only 1%. This has a very significant implication as it changes the real rate of return on the bond. Since, the real rate of return is 3%, this means that the lender (the holder of the bond) benefited by receiving a real compensation of 3%. However, the borrower (the issuer of the bond) ended up paying a real rate that is three times higher than what they had anticipated at the time of the bond sale. In this case, inflation redistributed wealth from the borrower to the lender. This redistribution occurred because inflation proved to be unanticipated.

unexpected inflation

| Cost 1: Redistribution of Wealth | As the prior discussion illustrated, inflation is capable of redistributing wealth from borrowers to lenders. Indeed, the process can also work in reverse. For instance, consider a slightly different

---

[26] In microeconomics, real rate of return can be defined as the rate of discount of future consumption by the marginal borrower or lender. Note that it is the marginal participant that determines the real rate of return.

scenario where an individual purchases a house and borrows 100% of the home's value in an interest only loan (this assumption is not necessary to illustrate our point, but it makes it easier to see the main point). Let us also assume that the mortgage interest rate is 5% with an inflationary expectation of 2%. We can immediately conclude that the expected real rate of return is 3%. Let us now assume that during the first year of the mortgage, the economy experiences 10% inflation and the price of the house increases by the rate of inflation. Since this is an interest only mortgage, the homeowner paid zero towards repayment of the principal balance. This means that no equity was built through a reduction of principal on the loan, and yet equity was formed. By the end of the first year, the home's value exceeded its loan value by 10%, which created 10% equity for the homeowner. In essence, the homeowner's wealth increased just because of inflation. In this case, inflation resulted in the real rate of the mortgage to be negative 5%.

Note that inflation cannot create wealth, only production creates wealth. Inflation can merely redistribute the existing wealth. In our example, one can almost say that inflation acts like Robin Hood who takes from the rich (in this case the bank that issued the mortgage) and gives to the poor (in this case the homeowner). However, inflation is no Robin Hood. The only reason the bank was able to create a 5% mortgage is because the cost of money to the bank was less than 5%. A bank is simply a market maker that allows borrowers to be matched with lenders. A bank pulls together the savings of lenders into a large pool from which it lends to borrowers. If the bank was able to create a 5% mortgage, then that means that the rate it paid to its lenders (depositors) was less than 5%. This means that inflation redistributed wealth not from the bank to the homeowner but from the bank's depositors to the homeowner.

Indeed, in this example inflation is far from acting as Robin Hood. If we consider the average depositor and the average borrower, then we will see inflation in a slightly different way. To understand this, we must examine how an individual's wealth evolves during their lifetime. Typically, when one is young, one tends to dive into debt. The moment one enters adulthood, debt usually becomes the reality of life. First, it might be borrowing for college, then for a house and so forth. Then during the period of participation in the labor market, the debt gradually gets paid off and wealth starts to accumulate. This process typically peaks right before retirement. This means that it is the individuals, about to enter retirement or early in their retirement, who tend to be depositors in banks and therefore the ultimate lenders. Since an unanticipated acceleration in inflation redistributes wealth from lenders to borrowers, unanticipated inflation is capable of redistributing wealth across generations. A tragic illustration of this nature of inflation was experienced by the Russian economy in the 1990s. Russia experienced hyperinflation throughout the mid 1990s that wiped out the savings of older generations, resulting in a sharp increase in their mortality rates and a rapid decline in their average life expectancy. As a young college student, you may not consider the benefit of having a wealthier older generation, but you do benefit from it. Your grandparents, and later in life, parents are usually financially independent of you in their retirement. If the process of wealth accumulation is disrupted (including by inflation), then this independence may be lost.

Cost 2: Uncertainty One of the key problems with unanticipated inflation is the uncertainty it creates. The preceding discussion constitutes a specific implication of such uncertainty – wealth redistribution. However, there are more serious implications of this uncertainty, including the possibility of an economic slowdown. As inflation starts to change, the uncertainty associated with future inflation is likely to increase. Just consider a simple example of two economies: A and B. In economy A, the rate of inflation has been 2% for each of the past three years, while in economy B, this rate assumed three different values: 2%, 0%, and 4%. Note that both of these economies had the same average rate of inflation over the course of the past three years, but the volatility of inflation was different. In the case of economy A, the standard deviation is simply zero, while in the case of B it is 2. This past volatility can create more uncertainty about future expectations. If such an uncertainty increases, then the amount of investment may decline.

For instance, consider borrowing for investment purposes in country A. Borrowers and lenders in economy A have an easier time agreeing on the rate of expected future inflation. If the market participants agree on the expected rate of inflation being 2%, and assuming the real rate is 3% (this is an assumption for the purpose of illustration), then the nominal rate on this type of loan becomes 5%. In economy B, the situation is more difficult. Assuming that the real rate is still 3%, the rate of expected inflation is much more difficult to agree on. For instance, the lenders would want to protect themselves from a possible acceleration in inflation and thus ask for a higher rate. On the other hand, the borrowers would want to protect themselves from a decline in inflation and ask for a lower rate. This uncertainty about future inflation can cause the amount of borrowing to decline, which in turn can cause a drop in the level of economic activity.

Cost 3: Menu Cost   This cost is present in either anticipated or unanticipated inflation cases. Menu cost simply refers to the cost of using real economic resources in the process of changing prices due to inflation. Inflation forces business to change price labels, advertising, signs, and so on. This process consumes real resources, including labor, and therefore has a cost to the economy. In an economy that experiences a higher rate of inflation, these re-pricing activities may have to be undertaken more frequently, thereby resulting in higher costs. Historically, menu costs were important. The term originated in the restaurant business where inflation would cause frequent reprinting of menus. In countries with high inflation, some restaurants choose to provide price inserts or price lists into their menus rather than list the prices in the menu as that would require frequent changes of menus. However, in a modern economy, menu costs play an increasingly less important role. This is due to technological progress and the adaptation of electronic pricing mechanisms.

In the late 1990s, at the dawn of online commerce, a professor and a Ph.D. student from MIT conducted a study of online commerce (Brynjolfsson, and Smith, 2000) that compared the pricing behavior of online retailers with that of brick-and-mortar retailers for a number of products. One of their findings indicated that online stores changed prices more frequently and in smaller increments. This implied that the cost of re-pricing online was considerably lower than in brick-and-mortar commerce. In essence, the results suggested that the adaptation of online commerce reduced menu costs. Once sizable, menu costs have become a minor implication thanks to technological progress.

Cost 4: Persistent Inflation Changes Expectations   Persistent inflation can also change the expectations about future inflation making it difficult for a central bank to alter inflation through policy. Persistent inflation induces businesses to adapt inflation indexation where prices are adjusted by the prior period's inflation. This process makes inflation self-perpetual as the past period's inflation effectively enters into the current period's price adjustments.

$\boxed{\textit{Cost 5: Impact on Foreign Exchange}}$ In an open economy, domestic inflation can impact the value of the exchange rate. An open economy is one that is open to the rest of the world as opposed to a closed economy that does not participate in international markets (capital, labor, goods and services). If an open economy experiences inflation that is higher than that of its trading partners, then its goods and services gradually become less competitive internationally. This results in a worsening trade balance. A drop in exports translates into a decline in the demand for domestic currency, while a rise in imports implies a rise in the supply of domestic currency in the forex market (recall Appendix B of Chapter 4). As a result, the domestic currency depreciates, all else held constant. This relationship is referred to as the purchasing price parity (relative).

The relationship between the exchange rate and inflation works both ways. Currency depreciation creates inflation, and inflation can lead to currency depreciation.[27]

IS INFLATION ALWAYS A BAD THING?

Is inflation always a problem? Since inflation tends to redistribute wealth, some individuals may actually benefit from inflation. An unanticipated increase in inflation will redistribute wealth from lenders to borrowers (assuming the borrowing is done at fixed, inflation unadjusted rates). Similarly, an unanticipated decline in inflation will redistribute wealth from borrowers to lenders under the same assumption.

There is one other implication of inflation that is often considered as a positive factor in economics. Inflation (CPI inflation), tends to reduce real wages and therefore reduce the real cost of labor to businesses. Consider a simple example that occurred during the last recession when the Board of Regents of the University System of Georgia decided to freeze all pay increases in public universities and colleges. However, tuition costs continued to increase during that time. Over time, this process would result in lower real wages paid by the public universities and colleges and would improve their financial standing.

---

[27] Currency depreciation would increase the prices of imported goods. It would also reduce the prices of exported goods in foreign markets resulting in an upward pressure on these goods in the domestic market.

INFLATION: SUMMARY

The key problem with inflation is its instability and uncertainty. These two characteristics of inflation make it difficult to enter into a forward looking financial arrangement. Such arrangements include loans, annuities and pensions, investments, etc. It is interesting to note that it is not the rate of inflation that matters but its stability and predictability. At higher rates, the instability naturally increases in part because the central monetary authority is likely to intervene.

SURVEY NATURE OF DATA

Pope Julius III is accredited with the following phrase: "Do you know, my son, with what little understanding the world is ruled?" Unfortunately, this phrase seems somewhat appropriate in the context of this chapter. We discussed the three most important criteria of measuring economic activity: output, employment, and inflation. In all of those cases, we saw the use of surveys in obtaining the information. Some data require multiple revisions as additional survey participants report their data, or further recalibration is needed. In some cases, it may take over a year to complete the revisions and to finally understand what happened. This implies that we not only do not know what will happen, but in some cases we do not know what is happening or even what has already happened. This creates the need to not only forecast the future but to actually estimate the current environment. One excellent illustration of this is the GDP data for 2001. At the end of 2001, the BEA data showed that the U.S. economy contracted in the first three quarters of the year. Later, the revised data showed that the economy expanded in the second quarter. The revision didn't just change the rate, but the sign!

References

Bloomberg News 2012, Caroline Salas Gage, "Fed Shifts Focus to Jobs as Unemployment Stalls Above 8%." Published on July 17, 2012. Available online at: http://www.bloomberg.com/news/2012-07-16/fed-shifts-focus-to-jobs-as-unemployment-stalls-above-8-.html

Brynjolfsson, Erik, Michael Smith. 2000. "Frictionless Commerce? A Comparison of Internet and Conventional Retailers." *Management Science*, 46(4) 563-585

NBER, 2013a, "Statement of the NBER Business Cycle Dating Committee on the Determination of the Dates of Turning Points in the U.S. Economy." Accessed on March 27, 2013. Available online at: http://www.nber.org/cycles/general_statement.html
NBER, 2013b. "US Business Cycle Expansions and Contractions." Accessed on March 27, 2013. Available online at: http://www.nber.org/cycles/cyclesmain.html

Slavin, Stephen L., Economics. 11th edition, McGraw-Hill Publishing, 2014.

Steindel, Charles, 1995, "Chain-weighting: The New Approach to Measuring GDP." Current Issues in Economics and Finance, by Federal Reserve of New York, Vol 1, N 9. Available online at: http://www.newyorkfed.org/research/current_issues/ci1-9.pdf

The New York Times, 2012, Binyamin Appelbaum, "Fed Ties Rates to Joblessness, With Target of 6.5%." Published on December 12, 2012, also available online at: http://www.nytimes.com/2012/12/13/business/economy/fed-to-maintain-stimulus-bond-buying.html

U.S. Bureau of Economic Analysis, 2013, *National Income and Product Accounts, Gross Domestic Product, 4th quarter and annual 2012 (third estimate)*. Released on March 28, 2013. Available online at www.bea.gov.

U.S. Bureau of Economic Analysis, 2012. NIPA Handbook: Concepts and Methods of the U.S. National Income and Product Accounts. Available online at: http://www.bea.gov/methodologies/index.htm#national_meth

U.S. Bureau of Labor Statistics, 2013a. Employment Situation Summary for February 2013, released on March 8, 2013. Available online at: http://bls.gov/news.release/empsit.nr0.htm

U.S. Bureau of Labor Statistics, 2013b, Current Employment Statistics – CES (National), available online at: http://www.bls.gov/ces/cesrevinfo.htm

U.S. Bureau of Labor Statistics, 2004. *Understanding the Consumer Price Index: Answers to Some Questions*. Available online at: http://www.bls.gov/cpi/cpifaq.pdf

U.S. Department of the Census, 2013, Current Population Survey (CPS). Available online at: http://www.census.gov/cps/

Chapter 13

BASICS OF AGGREGATE FRAMEWORK

A market economy exhibits cyclical fluctuations known as the business cycle. The business cycle is characterized by periodic fluctuations in the level of general economic activity and consists of two stages: expansions and contractions. Expansions are defined as the periods of time when the economy experiences a rise in the level of economic activity, while contractions represent the periods of decline in economic activity.[28]

Since economic activity is best represented by production, it is only natural to use a measure of output such as real Gross Domestic Product to track the level of economic activity. However, it is important to understand that real GDP may not fully capture the overall state of the economy, and hence other measures of economic activity including employment may need to be considered. Indeed, the NBER (National Bureau of Economic Research) does not limit its consideration to the U.S. GDP alone when declaring recessions. One example is the recession of 2001. The NBER defines that recession to have spanned between March and November of 2001 even though the contraction in the real GDP was not continuous throughout that period. The real GDP contracted in the first quarter of 2001 and then again in the third quarter but rebounded in the second quarter. However, the overall economic performance remained weak throughout this period, which was seen in its rising unemployment.

Since our focus is on the basics of economic theory, we have the luxury to define the business cycle solely in terms of the fluctuations in the level of output; the other relevant measures of economic activity are assumed to be correlated with changes in output. However, the reality is not as perfect, and as a result it is possible to have a situation where output, incomes, and employment may not jointly move in an expected manner.

---

[28] For the complete history of the US business cycle please see the National Bureau of Economic Research (www.nber.org).

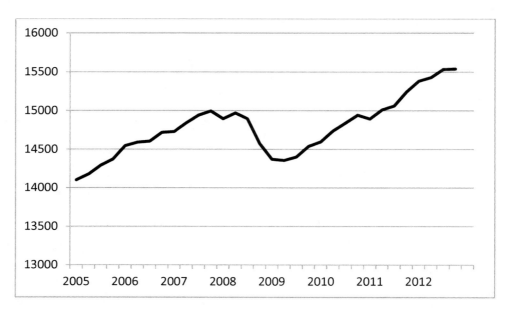

Figure 13.1, U.S. Real GDP: 2005 – 2012, in billions of 2009 chained dollars.
Source: U.S. BEA

Figure 13.1 illustrates the cyclical fluctuations of the U.S. real GDP during 2005 – 2012. This period includes a severe recession and an economic recovery. The observed pattern repeats itself over time as expansions end up being replaced with contractions. This pattern constitutes a cycle, hence the term – business cycle. Economists often refer to contractions as recessions. A recession is a period of contraction between the peak and the trough of the business cycle.

THE DYNAMICS OF A RECESSION: 2007-2009

The preceding chapter focused on the three fundamental criteria of evaluating economic activity: output, employment, and prices. It is beneficial to investigate the possible existence of any relationship between them. Figure 13.2 captures data of the three indicators during 2006-2010. There are several interesting observations that can be concluded from Figure 13.2:

- During a contraction (contraction of real GDP), the unemployment rate increases.
- The unemployment rate continues to increase for a short period of time following the end of a contraction in real GDP.
- Inflation decreases during a period of contraction of real GDP.

- It also appears that higher unemployment is correlated with lower inflation (the Phillips Curve relationship).

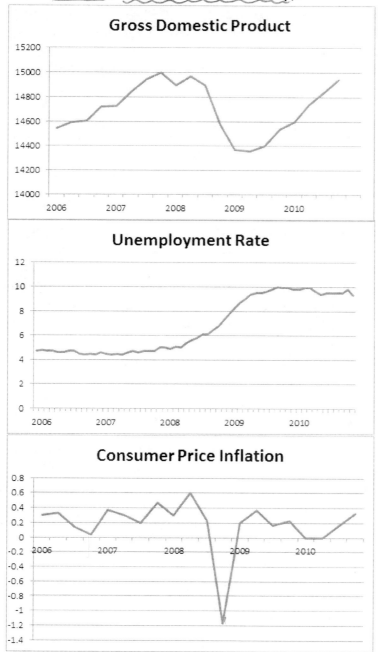

Figure 13.2. Sources: U.S. BEA and U.S. BLS. Real GDP is in billions of chained 2009 dollars.

Each of these observations is relevant to our understanding of the business cycle. The first observation is rather straight forward; as the level of economic activity declines, the level of unemployment naturally increases. Recall from our earlier discussion on the value of the marginal product of labor that the demand for labor is a derived demand. It is derived from the demand for the output produced by labor.

The second observation is much more interesting in that the unemployment is slightly out of phase with the output cycle, and it reaches its peak not at the end of a recession but rather into the recovery that follows. For this particular observation, the last two recessions (2001, 2007-2009) do not provide much in the way of empirical support because they were followed by relatively low employment growth early in the recoveries, i.e. jobless recoveries. As a result, the unemployment rate continued to increase for an extended period of time. In the case of the recession of 2001, the recession was declared to be over in November of 2001 by the NBER, but the unemployment rate did not peak until June of 2003. Similarly, the recession of 2007-2009 ended in June of 2009, while the unemployment rate continued to increase until November of 2009 and the labor force participation rate continued to decline for years. The reason these two recoveries tend to be considered as "jobless" recoveries is because the payroll growth remained rather subdued early in the recoveries. For example, steady, sustainable, positive employment growth did not return until September of 2003 following the recession of 2001. In the case of the 2007 – 2009 recession, steady sustainable job creation returned only in the last quarter of 2010.

Generally, an economic recovery brings with it positive job creation, which in turn gives hope to discouraged workers. This reentry of discouraged workers back into the labor force increases the labor force participation rate. This causes the unemployment rate to increase if the number of returning workers exceeds job creation. This temporary rise in the unemployment rate is accompanied by positive and sustainable job growth. It is temporary because the pool of discouraged workers is limited, and inevitably the economic recovery will start to pull the unemployment rate down. This behavior of the unemployment rate makes it a lagging economic indicator as it does not reflect what is happening but rather what has already happened.

The last two observations should be examined together. In so doing, it appears that inflation is affected by the unemployment rate. The logic behind it is rather simple; as individuals lose their jobs their incomes decline, causing them to reduce their consumption spending. Effectively, the unemployed cannot "bid up" prices as the purchasing power of their incomes declines. In economics, this relationship is represented by the Phillips curve, named after Alban William Phillips, who estimated it in his groundbreaking paper (Phillips, 1958). Because unemployment is derived from output fluctuations, the Phillips curve enables us to view inflation as a function of the difference between the current output level and the potential output level. This is an important observation as it suggests that inflation can be generated by the economy, and that there may be a tradeoff between inflation and the output gap.[29] We will briefly touch on this point in the discussion below. For further illustrations and possible implications of this relationship on policy, see Carlstrom and Fuerst (2008).

PUTTING THE THREE INDICATORS TOGETHER: THE PICTURE OF THE BUSINESS CYCLE

Note that scientifically, no relationship can be constructed from a single recession as there is simply not enough data. Figure 13.2 can be used to justify Figure 13.3, which summarizes the standard approach to the relationship between these three variables in macroeconomics (for further discussion, see Robert Gordon, 2011). Figure 13.3 groups these three important measures of economic performance into one framework. In the real GDP diagram, the dotted line represents the natural expansion path of the economy (one can think of it as a multi-year moving average). The natural expansion path represents the economy at full employment (or capacity). The dotted line is upward slopped as we expect the economy to grow over time. The solid curve represents the actual real GDP behavior over time.

Note that it is possible for the economy to outperform relative to the full employment level, but such a performance is likely to lead to inflation and a pullback in growth. When the economy overperforms relative to the full employment level, the economy experiences a positive output gap (the difference between the actual and potential output levels). When the economy underperforms relative to the full employment level, the gap is negative.

---

[29] An output gap is defined as the difference between the actual real output (Real GDP) and the potential (or full-employment) real output level.

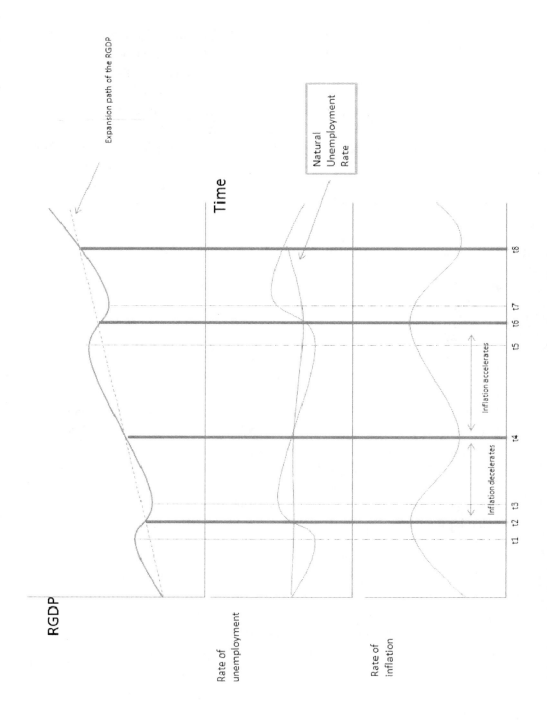

Figure 13.3

226

Using the diagram in Figure 13.3, we can illustrate the different stages of the business cycle. We will define the business cycle in terms of movements in the real output (real GPD), in which case a contraction in the level of economic activity occurs between the peaks and the troughs of the real GDP cycle. An example is the time period between t1 and t3. An expansion is a period of positive growth in real GDP as is observed between t3 and t5. However, in our discussion, the important time points will be t2, t4, t6, and t8. At all of these points in time, the actual real GDP equals the potential real GDP, i.e. the economy experiences no output gap. Later in our discussion, we will define this situation as the long-run equilibrium where the long-run aggregate supply equals the long-run aggregate demand.

It is important that we associate the real GDP diagram to that of the unemployment rate. The unemployment rate is almost countercyclical to real GDP because it peaks slightly after the end of a contraction. Otherwise, it would be completely countercyclical. During contractions, the unemployment rate rises drastically. The last two U.S. contractions are no exception to this rule. During the recession of 2001, the unemployment rate increased from 4.3% (March) to 5.5% (November). Between December of 2007 and June of 2009, the unemployment rate increased from 5.0% to 9.5% (for more details please see the U.S. BEA, www.bea.gov).

If we consider the full employment output level as ideal, then it is the unemployment rate at times t2, t3, t6, and t8 that is the preferred rate. In Figure 13.3, this rate is roughly constant over time and is labeled as the Natural Unemployment Rate because it corresponds to the economy being on the natural expansion path of real GDP. One way to define the natural unemployment rate is to tie it to real GDP and argue that it is the unemployment rate that corresponds to the full employment level. Since the full employment level is a long-run equilibrium, the natural unemployment rate is a long-run unemployment rate. The concept of natural unemployment rate was formulated by Milton Friedman (see Friedman, 1968).

It is interesting to note that the natural unemployment rate does not need to remain constant over time. For instance, at the start of the 1990s, most economists believed that the natural unemployment rate for the U.S. economy was about 6%. By 2000, that target moved into the 4 – 4.5% range. Today, it is probably closer to 6 – 6.5%. Government policies, reservation wages, labor mobility, capital stock, and productivity all impact the natural unemployment rate.

Since the long-run in economics is defined as a time period it takes to undergo a complete adjustment including a complete adjustment in prices, the long-run equilibrium is characterized by a constant rate of inflation. Note that any acceleration or deceleration of inflation by definition is an adjustment and therefore is not a characteristic of the equilibrium. This implies that the natural rate of unemployment is connected to inflation as it is the rate of unemployment that keeps inflation constant. This allows us to connect the discussion to the last aspect of Figure 13.3 - inflation.

CONNECTING INFLATION TO UNEMPLOYMENT

The lower section of Figure 13.3 presents the diagram of inflation. As discussed earlier, in the context of the Phillips curve, there exists a relationship between inflation and unemployment. If the economy starts to operate beyond its capacity level, the unemployment rate will decline below the natural unemployment rate and inflation will start to accelerate. In this situation, businesses start to compete for economic resources (including labor), and the prices of these resources start rising above the growth in their productivity. This process is typically referred to as overheating. In Figure 13.3, we see overheating in the later stages of an expansion and at the start of a contraction when the actual unemployment rate falls below the natural unemployment rate. During this stage of the business cycle, inflation is likely to increase. The last time the U.S. economy experienced overheating was 1999 – 2000.

When the actual unemployment rate exceeds the natural unemployment rate, the situation is reversed. The growth in input prices (including wages) slows down and as a result inflation decelerates. This implies that the natural unemployment rate is the rate that keeps inflation constant.

Note that there is no such thing as a natural rate of inflation. Figure 13.3 shows there are at least two different constant rates of inflation that correspond to the natural unemployment rate. The first is seen at t2 and the second is observed at t4. This means that the rate of inflation itself is not as important as the rate of change in inflation.

In our discussion, we stated that it is not the rate of inflation but its stability is what matters. Figure 13.3 demonstrates that when the economy reaches its full employment, regardless of the inflation rate, inflation becomes constant. However, a higher rate of inflation may itself contribute to uncertainty. It is because businesses and households might anticipate a future change in the monetary policy of the central bank. Businesses and households might expect the central bank to intervene during high inflation, all else held constant.

THE BASICS OF THE AGGREGATE FRAMEWORK

This section provides a rudimentary foundation of macroeconomic analysis. Although the analysis in this section is basic and limited to graphical framework, it does offer useful insight into the different types of recessions and the long-run adjustment mechanism. We simplify our discussion by beginning with an already defined aggregate demand, which presents a significant simplification, and as a consequence limits the framework. For the derivation of aggregate demand from the IS/LM model and a basic construction of the IS/LM model, please see Appendix A at the end of this chapter. The discussion in Appendix A presents a basic overview at the level of an intermediate macroeconomics college course.

Aggregate demand represents demand for domestically produced final goods and services aggregated across all economic agents in all sectors. In essence, aggregate demand is simply demand for real GDP. Thus, it can be represented by the GDP identity:

13.1) $GDP = C + I + G + x - m$

Similarly to the demand functions discussed at the beginning of this book, an aggregate demand curve is plotted in the output/price space. Since aggregate demand represents demand for real GDP, it is only natural to use real output (real GDP) as the measure of output. The role of price is assumed by the price level (or price index, see the discussion in the preceding chapter). The price level represents the average price in the economy. GDP has a corresponding price level called the GDP deflator, which is an appropriate measure for the price axis in the aggregate demand diagram (see Figure 13.4).

The negative relationship captured by the aggregate demand in Figure 13.4 between the price level and real GDP is not immediately obvious. In the context of a single market, demand is downward slopped because of two effects: substitution and income. Similar effects exist in the context of aggregate demand such as an open economy effect, a real balances effect, and an interest rate effect

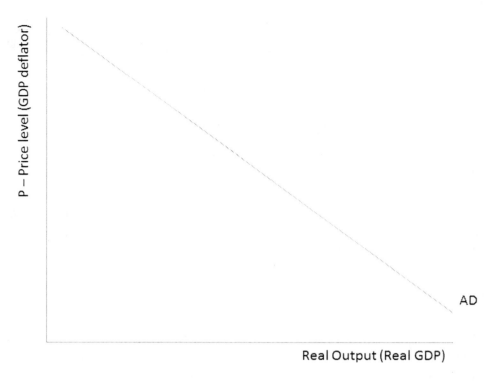

Figure 13.4

The first of these, the open economy effect, is very similar to the substitution effect in the context of a single market demand. At higher domestic output prices, net exports should be lower, with all else held constant. A higher domestic price level makes domestic goods relatively more expensive compared to foreign goods, and as a result exports decline, while imports increase.

Real Balance effect The second effect is somewhat similar to the income effect in a single market demand. A higher price level reduces the purchasing power of any savings held in the form of money, and thus the wealth of households declines, causing them to reduce their spending on all normal goods.

interest rate effect The third effect has no analogue in a single market demand. In the case of aggregate demand, the money supply is one of the factors that shifts the curve. Thus, when a given curve is drawn, the assumption is made that the money supply is fixed. A rise in the price level increases the need to hold more money for transaction purposes. One of the key determinants of money demand is the need to use money for ongoing transactions (see Appendix A). A rise in the

230

transactional demand for money causes the price of money, the interest rate, to increase. A higher interest rate makes investment and consumption more costly, causing these interest-sensitive aggregate expenditures to fall, thus taking the economy to a lower level of output.

SHIFTS IN AGGREGATE DEMAND

Other than the price level, anything capable of changing any of the aggregate expenditures can shift aggregate demand. The discussion below presents some examples of factors that would shift an aggregate demand curve.

Consumption   A rise in consumption spending would cause aggregate demand to increase (shift to the right in Figure 13.4). Factors that would cause consumption spending to increase include:

- A rise in consumer confidence (i.e. improved consumer expectations about the future income)
- A reduction in personal taxes (e.g. income, sales, property)[30]
- A rise in transfer payments from the government[31]
- A rise in household wealth (for factors other than a decline in the price level as the effect is captured in the slope)
- A reduction in interest rate

Investment   A rise in investment spending causes an increase in aggregate demand. Factors that cause such a change in investment spending include:

- A rise in business sector confidence (i.e. improved expectations about the future profitability)
- A reduction in business taxes
- A reduction in interest rate (recall that interest rate represents a cost of investment)[32]

---

[30] A change in the income tax rate (see Appendix A) would actually rotate aggregate demand, changing the slope as well.

[31] Transfer payments are payments that do not require anything in return. Examples of public sector transfer payments include welfare payments, food stamps, etc.

[32] Recall from the discussion in Chapter 1 that capital equipment includes two cost components: interest rate and economic depreciation.

Government Government fiscal or monetary policy can stimulate aggregate demand. Some stimulus directly enters aggregate demand as is the case with government spending (G). Some instruments of government policy work indirectly by influencing the behavior of private economic agents through taxation, transfers, and interest rate changes. The following changes cause aggregate demand to increase (some of these were previously listed as part of consumption and investment):

- A rise in government spending
- A reduction in taxes
- A rise in transfer payments
- A rise in money supply (which leads to a lower interest rate)

Net Exports Below are some of the main factors that lead to a rise in net exports (i.e. a rise in exports and/or a decline in imports):

- A decline in the value of the domestic currency
- An improvement in the economic conditions of trading partner economies

However, one has to be careful with the first statement. It is true that a declining domestic currency effectively lowers the prices of domestic goods in foreign markets while it simultaneously increases the prices of imports. Depending on what the economy imports, the consequences might be different. We will return to this argument later when we examine short-run aggregate supply.

SUPPLY SIDE

The supply side in aggregate framework has to differentiate between two different states: one in which all prices adjust fully and another where some prices are fixed or as Keynes put it are "sticky". This distinction allows us to differentiate between the long-run and the short-run macroeconomic frameworks. The short-run will be defined as the framework where some prices are fixed. The long-run will be defined as a time period that it takes to fully adjust all prices. Since the Classical Economic model assumes full price flexibility, the long-run discussion simply becomes an application of the Classical model.

LONG-RUN VERSUS SHORT-RUN AGGREGATE SUPPLY

Recall from our earlier discussion on the costs of production in the long-run; in economics, the long-run is defined as a time framework where economic agents are not constrained in their decisions. The same logic applies in the aggregate framework where the long-run is defined as a time period needed to achieve full flexibility in all prices, including input prices. If full price flexibility exists, then economic agents, such as households and firms, become fully flexible in their decisions to supply/demand all goods and services, including inputs. In this environment, all economic agents will select their desirable quantities. This implies that workers will supply the desired number of hours of labor, firms will hire the desired number of workers, consumers will purchase the desired level of output, and so on. This describes an economy that operates at its capacity.

Consider a situation where you are self-employed and produce one unit of output for each hour of work. You could be an accountant performing tax return filings for your clients, with the assumption that it takes you one hour to complete one tax return. This assumption is purely for simplification purposes and is not essential since all it accomplishes is that it allows us to set the hourly wage to the price of tax returns. Let us assume that you desire to allocate eight hours to work each day. The eight hours serve as your desired employment level. For the sake of the example, let us assume that the price at which the output is sold is $30. This implies that your daily income is $240. This situation is depicted by point A in Figure 13.5. The fact that you are capable of charging $30 and selling 8 units of output, without shortage or surplus, implies that the demand for your services goes through point A. The actual shape of the demand is irrelevant; the important point is that the price of $30 and the quantity of 8 constitutes the current equilibrium.

Let us now create a recession and assume that the demand for your services decreases to D2. You have two options: to keep the price fixed, or start lowering the price. If you decide to keep the price at $30, you would effectively need to fire yourself as your work day would decrease from 8 hours to only 3. If you start lowering the price, you can still keep yourself employed for the desired number of hours. To keep yourself employed for 8 hours, the price needs to fall to $24. Obviously, this is a disaster as your nominal income decreases by 20%. However, what if this decline in the demand is not just observed by you but across the entire economy, including those markets where you are a consumer? What if the suppliers in those markets also reduce their prices to keep themselves fully employed? As a result, if all prices decline by 20%, the drop in income you observe is only nominal because in real terms nothing happened. This is actually

233

a very important observation because it implies that a recession, specifically a demand driven recession, simply translates into deflation in the long-run.

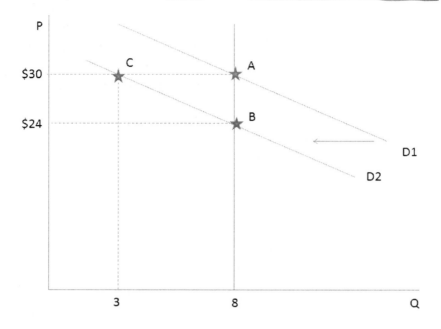

Figure 13.5

If we connect points A and B in Figure 13.5, we will construct your long-run supply function. Your long-run supply function is vertical, and it is determined by your capacity to produce output and not the price level. From the long-term perspective, the price is irrelevant because it adjusts to where it needs to be. A recession is like pressure on the system, and in the long-run, the entire pressure is absorbed by prices, leaving employment and output unchanged.

Next, let us now slightly modify this scenario by introducing a hired unit of labor. We still start at point A, but instead of doing the work yourself you hire a worker whom you pay $30/hour, where the wage is subject to a contract between you and the worker. Just as before, the demand decreases to D2. The two scenarios seem similar but actually they are very different. In the latter case, you have no ability to lower the wage rate to $24 because the contract does not permit it. It becomes simpler to reduce the level of employment and cut the worker hours to 3 instead of lowering the wage. This leads to an actual reduction in employment and output, or recession. Instead of moving to point B in Figure 13.5, you therefore move to point C, tracing a horizontal supply curve.

The irony is that as time passes you will be able to move to point B. The reason for this move will be due to a reduction in the wage rate of the worker you hire. It might be difficult to renegotiate the wage down from $30 to $24, but after a period of unemployment (or underemployment as it is in this scenario) the worker might be more willing to accept the wage reduction to return to their full employment. This is the difference between the short-run and the long-run. In the short-run, input costs (including the wage rate) are fixed, but in the long-run, input costs are fully flexible. When input costs are fixed, any fluctuation in demand for output results in changes in employment because the recessionary pressure cannot be absorbed by an inflexible wage; therefore, the impact falls on a more flexible level of employment. Over time, as the wage becomes more flexible, employment returns to its pre-recession level.

In essence, the short-run is characterized by inflexible input prices, forcing input quantities to become flexible, while the long-run is characterized by flexible input prices and fixed input quantities. Earlier, we argued that a recession is similar to pressure being applied on an economy. In the short-run, this pressure is absorbed by input and output changes, while in the long-run, it is completely absorbed by changes in prices.

SHIFTS IN AGGREGATE SUPPLY CURVES

Since the long-run aggregate supply represents the economy at its capacity level, the long-run aggregate supply curve is impacted by economic growth. The curve would shift outwards (increase) if the quantity of inputs or their productivity were to increase.

The horizontal line (going through points A and C) that represents the short-run aggregate supply function in Figure 13.5 is drawn given a constant wage rate. This implies that changes in the wage rate and other input costs will cause the short-run aggregate supply curve to shift. Increases in input costs will cause it to shift upwards (decrease), and declines in input costs will cause it to shift downwards (increase).

Would a real world example be as pessimistic as our scenario where the movement from point C to point B requires a wage reduction? Luckily, the answer is no. There is one additional mechanism, an increase in productivity. For instance, in our scenario, a rise in labor productivity will cause both curves to shift. If labor productivity were to increase by 50%, then the long-run curve

235

would move from 8 to 12 units of output (tax returns), and the short-run curve would shift down from the horizontal line at $30 to one at $20. The shift in the short-run aggregate supply would occur because the per unit cost of output (the horizontal axis measures output) would now be $20. The decline in the per unit cost is due to the fact that the worker can now perform one and a half tax returns per hour.

AGGREGATE DIAGRAM

If we combine the two aggregate supply functions with the aggregate demand, we would have the complete picture of the aggregate framework. Note that in Figure 13.6, the short-run aggregate supply is upward slopped and becomes steeper as the economy exceeds its capacity.[33]

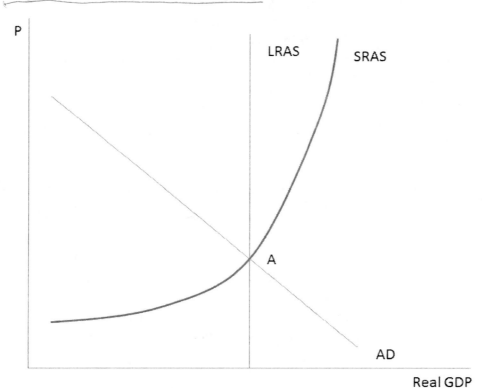

Figure 13.6

---

[33] Unlike the constant returns function of Figure 13.5, this function assumes diminishing returns.

236

Point A in Figure 13.6 represents both the short-run and the long-run equilibrium. It is important to understand that the economy is always in a short-run equilibrium. A short-run equilibrium occurs when aggregate demand equals short-run aggregate supply. The short-run equilibrium from Figure 13.6 corresponds to being on the actual path of the real GDP in Figure 13.3. A long-run equilibrium occurs at the point where aggregate demand meets long-run aggregate supply. Note that since the economy is always in its short-run equilibrium, a long-run equilibrium can only be observed when all three curves intercept, as is illustrated in Figure 13.6. A long-run equilibrium corresponds to being on the expansion path of the real GDP, as seen in Figure 13.3.

RECESSIONS

Recessions can originate on either the supply or demand side. Demand driven recessions are much more common and represent the typical recession in the US. The last two U.S. recessions (2001, 2007-09) are examples of demand driven recessions. In a demand driven recession, the aggregate demand decreases, causing the short-run equilibrium to move from point A to point B as demonstrated in Figure 13.7.

A demand driven recession results in a lower output level and a lower price level as is seen from a comparison between points A and B in Figure 13.7.

Supply driven recessions are considerably less common. The U.S. experienced a supply driven recession in the 1970's as a result of the oil embargo that drove up the price of oil. A supply driven recession is caused by a rise in cost of production. Typically, this is induced by a resource crisis that leads to higher commodity prices and causes the short-run aggregate supply function to decrease (shift upwards) as shown in Figure 13.8.

The short-run equilibrium moves from point A to point D. As the figure illustrates, a supply driven recession is accompanied by a rise in the price level. Initially, such a recession is characterized by stagflation (i.e. stagnant growth accompanied by inflation).

Demand
Driven
Recession

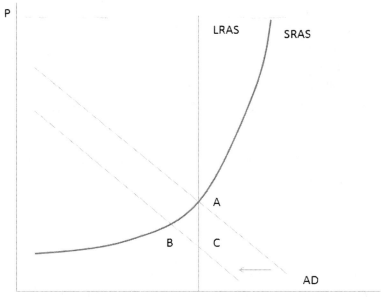

Figure 13.7

Supply
Driven
Recession

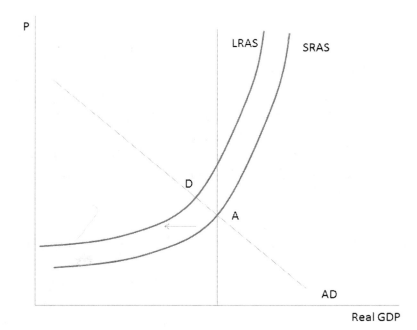

Figure 13.8

Both types of recession are self-correcting. In the case of a demand driven recession, like the one depicted in Figure 13.7, the likely correction will come in the form of a decline in real input costs over time; this will result in the short-run aggregate supply shifting down and the equilibrium moving to point C. The supply driven recession depicted in Figure 13.8 is also self-correcting. In this case, the short-run aggregate supply will likely return to its original position bringing the equilibrium back to A.

To better understand the corrective mechanism of a supply driven recession, one can examine the U.S. airline sector between 2004 and 2008: a period of rising fuel prices. During this period several U.S. passenger airlines, beginning with American Airlines in 2004, significantly renegotiated their labor contracts. Generally, these renegotiations resulted in lower labor costs (including the nominal wage rates). Consequently, the higher fuel costs caused the shareholders and the workers to receive lower compensation for capital and labor. The lower compensation to these inputs helped offset the higher fuel cost and thereby reversed at least some of the effect the higher fuel cost exerted on the supply function. The same logic applies to the short-run aggregate supply function. After the economy reaches point D, high unemployment begins to suppress wages (nominal wages), and as these wages decline, the aggregate short-run supply function rolls back to its original position.[34]

The previously described corrective mechanisms can potentially take years to run their course. Keynes, easily one of the most well-known and influential economists, is credited with a very depressing statement: "In the long-run, we are all dead." Unfortunately, this statement applies to Figures 13.7 and 13.8. While waiting for the adjustment to run its course, the population undergoes significant economic suffering. Recessions can cause political instability since they create poverty, which in turn can act as an important ingredient for social unrest. Social unrest leads to greater uncertainty about the future and therefore reduces investment. This further fuels recessions, creating a vicious cycle.

Although it is possible for a short-duration spike in unemployment to lead to human capital formation as the opportunity cost of education decreases, a prolonged unemployment is highly destructive to human capital. This implies that a prolonged recession is capable of lowering the level of economic development.

---

[34] Real wages can also be reduced through inflation in output prices. If output prices rise while input costs remain constant, then the real input costs decrease.

Given the length of time needed to undergo the adjustment and the amount of damage a recession and underproduction create, there may be a desire to deploy public sector policies aimed at stimulating the level of economic activity.[35]

ROLE OF GOVERNMENT

Government has two broadly defined approaches to the economy: a short-run approach to economic stabilization and a long-run approach to economic growth. An economy is like a sailing ship where there are two important things to consider: the motion of the ship side to side and its forward speed. Stabilization focuses on avoiding capsizing the ship, while development concentrates on the forward moving speed. Economic development policies are long-run policies aimed at enhancing the level of economic growth.

An example of a development policy is education. The classroom of today is where the competition for future exports takes place. Countries with better educational systems will be able to enhance the productivity of their future labor force to better compete in the global economy. Thus, spending on education can be perceived as a long-run economic development policy. However, like any economic policy, it is very complex. One simple illustration of such complexity would be a basic comparison of the German or Russian educational models to that of the U.S. In Germany and Russia (although the Russian educational model is undergoing changes) specialization tends to begin earlier in a student's education. In these countries, the educational system puts high school students on a more specialized path at an earlier age, while most college level institutions offer highly specialized education from the start. The U.S. employs a rather different approach to education where specialization is not as encouraged early on. Most U.S. college students do not begin their professional specialization until their third year in college. These two approaches are rather different. It may seem that the German or Russian approaches are better as they allow the student to focus on what is important for their future profession and obtain the specialized skills earlier in life; thus, providing the student with more time to benefit from their skills in the labor market. However, the U.S. model creates a labor force that is more flexible and can easily be retrained at a later point in time, given the large investment into general educational skills. Depending on the economic model, a different educational model may be best suited. For example, the more

---

[35] Production at points B and D resulted in a negative output gap, which is the difference between the potential or capacity output and the actual output.

specialized skill set requires a more stable labor market as the occupational labor mobility cost is higher. A more flexible labor force is better suited for a dynamic labor market as the cost of shifting labor across occupations is lower.

In our discussion, we should focus on stabilization policies and not on development economics. Stabilization policies are aimed at reducing the volatility in the business cycle. The best business cycle is one that actually does not exist so that the economy advances along the potential expansion path. There are generally two types of domestic stabilization policies: fiscal and monetary.

FISCAL POLICY

Fiscal policy is simply a change in the budget of the public sector. A fiscal expansion means the public sector injects more into the economy than it takes from it, which means it must run a budget deficit. A fiscal contraction means the public sector injects less into the economy than it takes from it, which means the budget must be in surplus. The instruments of fiscal policy are simple and include: government spending (G), taxation (Tax), and transfers (Tr). A fiscal expansion is a combination of one or more of the following policies: increases in government spending, decreases in tax collection, and increases in transfer payments. A fiscal contraction is simply a reversal of the previous statement. Theoretically speaking, the public sector can serve as a stabilizer to the economy and inject into the spending flow when the private sector is soft, and later it can compensate for the debt accumulated during the recession by collecting more from the private sector when the economy is overheating. This balances the public sector budget over time while stabilizing the level of aggregate spending in the economy.

Although generally the use of fiscal policy requires a decision on the part of public sector policy makers, some elements of fiscal policy can activate on their own when the economy needs them. Such instruments are called automatic fiscal stabilizers. Progressive income taxation and unemployment benefits are examples of automatic stabilizers. Progressive income taxation is characterized by a rising marginal tax rate structure, which implies that the average tax rate increases with income. When the economy falls into a recession, household incomes decline, and as a result households move into lower marginal tax brackets. Households with falling incomes not only pay less in taxes, but more importantly, they face lower marginal tax rates. This effectively amounts to a tax decrease exactly when it is needed, during an economic downturn. Similarly, unemployment benefits increase when the economy is weak and decline when it is strong. This makes the transfer payments somewhat countercyclical to GDP, which is exactly what we would want from a stabilization policy.

Advantage: There are numerous benefits to fiscal policy. If an economy suffers from high unemployment, the public sector can increase the government payroll and hire more government employees. This solution would directly reduce the ranks of the unemployed. Therefore, fiscal policy can go directly to the core of the problem. Another benefit is that fiscal policy can be regionally targeted (although with a spillover effect). For instance, we typically think of fiscal policy at the national level, but it can be run at a regional and even a local level. This is particularly valuable in a larger economy where an economic downturn can be localized.

Disadvantage: However, fiscal policy is not without its drawbacks. A fiscal expansion can result in a rise in interest rates which can in turn crowd-out private investment. Economists refer to this as an indirect crowding-out effect. When the public sector runs an expansionary policy it borrows in financial markets. An expansionary policy leads to deficits, which are then financed by issuing new government bonds and selling them in the open market. Since the public sector is a relatively large market participant, a fiscal expansion can result in a sizable change in interest rates, leading to a higher cost of investment for the business sector. Appendix A develops a basic view of the IS-LM model.[36] In the context of the IS-LM model, a fiscal expansion causes an outward shift of the IS curve which moves the equilibrium along an upward slopped LM curve. The steeper the LM curve, the weaker is the effectiveness of fiscal policy as the interest rate adjustments become larger.

Another drawback related to the indirect crowding-out effect is the open economy effect. A rise in interest rates induced by government borrowing leads to an increase in foreign investment entering the economy. Such a rise in foreign investment causes the value of domestic currency to increase, thereby negatively impacting the economy's international trade balance.

---

[36] IS – Investment and saving, LM – liquidity and money. The IS/LM model simultaneously captures three important markets: the market for goods and services, the market for loanable funds, and the market for money. The model is used to study general equilibrium in the short-run. For more details on the IS/LM model, please see Appendix A at the end of this chapter.

Fiscal policy can even directly crowd-out the private sector, which occurs when the public sector directly competes with private enterprises. An example of this can be found in public education. Public schools reduce enrollment in private schools. When a state increases spending on publically run colleges, the demand for private schools is negatively impacted.

MONETARY POLICY

To understand monetary policy in a modern economy, one must first understand the fractional reserve banking system. However, it is also important to point out that monetary policy, the way it is practiced today, is a rather new tool. Today, central banks can print unlimited supplies of money and use instruments such as quantitative easing to stimulate the economy. This is made possible by the fact that central banks are not required to back their domestic money supply with any reserves, such as an actual commodity like gold. A central bank that follows a gold standard and maintains convertibility of paper currency (convertibility into gold) is in a more restricted position. Under a gold standard, the convertibility requirement limits the ability of a central bank to change money supply. In the US, the role of the central bank is performed by the Federal Reserve, which was established only one hundred years ago in 1913. The Federal Reserve Act of 1913 required the Federal Reserve to honor convertibility and maintain 40% gold reserves against the currency in circulation, which significantly restricted its ability to vary the domestic money supply (see Friedman and Swartz, 1960; Bernanke and James, 1991).

It is interesting to note that the Federal Reserve does not have the words "central bank" in its title. Instead, it is called the Federal Reserve System. The Federal Reserve was established as a stabilizing mechanism for the banking sector. A major lending institutions' crisis of 1907 underscored the need for establishing a system of reserves to stabilize the nation's banks (see Tallman and Moen, 1990)). This lead to the establishment of the Federal Reserve System that required all member banks to maintain a certain percentage of all deposits in reserve.

Today, the reserve requirement for virtually all member banks is set at 10% against all demand deposits. A member bank has two ways in which the required reserves can be kept: cash in their own vault and in the bank's reserve account with the Federal Reserve. This has several important implications. Firstly, the amount of lending a bank can originate is limited to 90% of the funds in their demand deposits. Secondly, every bank must continuously meet the reserve

243

requirements and the reserve requirements are checked weekly. The first implication helps stabilize the banking sector, and the second implication creates a market for reserves as banks with low reserves are forced to borrow them from those banks that experience excess reserves.[37] It is this market for reserves that provides the Federal Reserve with the most commonly used target for monetary policy, the Federal Funds Rate.

| *Open Market Operations* | Monetary policy involves changes in money supply that lead to changes in interest rates and therefore impact the cost of autonomous consumption and investment. Unlike fiscal policy, monetary policy cannot be targeted regionally as it affects all who use the domestic currency.[38] Monetary policy also depends on the sensitivity of household and business spending to interest rate changes. An old saying comes to mind: "You can lead a horse to water, but you can't make it drink." The central bank can reduce interest rates, but it will be up to private borrowers to actually respond to the lower rates. The general structure of monetary policy is rather simple and should probably be analyzed backwards as the proceeding discussion demonstrates.

Consider a monetary expansion where the ultimate objective of the policy might be to reduce unemployment and to increase real GDP. Such a goal makes these variables the ultimate objectives of the policy. However, we do not see money supply anywhere in our GDP identity, so what can the central bank do to affect the real output? GDP includes two expenditure categories that are functions of interest rates: consumption and investment. Both of these are decreasing functions of the interest rates at which households and businesses borrow. Thus, in order to increase GDP, the central bank needs to lower these interest rates. Since the interest rate represents the price of money, to lower the interest rate the central bank needs to increase the supply of money. A higher money supply would reduce the scarcity of money and therefore reduce its price, the interest rate. This means that the policy target becomes a change in the relevant interest rate, while a change in the money supply becomes the tool. [39]

---

[37] Member banks can also borrow reserves overnight directly from the Federal Reserve at what is known as the Discount Rate.

[38] Recent addition of new monetary policy instruments such as purchases of assets other than U.S. Treasury bonds may offer some very limited regional targeting.

[39] There is a subtle difference in terms here. The policy objective is a change in GDP, the policy target is a change in the interest rate (the Federal Funds rate), and the instrument is a change in the money supply. Changes in GDP take time to materialize, and therefore they can't serve as a measurable policy target. On the other hand, a change in the

244

This immediately brings up two important questions. First, which interest rate should be targeted? Second, how can money supply be changed? The first question is a more complex one. An advanced economy has an array of interest rates. There is the rate on a 30 year mortgage, the rate on a 5 year AAA corporate bond, the rate on a car loan, etc. However, despite this complexity, the system is actually a bit simpler. Think of all these interest rates as simply floors in a multistory building. The highest floor may be the interest rate on a credit card where the securitization of the loan is rather poor and the risk of default might be high. Below that there are some low investment grade corporate bonds. Further down the structure are mortgage rates where the securitization is somewhat stronger, and so on. The basement of this building is the rate on the most secure and shortest term loan. This loan is one that is made overnight by one major bank to another for the purpose of meeting the reserve requirement. In the U.S., the rate on these loans is called the federal funds rate, as it is the rate on funds required by the Federal Reserve. When the rate changes; all floors in the building adjust. The only issue is that the other rates don't have to move by the same amount or proportion. In other words, our strange building can have its floors change in height, but the general direction of the move tends to be the same.[40] As the Federal Funds rate decreases, all other rates tend to decline.

Changing the money supply is not all that difficult either. To expand the money supply, the Federal Reserve simply purchases financial assets from the public and in return pays for them with newly created money.[41] This new money gets deposited into the accounts of households and businesses who sold their financial assets to the Federal Reserve. As the money gets deposited into these accounts, the banking system experiences a rise in demand deposits and consequently a rise in reserves. Note that the rise in required reserves is only one tenth of the rise in the overall reserves, which means the excess reserves increase by 90% of the

---

interest rate can be achieved within a few minutes, and thus it becomes a workable policy target.

[40] Since the federal funds rate represents a rate on a short-term loan, the relationship between the federal funds rate and the short-term rates in the economy tends to be direct. The relationship between the federal funds rate and the long-term rates may not exhibit the same characteristics. One reason for this might be inflationary or recessionary expectations. For instance, a rise in short-term rates may induce expectations of lower inflation in the long-run and lead to a reduction in the long-term rates and a "flattening" of the yield curve.

[41] Although monetary policy implementation typically involves purchases/sales of U.S. Treasury bonds mainly in the secondary market, exceptions can be made. In recent years, the Federal Reserve purchased a number of various assets including mortgage backed securities.

Federal Reserve's purchases.[42] These excess reserves lead to more funding available for lending and also to a decline in the price of reserves, the federal funds rate. Once the interest rate target is reached, some periodic purchases/sales might be needed to maintain the target rate. At this point, the effect of the policy begins to materialize as the household and the business sectors start responding to lower interest rates in the economy.

The effectiveness of the policy rests on the sensitivity of household and business spending to changes in interest rates. The greater the sensitivity, the greater will be the response in consumption and investment expenditures. In the context of the IS-LM model presented in Appendix A, the slope of the IS curve captures the effect of this sensitivity. The flatter the IS function, the greater is the effectiveness of monetary policy. On the other hand, an extremely low sensitivity of consumption and investment to interest rate changes may make monetary policy practically useless. This scenario would be captured by a nearly vertical IS function.

In addition to the open market operations method, the Federal Reserve can change the amount of lending in the economy by lowering the reserve requirement ratio. Lowering the ratio would free these reserves and allow banks to generate more lending. Using this instrument, as part of an expansionary monetary policy, has significant repercussions because reversing this policy at a later point in time might prove to be a significant shock to the banking system. Since the reserve requirement ratio is easy to reduce but rather difficult to increase, it is an instrument that is rarely used.

Benefit:

There are certain benefits to monetary policy. Monetary policy does not add to the nation's debt. The open economy effect works in the direction of the policy. Reductions in interest rates lead to currency depreciation because they make foreign financial assets relatively more attractive than before. In turn, the depreciation helps net exports.

STABILIZATION POLICY

Fiscal and monetary policies tend to complement each other. A fiscal expansion tends to drive up interest rates, while an expansionary monetary policy reduces them.

---

[42] Excess reserves constitute the reserves above what is required by the Federal Reserve.

Perhaps the greatest benefit of both fiscal and monetary policies is simply that they exist. Their presence calms various economic agents. The fact that the Federal government has these powerful, corrective tools available can reduce the amount of uncertainty and risk about the future, thereby reducing volatility in the economy.

References

Bernanke, Ben, and Harold James. 1991. *"The Gold Standard, Deflation, and Financial Crisis in the Great Depression: An International Comparison."* Published in Financial Markets and Financial Crises, edited by R. G. Hubbard. University of Chicago Press. Available online at: http://www.nber.org/chapters/c11482 .

Carlstrom, Charles T. and Timothy S. Fuerst, 2008. *"Explaining apparent changes in the Phillips curve: trend inflation isn't constant,"* Economic Commentary, Federal Reserve Bank of Cleveland, issue Jan.

Friedman, Milton, and Anna J. Schwartz. 1963. *A monetary history of the United States, 1867-1960.* Princeton: Princeton University Press.

Friedman, Milton. 1968. *"The Role of Monetary Policy".* American Economic Review 58: 1–17.

Robert Gordon, Rober J. 2011. Macroeconomics, 12th Edition. Pearson/Addison Wesley, Boston, MA.

NBER. 2013. U.S. Business Cycle Expansions and Contractions. Available online at: http://nber.org/cycles/cyclesmain.html .

Phillips, A. W. 1958. *"The Relationship between Unemployment and the Rate of Change of Money Wages in the United Kingdom 1861-1957".* Economica 25 (100): 283–299.

Tallman, Ellis W. and Jon R. Moen. 1990. *"Lessons from the Panic of 1907."* The Federal Reserve Bank of Atlanta, Economic Review 75.

APPENDIX A

BASICS OF AGGREGATE FRAMEWORK

This discussion develops the basics of an aggregate framework of analysis in macroeconomics. Perhaps the best point to start the aggregate framework discussion is with the GDP identity:

1A) $\quad GDP = Y = C + I + G + x - m$

In equation 1A, we make an assumption that income and output are identical, which allows us to equate GDP to income (Y). We designate it with Y as I already designates investment in macroeconomics. We will also refer to the individual GDP components, such as C, I, G, x, and m, as expenditures. These are aggregate expenditures as they are aggregated across all consumers (C), businesses (I), etc. and represent spending on domestically produced final goods and services.

To proceed, we need to differentiate the expenditures along two different criteria. First, we need to separate those expenditures that are induced by current income from those that are influenced by other factors. Induced expenditures will be a function of Y (current Y), while expenditures that are not a function of Y will be referred to as autonomous (i.e. independent of current income). This distinction needs to be made for one simple reason; we need to identify Y. The identity listed in 1A actually is not solved for Y (or GDP); this is because some expenditure components such as consumption may depend on the current income, making Y appear on both sides of the equality sign. Solving for Y requires that we solve expression 1A for Y. Second, we will need to differentiate between unplanned and planned expenditures. Luckily for us, the last differentiation is very simple to accomplish as it will only involve one expenditure category - Investment.

One of the difficulties in this discussion is that unlike the microeconomic models discussed earlier, a macro model is a general equilibrium one. Micro models tend to be partial equilibrium models, meaning that only one market is being analyzed, and there is no need to consider how the other markets are being impacted or how the equilibrium in one market impacts other markets. A general equilibrium model requires multiple markets to be simultaneously in equilibrium. The model we are about to discuss will be an example of such a general equilibrium model. We will have three separate markets being simultaneously in equilibrium: the market for goods and services, the market for loanable funds, and the market for money.

Even though this is a general equilibrium model, we will start its development with a single market, and then gradually incorporate the other two markets into the framework. We will begin with the market for goods and services, which is already identified by the GDP (income, Y) identity. This will enable us to understand how income (output) is being determined. Because we are starting with the market for goods and services, we need to assume that the other two markets (the market for loanable funds and the market for money) remain in equilibrium and the variables determined by those markets remain constant. This requires us to assume a constant price level (the price level is determined by the market for money) and a constant interest rate (the interest rate is determined by the loanable funds market). Later, we will relax these assumptions.

INDUCED VERSUS AUTONOMOUS: INCOME DETERMINATION

As previously mentioned, we replace GDP with Y in Equation 1 (or Equation 1A), where Y represents income. Since GDP generates income for all domestic economic agents, there is no logical error in using this substitution. The expenditures listed in Equation 1A may themselves be influenced by the current income. Such functions will be called "induced" because they are influenced or caused by the current income. Expenditures that are independent of the current income will be referred to as "autonomous". With this in mind, we need to examine each of the expenditure components of Equation 1 (or Equation 1A).

CONSUMPTION FUNCTION (C)

Consumption expenditure is a function of multiple variables. Just think about what factors might influence your own consumption behavior. When you purchase new goods and services produced in the U.S., you directly contribute to the aggregate consumption expenditure, C.

Induced Consumption: Income

Among the factors that are expected to influence consumption spending, the first that comes to mind is current income (Y). Consumption is indeed influenced by the current income of households. For instance, a decline in household incomes can cause demand to decline for such things like eating out, vacations, airfares,

249

etc. We refer to the part of the consumption function that is a function of current income as induced consumption. It is important to note that consumption is actually a function of personal disposable income (PDI), which in turn is a function of any taxes paid and transfers received. The current income (Y) is not the only factor that influences C and the proceeding discussion lists some of the other factors capable of changing consumption spending.

Autonomous Consumption: Independent of Current Income

- Expected Future Income (Consumer Confidence)

For instance, a decision to purchase a new car may be in part based on expected <u>future</u> income. A household may increase their consumption spending today because they expect a higher stream of income in the future. One proxy for household expectations about the future is consumer confidence. An improvement in consumer confidence will cause consumption spending to rise, all else held constant. In the U.S., there are two widely used measures of consumer confidence. One such measure is reported by The Conference Board and another by the University of Michigan. Both measures are survey based and are conducted monthly. For further information please refer to the Consumer Confidence Index of The Conference Board (http://www.conference-board.org) and the University of Michigan's Index of Consumer Sentiment (http://www.sca.isr.umich.edu/).

- Real Interest Rate

Consumption is also influenced by the economy's real interest rate. This is particularly true for higher valued goods such as cars, appliances, and so on. A higher interest rate would cause consumption spending for these products to decline.

- Wealth

Consumption is also affected by wealth. Changes in household wealth can significantly impact consumption spending. In recent years, we have seen several examples of the wealth effect at work. In the late 1990s, the rising stock market increased household wealth, which in turn lead to a rise in the level of consumption spending. While the meltdown in housing values during 2008 – 2010, created a negative wealth effect on consumption spending.

CONSUMPTION FUNCTION: ALGEBRAIC FORM

We can represent the above discussion in an algebraic form:

$$2A) \quad C = f(Y, Tax, Tr, Expectations, W, r)$$

Y – current income
Tax – all personal taxes
Tr – transfer payments
$Expectations$ – Expectations about future income (i.e. consumer confidence)
W – wealth
r – real interest rate

We can simplify the discussion by grouping the effects of $Expectations$, W, and r into one component and refer to it as autonomous consumption (a):

$$3A) \quad a = f(Expectations, W, r)$$

Personal disposable income (PDI) is defined as the after tax and transfer income:

$$4A) \quad PDI = Y - Tax + Tr$$

Combining 3A and 4A, we can construct the consumption function:

$$5A) \quad C = mpc(Y - Tax + Tr) + a$$

Expression 5A introduced a new term, Marginal Propensity to Consume (mpc), which represents the change in consumption that results from a change in personal disposable income:

$$6A) \quad mpc = \frac{\Delta C}{\Delta PDI}$$

For instance, if we were to assume that mpc is 0.8, then that would mean that 80% of any addition to (or subtraction from) the PDI would be directed to (or taken from) the consumption spending.[43]

We can complicate things further by assuming that the tax structure can in part be income based. For example, the U.S. deploys a variety of taxes, some of which are income based. The Federal government derives the bulk of its revenue from the Federal Income Tax, which is a function of income. State and local governments tend to rely on non-income tax bases such as sales and property taxes, and activities (e.g. speeding tickets, lotteries, and so on). With this in

---

[43] MPC is simply the derivative of the consumption function with respect to the PDI.

mind, we can rewrite the tax term (*Tax*) in the consumption function as a combination of autonomous of income taxes (*T*) and induced taxes (*tY*), where the lower case *t* represents the income tax rate:

$$7A) \quad \begin{aligned} C &= mpc(Y - T - tY + Tr) + a = mpc(Y(1-t) - T + Tr) + a = \\ &= mpcY(1-t) + mpc(Tr - T) + a \end{aligned}$$

In the above expression, we have clearly defined the induced component of consumption as *mpcY(1-t)* and the autonomous component (the rest of the expression).

We need to examine the other components of aggregate demand in a similar manner. The primary objective is to determine the variables that affect each of the components and differentiate between the autonomous and induced expenditures. Luckily for us, the most complex component of GDP in our discussion is consumption. The other components will tend to be mostly autonomous.

INVESTMENT FUNCTION (I)

Investment is a function of its expected benefit and cost. Chapter 1 defined the opportunity cost of money as the interest rate at which the money would otherwise be invested. Since investment involves an allocation of financial capital, the opportunity cost of money becomes its cost.[44] It is easy to see the connection between the interest rate and the cost of an investment when a firm undertaking an investment project borrows to finance it. For instance, businesses often issue bonds to raise funds to finance their capital expenditures. In this case, the interest rate on the bond is an explicit cost of the investment project that is being financed through the issuance of the bond. If the firm uses its own funds to finance an investment project, then the interest rate becomes the implicit cost of investment as the firm forgoes an opportunity to earn the interest rate. The expected benefit of investment depends on its expected future return. This expected return is a function of future income (future *Y*), or the future GDP of the economy.

---

[44] Cost of capital consists of interest cost and economic depreciation. There may also be some additional costs involved in purchasing and maintaining capital equipment such as property taxes, insurance, etc.

Since investment is a function of future income and the current real interest rate, we can consider it as an autonomous function, i.e. a function that does not depend on the current income:

8A) $I = f(r, Y^{F})$

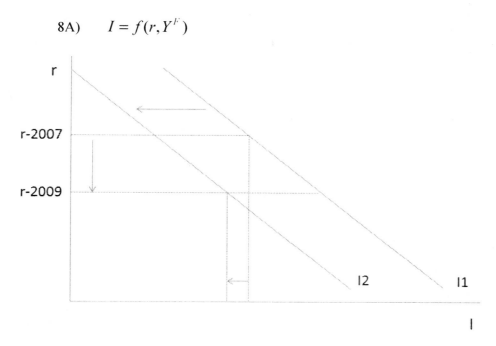

Figure 1A

Figure 1A projects investment as a function of real interest rate. Investment is a decreasing function of real interest rate. A lower interest rate allows businesses to invest into projects with a lower expected rate of return, thereby expanding profitable investment opportunities. The investment function depicted in Figure 1A is typically referred to as Investment Demand. Like any demand, it projects the level of investment as a function of its cost (interest rate), all else held constant. It is important to understand that changes in other investment decision factors can cancel out the effects of interest rate changes.

The 2007-2009 U.S. recession is an illustration of the importance of such other factors relevant in the investment function. Between September of 2007 and December of 2008, the Federal Reserve lowered the Federal Funds Rate from 5.25% to 0%. Even if we were to assume that the inflationary expectations declined by 3% during this period, the expected real rate of return still dropped by a sizable 2.25% (recall that r represents the real rate of interest, or real rate of return). Yet, despite this reduction in both nominal and real rates, the level of investment in the U.S. decreased. This observation does not imply that the relationship between the real interest rate and the level of investment is positive, but rather that there are other factors changing at the same time. The expectations about the future profitability of investment in the U.S. declined sharply during the course of 2007 – 2009, resulting in the combined effect (the reduction in business confidence about the future and the decline in interest rates) being negative. This is illustrated in Figure 1A by the shift in the demand for investment (investment function) from I1 to I2.

Our investment function is independent of the current income (Y), therefore it is completely autonomous. There is no reason to think that the current income is a determinant of an investment decision since the return is expected to materialize in the future.

GOVERNMENT SPENDING (G)

Government spending is primarily a function of government policy. Because it is a function of policy and not the current income, it is an autonomous expenditure. Even if government policy responds to changes in income, it does not justify government spending to be structured as a function of the current income. Some aspects of government spending such as automatic fiscal stabilizers may tie government spending to current income, but broadly defined, government spending is independent of the current income. Automatic fiscal stabilizers are discussed in the main body of the chapter.

NET EXPORTS (x-m)

Exports (x)   We also treat exports as an autonomous expenditure. Exports are a function of many variables including the value of exchange rates, and the economic conditions in the economies of the trading partners, but not of our current domestic economic conditions. Assuming that the goods we export are considered by foreign consumers as normal goods, a recession in the importing economies would cause our exports to decrease. This process makes recessions a contagious economic condition.

Imports (m)   Similar to exports, imports are a function of exchange rates. In addition, imports are in part induced by the current domestic income (Y). How much we purchase from overseas depends on our incomes. As domestic economic activity improves, imports of normal goods (perceived as normal by domestic consumers) increase. Thus, the net exports function can be expressed as:

9A) $\quad x - m = nx - pm \times Y$

Where pm represents the marginal propensity to import and nx represents the autonomous net exports.

MULTIPLIER EFFECT

If we combine all of the individual expenditure components from the preceding discussion we will have:

10A) $\quad Y = mpcY(1-t) + mpc(Tr - T) + a + I + G + nx - pm \times Y$

Solving the above expression for Y (i.e. identifying the current income):

11A) $\quad Y = \left[\dfrac{1}{1 - mpc(1-t) + pm} \right] \left(mpc(Tr - T) + a + I + G + nx \right)$

It is easy to see why the term in the square brackets is referred to as the multiplier. It multiplies each of the autonomous expenditures. In other words, the derivative of income with respect to any of the autonomous expenditures (except $(Tr-T)$) is the multiplier. With regard to $(Tr-T)$, it is the product of the multiplier and the marginal propensity to consume.

UNDERSTANDING THE MULTIPLIER

The role of the multiplier is simple as it just multiplies a change in an autonomous expenditure to obtain the effect on the economy's income level under the assumption of fixed prices.

For example, let's assume that mpc is 80% meaning that households, after purchasing foreign goods, allocate 80% of any change in their personal disposable income to consumption and 20% to saving.[45] Let us also assume that

---

[45] Note the use of the word "saving" as a noun. The word "savings" refers to the total accumulated savings of a household, while "saving" designates the behavior. For

the marginal propensity to import is 5% and the income tax rate is 20%. Under these assumptions the multiplier would be:

12A)

$$Multiplier = \frac{1}{1 - mpc(1-t) + pm} = \frac{1}{1 - 0.8(1-0.2) + 0.05} = \frac{1}{0.41} = 2.44$$

The implications are rather simple. If the government sector were to increase government spending by 10, then income would expand by 24.4. If the economy of one of our trading partners were to slide into a recession and as a result reduce its purchases of our exports by 5, then our aggregate income would decline by 12.2. If our businesses were to increase their investment spending by 20, then income would increase by 48.8. If the government were to increase the transfer payments by 10, then income would increase by 19.52.

The multiplication effect can be easily visualized. Assume that you get a pay raise at work and your PDI increases by $10,000 (for simplicity, assume zero marginal propensity to import and no income taxes). If we assume that your marginal propensity to consume is 80%, then your consumption spending increases by $8,000. Your consumption spending becomes the income of those individuals from whom you purchased goods and services. This implies that the aggregate income change in the economy is now $18,000 (the original $10,000 that your income increased by plus the $8,000 that your consumption spending created). If we assume that the individuals from whom you purchased goods and services have the same marginal propensity to consume, then their consumption spending increases by $6,400; therefore, generating an income of $6,400 for other individuals in the society and thus bringing the change in the aggregate income to $24,400. This process continues on, resulting in a multiplier effect of the original injection in spending.

We need to briefly examine the factors that influence the multiplier itself. The list of these is short and includes: marginal propensity to consume, income tax rate, and marginal propensity to import. A rise in the marginal propensity to consume would magnify the multiplier. For instance, if we were to increase the marginal propensity to consume to 0.9 while keeping all else constant, our multiplier in

---

example, a household might have 20,000 in savings and saving only 20% of their income a year.

Equation 12A would increase to 3 from the previous level of 2.44. And vice versa, if households were to become savers, then the multiplier would decline not only causing income to decrease but making the instruments of fiscal policy (taxes, transfers, and government spending) less effective. This is why a rise in the saving rate of U.S. households, similar to the one in response to the wealth meltdown of 2008, has a negative effect on the economy and the effectiveness of fiscal policy.

Note that a rise in the income tax rate would also cause the multiplier to decrease. For instance, if we continue with our prior computation and the assumption that *mpc* is 0.8, but use the income tax rate to 30% instead of the previous 20%, then the multiplier value would change to 2.04 (from 2.44). Later in the chapter, we discuss progressive income taxation, which allows the multiplier to change automatically with changes in income. This makes progressive income taxation an automatic fiscal stabilizer.

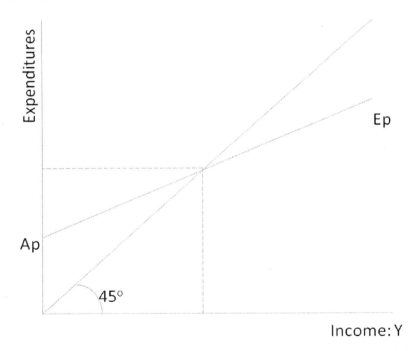

Figure 2A

Expression 10A identifies income, but under restrictive assumptions. The key assumption is that the price level is fixed. Economics textbooks frequently plot the expression in 10A against a 45 degree line and label the diagram as the Keynesian Cross. The diagram is insightful in that it models the short-run adjustment mechanism through unplanned investment, i.e. changes in business inventories.

SHORT-RUN ADJUSTMENT MECHANISM: CHANGES IN BUSINESS INVENTORIES

Figure 2A illustrates the Keynesian Cross. The economy is always in its short-run equilibrium, meaning that the sum of the expenditures adds up to the total output. Figure 2A has expenditures depicted on the Y-axis and output (income) on the X-axis. Generally speaking, the economy is always in a situation where the value on the Y axis must be equal to itself on the X-axis. That is to say, that the GDP identity of Equation 1 holds, because the X-axis represents GDP or Y, and the Y-axis represents the sum of the expenditures ($C+I+G+x-m$). Thus, the short-run equilibrium point must be located on the 45 degree line.

The line labeled Ep (Planned Expenditures) in Figure 2A is derived from Expression 10A. It is upward slopped, with a slope of less than one since the slope is equal to the inverse of the multiplier. This is not obvious from the diagram because the dependent variable axis is assigned to expenditures, and the independent variable axis is assigned to income. Note that Expression 10A represents the inverse of the variable assignments in Figure 2A (Y is a function of the expenditures). Thus, the Ep line in the Keynesian Cross is simply the inverse of Expression 10A, and its slope is simply one over the multiplier:

$$13A) \qquad \frac{1}{multiplier} = 1 - mpc + mpc \times t + pm = mps + mpc \times t + pm$$

Expression 13A introduces a new term, mps (marginal propensity to save). Marginal propensity to save is just the opposite of marginal propensity to consume. In our setup, households only have four uses of their pre-tax income. First, some of their pre-tax income has to be given away in the form of taxes. Then, this after tax income can be disposed of in three ways: spent on foreign goods, spent on consumption of domestic goods, and saved. Three of these activities represent leakages from the consumption cycle: taxes, imports, and savings. The multiplier is simply one over the sum of the marginal rates of leakage from the consumption cycle, which is expressed in Expressions 12A and 13A.

Ap represents autonomous planned expenditures, while *Ep* represents all planned expenditures (the sum of autonomous and induced planned expenditures). In terms of Expression 10A, *Ep* is the entire right hand side of the equation, while *Ap* is the term inside the parenthesis of Expression 11A. In the Keynesian Cross diagram, *Ap* serves as the intercept for the *Ep* function.

At this point, we need to differentiate between planned and unplanned expenditures. Planned expenditures are the desired level of expenditures, given the available information. For instance, planned autonomous consumption is the level of autonomous consumption that households want to make given their expectations about the future, the interest rate, and all other relevant economic conditions. Luckily for us, our model has only one unplanned expenditure, an unplanned investment, i.e. an unplanned change in business inventories. The model uses changes in unplanned investment as a signal for adjustment. The discussion below focuses on unplanned investment.

We first need to return our attention to the short-run equilibrium and the adjustment mechanism. To illustrate the short-run adjustment mechanism, we need to introduce a shock, a change to one of the planned expenditures. Figure 3A illustrates a scenario where one of the expenditure components (autonomous expenditures) decreases.

For instance, let us assume that consumer confidence, or rather consumer expectations about the future deteriorate, causing autonomous consumption (*a*) to decrease. Since autonomous consumption (*a*) is a planned autonomous expenditure, *Ap* (the sum of all autonomous planned expenditures) decreases. This causes the short-run equilibrium to decrease from *Y1* to *Y2*. Figure 3A shows the adjustment process. As the planned expenditures decrease from *Ep1* to *Ep2*, the economy experiences an accumulation of business inventories, *BI1* (an unplanned investment). This is because the level of output (*Y1*) exceeds the new level of planned expenditures (after the decline in *a*). This increase in business inventories causes businesses to reduce production in the next time period, taking the output level down to *Y**. *Y** equals *Ep2* at *Y1* when the economy is at the start of the adjustment process. Unplanned investment continues to increase, although at a slower rate, *BI2* (the change in the business inventories). Rising business inventories continue to fuel the adjustment process as the economy moves past *Y**. The business sector continues to respond to this unplanned accumulation of business inventories by a further reduction in the output level. The process continues until there is no more pressure on business inventories to change, which is reached when *Y* declines to *Y2*.

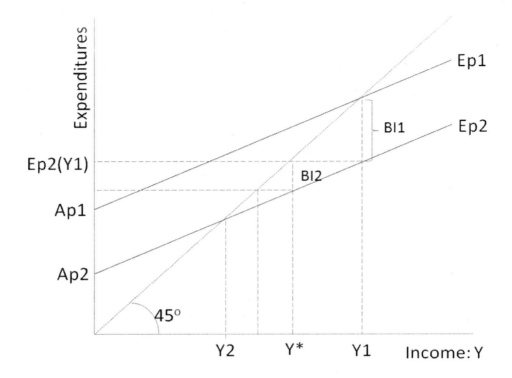

Figure 3A

The important conclusion from the Keynesian Cross is that unplanned changes in business inventories serve as a leading indicator for the future output level. If an unplanned change in business inventories is positive (accumulation), as it is in Figure 3A, then the economy is about to experience a decline in the level of economic activity. If an unplanned change in business inventories is negative (depletion), then the economy is about to experience a rise in the level of economic activity.

It is important to understand that the preceding argument applies to <u>unplanned</u> changes in business inventories. For instance, it is perfectly normal to see accumulation of business inventories in September and October in preparation for the holiday shopping season. It is also normal to see accumulation of business inventories if the business sector becomes optimistic about the future. Both of these are cases of planned business inventory accumulation and therefore are a part of the planned investment expenditure. In fact, we defined investment to be a function of business confidence earlier in our discussion. An unplanned change in business inventory occurs if the business sector collectively makes a mistake.

260

Unplanned changes in business inventory take place when the actual demand for goods and services materializes to be different from the one that had been expected by the business sector.

INVESTMENT AND SAVING: IS FUNCTION

Equation 10A includes two expenditure components that are functions of the real interest rate (r): Investment (I) and autonomous consumption (a). Both of these functions are decreasing functions with respect to the interest rate. Furthermore, the effects of any changes in investment and autonomous consumption get magnified by the multiplier (see the preceding discussion). The fact that two components of Y are decreasing functions of the real interest rate implies that Y itself is a decreasing function of the real interest rate, see Figure 4A.

Figure 4A

The IS function (Investment and Saving), plotted in Figure 4A, represents the combinations of output and the real interest rate for which the goods market and the market for loanable funds are simultaneously in equilibrium. Algebraically, the IS function is Equation 10A just expressed as a function of the economy's real interest rate through I and a. Other than changes in the real interest rate, anything that would cause any of the expenditures to increase in Equation 10A, would cause the IS function to increase or shift outwards. Examples would be a rise in transfer payments (*Tr*), a decline in taxes (*T*), a rise in consumer confidence (*a*), a rise in business confidence (*I*), an improvement in the economic conditions of the trading partner economies (*x*), etc. The slope of the IS function is determined by the sensitivity of the investment and autonomous consumption functions to changes in the real interest rate and by the multiplier. The more sensitive the investment and autonomous consumption functions are to changes in real interest rate the flatter the IS curve would be in Figure 4A. Similarly, the greater the multiplier, the flatter the IS curve.

LIQUIDITY AND MONEY: LM

Our discussion is still missing at least one more important market, the money market. The money market is relevant since it is where the interest rate is ultimately determined. On the demand side, households and businesses hold money balances. The holding of money balances is costly as money has an opportunity cost, interest rate. Note that we define money here in simple terms along the M1 and perhaps M2 definitions of money used by the Federal Reserve. M1 consists of currency in circulation (outside of bank reserves, U.S. Treasury, and the Federal Reserve), traveler's checks, and demand deposits, such as checking accounts. M2 includes everything in M1 plus savings accounts, small denomination time deposits, and retail money market mutual funds.

Thus, holding balances of M1 or M2 implies forgoing an opportunity to invest those funds into interest earning assets, such as bonds. If holding money is costly, why hold it? The answer is simple, households need money for transactional purposes. In economics, we refer to this part of money demand as the transactional demand for money, which is a function of output in the economy. In other words, economic agents hold money to pay for output. Thus, the real demand for money (*L*, liquidity) can be expressed algebraically as:

14A) $L = b \times Y - c \times r$

Where *Y* is output, *b* is the sensitivity of the demand for money to output changes, and *c* is the sensitivity to real interest rate changes. Since the interest rate represents the opportunity cost of money, the demand for money is a decreasing function with respect to the interest rate as is indicated by the negative sign in front of *c*.

The supply side of this market is rather simple as the supply of money is controlled by the central bank. The money supply is a function of monetary policy and not the real interest rate. Thus we can formulate the supply of money as some exogenously given constant M in nominal terms. Since our demand for money is expressed in real terms (recall that *Y* represents real GDP and *r* is the real interest rate), we need to convert supply into real money supply, which can be accomplished by dividing nominal supply by the price level (*P*): M/*P*. Graphically, the market for money is represented in Figure 5A.

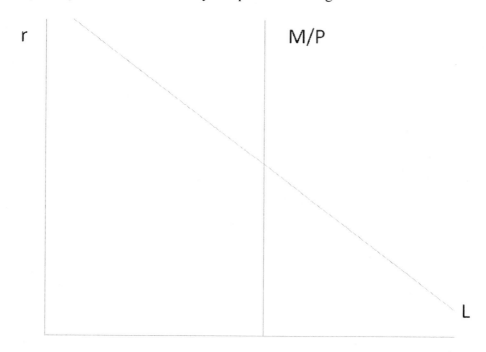

Figure 5A: Money Market (the horizontal axis represents real money balances).

The market for money provides us with an important conclusion: the interest rate is controlled by the central bank because it determines the level of the money supply. If the central bank decides to lower the interest rate, all it needs to do is increase the money supply and the equilibrium will move down along the downward slopped demand function.

In the previous section, we formulated the IS function. The IS function provided us with the equilibrium combinations of *Y* and *r* for which the market for goods and services is in equilibrium. At this point, we need to establish the relationship between *Y* and *r* for which the money market is in equilibrium. Together, these two functions will enable us to formulate the general equilibrium for the economy in the short-run. Luckily, Equation 14A and the money supply can easily define this relationship between Y and r for us. The market for money is in equilibrium when the real money demand and the real money supply are equal:

$$15A) \quad bY - cr = \frac{M}{P}$$

Expression 15A can be rewritten as:

$$16A) \quad Y = \frac{c}{b}r - \frac{1}{b}\frac{M}{P}$$

Expression 16A describes the LM function (LM – Liquidity and Money). This function represents the output as a function of the interest rate. Since we plotted the IS function in the Y-r space, we need to do the same for the LM function (we effectively plot the inverse of the function). In the Y-r space, the LM function will have a positive slope of b/c. Figure 6A shows the IS and LM functions in a single diagram.

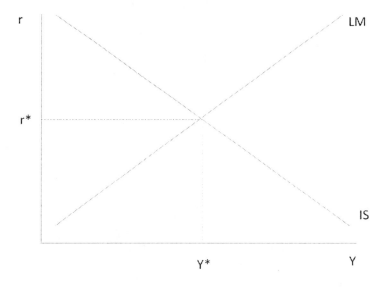

Figure 6A

Recall that everywhere along the IS curve, we have the combinations of Y and r for which the market for goods and services is in equilibrium. Similarly, everywhere along the LM curve, we have the combinations of Y and r for which the money market is in equilibrium. The intercept between these two curves produces the combination of Y and r for which both the market for goods and services and the money market are simultaneously in equilibrium. This is our short-run equilibrium. Figure 6A can be used to analyze the effects of monetary and fiscal policies, changes in expenditures, and so on. For example, consider the consequences of a decline in business confidence in the context of the IS-LM model. A decline in business confidence will cause investment spending to decline. In turn, this will cause the IS curve to decrease (shift towards the origin) and the short-run equilibrium to move along a downward slopped LM function to a lower Y and a lower r. Note that this decline in r reduces the impact on Y. Depending on the shape of the LM curve, the impact may be distributed differently between these two variables. For instance, a relatively steep LM curve would make the effect on Y rather minute because the interest rate adjustment absorbs most of the effect, while a flat LM curve would cause the output level to suffer a greater reduction. In an extreme case of a horizontal LM curve, the interest rate would remain constant.

DERIVING AGGREGATE DEMAND

At this point, we are ready to relax our assumption of fixed prices and move into the long-run. We already have the price level in our IS-LM model, so all we need to do is allow it to vary. The price level enters into the model only in one place, the money supply. We used the price level there to convert the nominal money supply into real. Figure 7A shows how a change in the price level changes the LM function.

Figure 7A illustrates a case where the price level increases from $P1$ to $P2$. In this case, the real money supply decreases (the nominal money supply (M) remains constant), resulting in a rise in the real interest rate as the equilibrium moves along the downward slopped money demand function. At the new equilibrium, we have the original output level (Y), corresponding to a higher interest rate. This causes the LM function to shift to the left, or decrease.

Plotting the shift in the LM function due to the change in the price level in the IS-LM diagram allows us to observe the effect on the general equilibrium. Figure 8A provides this illustration and derives the aggregate demand.

Aggregate demand is a function that consists of all equilibrium combinations of Y and P. Together with the IS-LM framework, we now have a model that allows us to connect output, prices, and interest rate to all of the main economic variables.

Furthermore, the model allows us to simultaneously solve for the equilibrium in all of the relevant markets, making it a general equilibrium model.

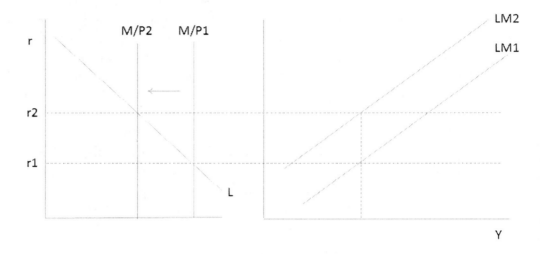

Figure 7A

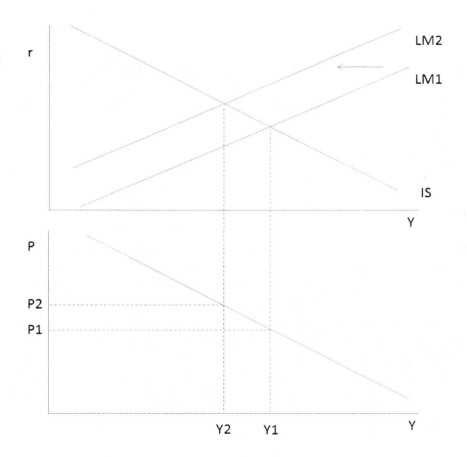

Figure 8A

Chapter 14

RECENT U.S. MACRO ECONOMIC HISTORY: FROM BUBBLE TO BUBBLE

In 2007, the housing bubble in the U.S. began to rapidly deflate, inducing major economic changes. The meltdown in housing values induced a wealth effect on the American consumer. The resulting loss of equity in housing values triggered a rise in foreclosures, which lead to a banking and financial crisis. The banking crisis in turn produced a liquidity crunch as the lending mechanisms of the financial system dried up. All of this translated into a rapid deflation of the global equity markets. In 2008, the stock market capitalization across the world's exchanges declined by nearly 30 trillion dollars or almost 46%, thereby hurting the household sector. [46] The impact was further amplified by the expansion in the use of financial derivatives that had taken place over the course of the preceding decade[47]. The meltdown led to an economic contraction which began in December of 2007 and lasted until March of 2009. This constituted the worst U.S. recession since the Great Depression.

The effect of the meltdown was not only felt by the U.S. economy but throughout the global economy. A question one can ask is, was the housing bubble a random event or was it a consequence of past economic policies? One can argue that the origin of the bubble was not even in the housing market, but rather it originated in the stock market of the late 1990s and then subsequently shifted into the housing market. To understand the recession of 2007-09 and the proceeding weak recovery, we need to look back to the last decade of the XX century.

---

[46] Source: World Bank.
[47] Instruments such as collateralized debt obligations, credit default swaps, enhanced the transmission mechanism of the crisis. Mortgage backed collateralized debt obligations allowed regional housing meltdowns to impact financial firms outside of their region.

THE 1990s

During the 1990s, the U.S. economy posted a phenomenal performance. The 1990s constituted the longest period of sustained economic expansion in U.S. history. According to the NBER, the expansion began in April of 1991 and lasted into February of 2001 (NBER, 2013). The economic performance was strong across all three fundamental criteria: output, employment, and price stability. Table 14.1 presents the summary of these fundamental measures of economic performance for the decade.

	1991	1992	1993	1994	1995	1996	1997	1998	1999	2000
Output (growth rates in real measures)										
Real GDP	-0.2	3.4	2.9	4.1	2.5	3.7	4.5	4.4	4.8	4.1
Consumption	0.2	3.4	3.6	3.8	2.7	3.5	3.7	5.2	5.5	5.1
Investment	-8.1	8.1	8.9	13.6	3.1	8.8	12.4	10	8.8	6.8
Non-residential	-5.4	3.2	8.7	9.2	10.5	9.3	12.1	12	10.4	9.8
Non-residential Structures	-11.1	-6	-0.6	1.8	6.4	5.7	7.3	5.1	0.1	7.8
Residential	-9.6	13.8	8.2	9.7	-3.3	8	1.9	7.7	6.3	1
Government	1.1	0.5	-0.8	0	0.6	1	1.9	2.1	3.6	2
Federal	-0.2	-1.8	-3.9	-3.8	-2.7	-1.2	-1	-1.1	1.9	0.5
Defense	-1.1	-5	-5.3	-4.9	-3.7	-1.3	-2.8	-2.1	1.9	-0.5
Exports	6.6	6.9	3.3	8.7	10.1	8.3	11.9	2.3	4.4	8.6
Imports	-0.2	7	8.6	11.9	8	8.7	13.5	11.7	11.5	13
Labor Market										
Unemployment Rate	6.85	7.49	6.91	6.10	5.59	5.41	4.94	4.50	4.22	3.97
Job Creation (monthly avg in 000's)	-71	97	234	320	180	234	283	251	264	162
Labor Force Participation Rate	66.20	66.45	66.25	66.58	66.63	66.78	67.10	67.10	67.10	67.08
Inflation										
CPI growth	3	3	2.8	2.6	2.5	3.4	1.7	1.6	2.7	3.4

Table 14.1 Sources: U.S. BEA and U.S. BLS.

As seen from Table 14.1, the real GDP posted growth of under three percent in only three years of the 1990s (1991, 1993, and 1995). Investment spending proved to be one of the main engines of growth during the decade. Within the investment component, it was the non-residential investment that expanded the fastest. This led to higher labor productivity and a greater demand for labor.[48] Between 1993 and 2000, the growth in non-residential investment averaged 10.25%. Since growth in non-residential investment is a requirement for job creation, the labor market expanded during the decade. In six of those years, the average monthly job growth exceeded 200 thousand a month. The unemployment rate steadily decreased and ended the decade under 4%. Simultaneously, the labor force participation rate increased. It is also interesting to note that the U.S. economy became increasingly more integrated into the global economy as both exports and imports expanded at much higher rates than the overall output.

Table 14.2 contrasts the fundamentals of economic performance of the 1990s with other recent periods.

	1971-1980	1981-1990	1991-2000	2001	2002-2007	2008-2009	2010-2012
OUTPUT (growth rates in real measures)							
Real GDP	3.21	3.27	3.42	1.1	2.58	-1.7	2.13
Consumption	3.26	3.51	3.67	2.7	2.90	-1.25	2.07
Investment	4.94	3.83	7.24	-7	2.93	-17.5	9.57
Non-residential	5.56	3.31	7.98	-2.8	3.48	-9.45	5.77
Non-residential Structures	3.65	0.69	1.65	-1.5	0.72	-7.35	-0.70
Residential	3.74	3.33	4.37	0.6	0.57	-23.15	2.33
Government	7.34	5.72	1.2	-5.6	5.68	-1.5	7.07
Federal	4.21	7.1	-1.33	-2.8	5.58	-8.1	6.57
Defense	0.97	3.25	-2.48	3.8	1.88	3.15	-1.40
Exports	-0.31	3.75	7.11	4.1	3.77	6.65	-0.17
Imports	-1.71	4.46	9.37	3.8	4.52	6.75	-0.90
LABOR MARKET							
Job Creation (monthly avg in 000's)	168	152	196	-146	100	-361	148
Labor Force Participation Rate	61.82	65.08	66.73	66.85	66.17	65.70	64.18
INFLATION							
CPI growth	4.51	8.12	2.67	1.6	2.95	1.4	2.4

Table 14.2 Sources: BEA and BLS

---

[48] Recall from the theory of the firm discussion that both the average and marginal product of labor depend on the ratio of other inputs to labor. As the ratio increases, the average and the marginal products rise.

The 1990s, in many ways, were a unique decade in U.S. history. The U.S. economy benefited from a number of important factors during this period, and their unique combination helped shape the longest economic expansion in the U.S. history. Volumes of books can be written describing the reasons behind the success of the 1990s, but given our limited space here, we will focus on the most fundamental ones.

THE ECONOMIC POLICY OF THE 1980s

At the start of the 1980s, the U.S. went through a number of important policy adjustments that enhanced its long-run economic performance. One was the anti-inflationary policy of the Federal Reserve that began in 1976 and culminated in May of 1980 when the Federal Funds rate reached 20 percent (see NY Federal Reserve, 2013). This policy, along with a sustained growth in the economy (beginning with 1983) and growth in productivity, helped to bring down and stabilize the U.S. inflation rates during the course of the 1980s.[49] At the beginning of the 1990s, the U.S. inflation was between 4 and 6 percent. This represented a sizable contrast to the 12 to 13 percent that was observed in 1979-80. Under the leadership of Paul Volcker, the Federal Reserve was able to successfully rein in inflation and create the foundation for the price stability seen later in the 1980s and throughout the 1990s.

Another potentially important policy change from the economic development perspective was the simplification of the U.S. income tax system under the Tax Reform Act of 1986. The Tax Reform Act of 1986 played an important role in simplifying the existing Federal income tax system as it significantly increased the standard deduction, reducing the need to itemize deductions (see Rosen, 1999). Ironically, the effects of the 1986 Tax Reform Act were later negated by two forms of legislation: first in 1990 with the phasing out of the itemized deductions and later with the complexities introduced by the Taxpayer Relief Act of 1997, colorfully described in Rosen's text as "… as 'mind-numbing' and 'a nightmare of complexity.'" (Rosen, 1999). It is noteworthy to point out that a more complex tax system creates higher costs of compliance and therefore can have a negative effect on the activity that is being taxed. Since income, sales, and

---

[49] The monetary policy contributed to the economic downturns of 1980 and 1982. These downturns helped reduce inflationary pressure. The proceeding economic recovery and the growth in the productivity of resources helped to further stabilize the price level.

value added taxes all tax production (in one way or another), then any increase in their compliance costs can have a negative effect on economic growth.

THE COLLAPSE OF THE USSR AND THE END OF THE COLD WAR

The collapse of the USSR may not seem like a major economic factor, but it indeed played an important role in the U.S. economy. The collapse of the USSR and the end of the Cold War allowed the U.S. government to reduce its spending on defense. As is seen from Tables 14.1 and 14.2, the level of defense spending in the U.S. was reduced substantially during the course of the 1990s, which stands in sharp contrast with the preceding two decades and the decade that followed. The collapse of the USSR also lead to what is now known as the Transitional Recession in the former Soviet bloc member economies. This transitional recession along with a number of other economic weaknesses outside of the U.S. made the U.S. economy appear as the safe haven for investment in the 1990s. This helped reduce the cost of investment to U.S. businesses and further fueled the economic expansion.

OIL PRICE

The 1990s began with a brief spike in the price of oil after Iraq's invasion of Kuwait. Following operation Desert Storm and the liberation of Kuwait in 1991, the price of oil declined and then remained relatively low and stable throughout the decade. Given the U.S. economy's dependency on oil (particularly imported oil), a low and stable oil price was an important ingredient for sustained economic growth.

Table 14.3 shows the WTI (West Texas Intermediate) spot price per barrel, the U.S. imports of Petroleum, and production growth behavior during the 1990s (sources: U.S. Energy Information Administration, 2013; British Petroleum, 2009). While the U.S. production of oil declined during the decade, the U.S. imports of oil increased sizably, indicating an ongoing economic expansion. This resulted in an increased dependency on imported oil and made the economy more vulnerable to price fluctuations. Given this international dependency, the price of oil can be viewed as a levy on U.S. businesses and consumers. During the 1990s (1991-2000), the U.S. spent on average $68.076 billion dollars a year on imported petroleum and petroleum related products. For comparison, in 2008, when the price of oil reached its highest peak so far, the U.S. spent $453.280 billion dollars on imported petroleum and petroleum products (source: U.S. Bureau of Economic Analysis).

Table 14.3 also presents two other interesting points. Firstly, it shows the effect of the transitional recession on the former Soviet bloc. The level of petroleum production in the former USSR decreased sharply between 1992 and 1996. Secondly, the OPEC output expansion during the 1990s helped to offset the effect of reduced production in the former USSR member states and thus helped to maintain low prices.

COMMERCIAL ADAPTATION OF THE INTERNET

During the 1990s, we witnessed a rapid commercial adaptation of the internet. The internet did not just create another set of means to conduct commerce, but more importantly it stimulated productivity growth, reduced information search costs and therefore fundamentally changed the economy. We are still too close to the event to understand its full implication on the economy, but suffice it to say that it has impacted practically every business and consumer. From an economics perspective, the internet adaptation has produced at least two important effects: increased worker productivity and reduced information search costs. The first of these directly stimulated economic growth. Although at this point in time, we cannot say with certainty that the internet has modified the productivity growth. Such a modification would place the economy on a steeper long-term expansion path for real output. Alternatively, the internet could have placed the economy on a higher long-term expansion path but one with the same slope (i.e. no modification to productivity growth in the long-run). In other words, the productivity gains are short term as they are only observed while the economy adapts this new technology. Once the process of adaptation is completed, the economy will obtain a higher level of output per unit of labor, but the growth rate will return to the past normal. Notwithstanding, the effect of commercial adaptation of the internet during the 1990s further fueled the economic expansion.

273

	1991	1992	1993	1994	1995	1996	1997	1998	1999	2000
WTI Spot Price	21.54	20.58	18.43	17.2	18.43	22.12	20.61	14.42	19.34	30.38
US Imports of Petroleum (000's of barrels)	2,110,532	2,226,341	2,477,230	2,578,072	2,638,810	2,747,839	3,002,299	3,177,584	3,186,663	3,319,816
Petroleum Production Growth (%)										
US	2.12	-1.16	-1.70	-1.97	-0.14	0.48	0.17	-1.93	-3.07	0.72
OPEC	-0.15	5.85	3.23	2.97	2.70	1.88	4.88	4.01	-3.50	6.26
Former USSR	-8.74	-14.81	-10.48	-7.82	-1.52	-1.37	2.39	0.68	5.19	7.14
World	-0.15	0.32	0.82	2.29	2.43	2.39	3.10	1.97	-1.11	3.85

Table 14.3 Source: U.S. Energy Information Administration.

Perhaps the most important benefit of the internet adaptation is its ability to reduce information search and information transmission costs. This may potentially have economy-wide implications, including changes in labor mobility and consequently in the natural unemployment rate. In a market based economy, labor mobility (both geographically and across occupations) plays an important corrective role. The internet as a technology made it easier to match workers with jobs by reducing the search costs and expanding the geographical scope of the labor market. This effectively increased the geographic mobility of labor. Although it is too early to adequately measure this effect, it is likely that the internet reduced the unemployment duration, thereby reducing the natural unemployment rate. On a related note, one can argue that a meltdown in housing values may reduce the geographical labor mobility as it makes it more difficult for workers whose home equity declined to zero or a negative value to liquidate their homes and relocate.

SAFE HAVEN FOR INVESTMENT

Although the 1990s were a great decade for the U.S. economy, outside of the U.S., it was a rather turbulent period. For the former Soviet bloc countries, spanning across Eastern Europe and into Central Asia, the decade began with a severe economic downturn. In some cases, this downturn lasted practically throughout the entire decade. One of the worst impacted economies was that of Ukraine where the economic contraction began in 1990 and lasted until 1999 according to the data of the World Bank (World Bank, 2013). Although the transition progressed peacefully in most places, there were some exceptions, with the most tragic being the war that followed the disintegration of Yugoslavia. This was the first military confrontation on such a scale on the European continent since World War II. The currently stable Euro currency was not around in the 1990s. The European Union was still in its formative stages, and the common currency market only emerged at the end of the decade, on January 1 of 1999.

The Middle East entered the decade with a war between Iraq and Kuwait that quickly expanded into an international operation. Throughout the decade, the price of oil remained rather low, keeping the performance of the economies of the Persian Gulf region at a somewhat moderate level.

Currency crises in Latin American economies continued to unnerve investors. Perhaps one of the most interesting examples was the crisis of the Mexican Peso in 1994.[50] Mexico had just entered into the NAFTA (the North American Free Trade Agreement) when it experienced a large balance of payments crisis and required one of the largest bailouts to that day. Nearly 50 billion dollars was used to assist the Mexican economy in 1995.

In the second half of the decade, the magnitude of economic crises expanded drastically when the Asian Financial Crisis erupted in 1997. Prior to the crisis, many rapidly growing Asian economies were referred to as the "Asian Tigers," a term that seems to have disappeared during the crisis. The worst affected currency was the Indonesian Rupiah, which in the first six months of the crisis lost over 60% of its value against the U.S. dollar (BBC News, 1998). The contagious effect of the Asian Financial Crisis expanded to other emerging economies, most notably Russia. In August of 1998, a combination of factors, including the contagious effect of the Asian Financial Crisis, and the low price of oil led to a debt and a subsequent balance of payments crisis. The balance of payments crisis resulted in devaluation of the rouble.[51]

Generally, currency depreciations help the international trade sector. Currency depreciations help both the domestic exporters and domestic firms that compete against foreign imports in the domestic market. For instance, in the cases of Mexico and Russia their current accounts (international trade) of the balance of payments improved following the currency correction. Indeed, some central banks make currency depreciation a policy aimed at helping their domestic manufacturing sector. The Central Bank of Japan employed a currency depreciation policy in 2013 to assist Japanese exporters. However, currency depreciations also have numerous drawbacks, and the previously mentioned currency crises of Mexico, the Asian economies, and Russia had numerous victims. Any domestic resident (business or household) with debt denominated in foreign currency saw their debt expand rapidly.[52] Prices of imported goods

---

[50] A currency crisis is simply a sharp adjustment in the exchange rate. A currency crisis is a consequence of some other underlying serious issue. A currency crisis follows what is called a balance of payments crisis. Fundamentally, the balance of payments summarizes trade and investment activities. A balance of payments crisis represents an outflow of foreign exchange through either trade deficit or capital flight.

[51] Devaluation occurs when a country with a fixed exchange rate system changes the official exchange rate (reduces). Depreciation refers to a change (reduction) in the value of a floating currency.

[52] This tends to be particularly important for developing economies. Developing economies tend to be characterized by lower levels of capital equipment and subsequently a high ratio of labor to physical capital. Thus, these economies tend to observe capital influxes, which make their businesses borrowers in the international

increased, which contributed to inflation and a rise in the cost of living. Commodity prices tend to be denominated in the U.S. dollar, meaning that any currency depreciation against the dollar results in higher commodity costs, which can in turn adversely impact the costs of production.

The underlying effect of this turbulence was that the U.S. economy appeared to be a safe haven for investment. This helped fuel the expansion of the U.S. stock market and the U.S. economy. The global turbulence produced two additional side effects for the U.S. economy: low inflation and low cost of commodities.

The U.S. inflation of the 1990s was non-uniform. On average, it was relatively low and stable but that was in part due to the strong U.S. dollar and growing globalization (trade globalization) of the U.S. economy. The sectors of the economy that were exposed to foreign competition saw little inflation, but those areas of the economy where foreign competition was not present saw considerably higher inflation.

	Average Annual Inflation Rates: 1991 - 2000
CPI	2.4
Housing: Shelter	3.3
Furniture and bedding	1.1
Apparel	-0.1
Transportation: New Vehicles	1.3
Transportation: Gasoline (all types)	-0.4
Transportation: Motor vehicle maintenance and repair	3.1
Transportation: Motor vehicle insurance	3.9
Transportation: Airline Fare	3.5
Medical Care	4.6
Medical Care: Services	4.8
Medical Care: Hospital and related services	5.7
Education: Tuition	6.2

Table 14.4 Source: U.S. Bureau of Labor Statistics, computation by the author.

capital markets. Under these conditions, these businesses tend to have their liabilities in foreign currency, while their revenues are generated in the domestic currency.

Table 14.4 illustrates that those areas where international trade played a limited role recorded higher levels of inflation. For instance, tuition, medical care, housing, insurance, and vehicle maintenance all experienced relatively high inflation. Simultaneously, the areas of the economy that saw increasing participation of foreign competitors experienced relatively low inflation (e.g. furniture and bedding, apparel, new vehicles). However, the overall price inflation remained low and stable during the course of the decade.

FORMATION OF THE BUBBLE

Reflecting on the exceptional performance of the economy, the U.S. equity markets advanced rapidly during the 1990s, particularly in the second half of the decade. Between 1990 and 1995, the U.S. equity markets added nearly 3.8 trillion dollars, or 55% to the total domestic market capitalization (World Bank, 2013). In the next five years, the market capitalization expanded another 8.3 trillion dollars, or 120% (World Bank, 2013). This was a spectacular expansion that produced sizable effects on household, business, and public sectors.

For the household sector, this rise in equity values created a massive wealth effect, further fueling consumption spending. A wealth effect occurs when household assets appreciate in value, causing a rise in wealth, which in turn impacts a household's consumption and saving decisions. These assets include stocks, bonds, real estate, and so on. When a household's wealth increases, the household is likely to increase their consumption and reduce their saving. This is exactly what was observed during the course of the 1990s. The stock-market-induced wealth creation stimulated consumption and reduced saving. Daniel Larkins of the U.S. BEA stated in the 1999 February Survey of Current Business: "Personal saving rate—personal saving as a percentage of disposable personal income—decreased to 0.5 percent in 1998 (and reached zero in the fourth quarter of 1998). These decreases, which continue a two-decade long downtrend, are not surprising in light of the large gains in household wealth, the steady growth in income, and the high levels of consumer sentiment" (US BEA, 1999). However, wealth based decisions are interesting because wealth can be volatile. For instance, a gain in stock value becomes finalized only if the stock is liquidated, otherwise the owner of the stock continues to "gamble" and face the risk that any stock appreciation can be reversed.

The business sector was also affected by the rise in the equity markets. One obvious effect was through consumer demand. However, there was another effect as well; high share prices enabled many companies to raise capital by simply selling more shares.[53] This mechanism effectively reduced the cost of raising capital for businesses but exposed their shareholders to a greater potential risk.

In 1999 – 2000, the U.S. equity markets reached unprecedented levels; levels that were unjustified by corporate earnings or dividends. Shiller deemed the behavior that leads to the formation of an asset bubble as "irrational exuberance" on the part of investors (see Shiller, 2000). However, there can be other explanations. Miller, Weller, and Zhang (Miller, Weller, and Zhang, 2002) argued that the equity market bubble formed due to the moral hazard created by the policies of the Federal Reserve: "…the observed risk premium [in equity markets] may be reduced by one-sided intervention policy on the part of the Federal Reserve which leads investors into the erroneous belief that they are insured against downside risk."

Perhaps it is unfair to argue that the Federal Reserve did nothing to prevent the formation of the equity bubble in the later part of the 1990s. Starting in June of 1999, the Federal Reserve began to increase the interest rate in quarter point steps. Between June of 1999 and May of 2000, the federal funds rate was increased six times from 4.75% to 6.50%. However, this appears to have been too little too late as the multi-trillion dollar bubble was in its final stages of formation. In March of 2000, the myth of the new dotcom based economy evaporated and the bubble burst.

SHIFTING THE BUBBLE INTO THE HOUSING MARKET

In March of 2000, the NASDAQ market experienced a crash. The tech heavy NASDAQ reached its highest level (to this day) on March 10 of 2000 when it touched 5048.62[54]. For about two weeks, the index fluctuated reaching another lower peak of 4963 on March 24 and then the fall began. By the end of trading on March 30, the index was down to 4457.89, posting a ten percent decline in just six days. The fall continued, and on April 14 the index closed at 3321.29, falling over 34% since March 10. The collapse extended over the next two and a half years as the index rolled towards its lowest point of the XXI century so far. The trough was reached on September 30 of 2002 when the NASDAQ declined to

---

[53] Convincing the shareholders of diluting their equity is a tough task, and amongst other factors it is a function of the number of shares to be issued. As the price of the share increases, the number of shares needed to raise the same level of capital declines.
[54] Market data is obtained from Yahoo.com (http://finance.yahoo.com).

1139.90, representing a meltdown of nearly 77% from the peak of 2000. Between 2000 and 2002, the U.S. equity markets lost nearly four trillion dollars or about 26% of their valuation near their peak (World Bank, 2013). Such a meltdown in wealth, particularly in an economy where by the supplemental retirement system nearly every worker was in one way or another invested in the equity markets, could not have left the economy unaffected. Some of the very engines of the expansion that took place in the later part of the 1990s were now turning against the economy (i.e. the wealth effect).

The Federal Reserve preemptively jumped to the rescue, and it was this rescue that helped shift the bubble from the equity market into the housing market and in the process helped create the grounds for the next crash. The Federal Reserve began an aggressive monetary expansion on January 3 of 2001. During the course of January alone, the Federal Reserve lowered the federal funds rate by one full percent. By the end of 2001, the Federal Reserve had lowered the federal funds rate from 6.5% to 1.75%. The monetary expansion continued in 2002 and 2003 as the Federal Reserve remained focused on fighting the jobless recovery that followed the recession of 2000 – 2001. The last rate reduction was implemented on June 25 of 2003, bringing the federal funds rate to a mere one percent.

The massive monetary expansion of 2001 – 2003 helped stabilize the business cycle, but the effect was not confined there. The monetary expansion also created a moral hazard as it signaled the proactive position of the Federal Reserve. Fuelled by low interest rates the housing market started to expand. The capital that previously left the stock market now searched for the next big game, and the housing market seemed to fit the criteria. Between 2002 and 2004, investment into residential housing steadily increased. If in the 1990s it was the non-residential investment that lead the growth, then during 2002 – 2005 that role was overtaken by the residential investment (see Figure 14.1).

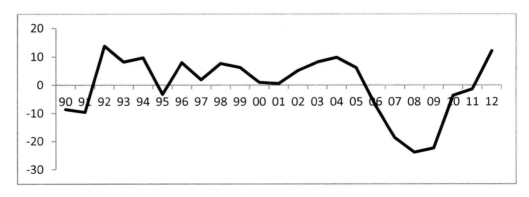

Figure 14.1: Residential Investment Growth in percentage (1990 – 2012).

The monetary expansion induced lower mortgage rates, which in turn stimulated demand for housing. As housing prices increased, the financial system widely adapted adjustable rate mortgages to further reduce the mortgage interest rate for at least an introductory period.[55] The adjustable rate mortgages further fueled housing expansion as they made housing temporarily more affordable.[56] One should not underestimate the effect of the interest rate on mortgages. For a $200,000 loan for 30 years, a change in the interest rate from 8.05% (the average for 2000) to 5.83% (the average for 2003) would mean a $297 (or about 25% relative to the monthly payment based on 5.83%) difference in the monthly payment.[57]

Other practices, such as no-down payment or low-down payment loans effectively required housing inflation in order for households to build sufficient equity and to be able to sell their properties shortly after buying them. Being able to sell one's home is an important condition for geographical labor mobility. In a zero price appreciation environment, a homebuyer with a no down payment loan at 5.83% would have to wait four years and four months to gain six percent equity. If we assume that the average transaction cost to sell a house (including the real estate commission) is about six percent of the property value, then the above homeowner would need to wait for over four years to avoiding owing money at closing.

The lending practices increasingly became dependent on ongoing appreciation of housing values. One can add here a discussion on mortgage backed securities, and the role they played in generating additional financing, and how they distributed the risk of the housing market throughout the financial system at large. One can also add a discussion on how the formation of mortgage backed securities created uncertainty about the level of risk associated with these securities. However, it seems that the important point is that the system increasingly became dependent on housing inflation, and when the inflation failed to materialize, the market crashed. When housing prices stopped rising, homeowners who had little or no equity (due to low down payments) found

---

[55] Adjustable rate mortgages allow the borrower to move "down" the yield curve. The traditional 30 year mortgage is correlated with the 10 year T-bond, while an adjustable rate mortgage with a three year fixed period would tend to follow the 3 year T-bond.

[56] In addition to these there were also interest-only mortgages.

[57] The average mortgage rates are obtained from Freddie Mac and are available online at: http://www.freddiemac.com/pmms/pmms30.htm

themselves in a situation where selling their property might require bringing more capital than just their home to the closing. Households who had adjustable rate mortgages found themselves in a situation where their mortgage rates would reset to higher rates, thereby making their shelter costs higher.[58]

Instruments, such as collateralized debt obligations and credit default swaps merely facilitated the transmission of the crisis across all financial markets and lead to a liquidity crunch; however, the underlying problem that caused the crisis was the increasing dependency of the lending practices on price appreciation. This was a standard bubble where the true valuation was increasingly falling below the market valuation. Nevertheless, it seems that this bubble did not form out of thin air, but rather developed as a consequence of the monetary expansion of 2001 – 2003. In essence, the housing bubble replaced the stock market bubble that burst in 2000.

HOUSING PRICES AND AFFORDABILITY

During the housing meltdown of 2008 – 2011, it seems that the mainstream media successfully painted the picture that home price decreases negatively impact households, especially those households that own the depreciating homes. This view is not exactly complete. To truly understand the role of housing prices on households, we need to differentiate between those households that invest into housing and those that derive housing services from their homes. The first category consists of real estate investors. These households clearly get hurt from any depreciation in housing values. The latter category consists of homeowners who live in their own homes. The impact on these households from housing price depreciation is not as straight forward. On the surface, these households may view their homes as an investment, but in reality their homes provide a service – shelter, thereby constituting consumption. To understand that a home is not an investment, one needs to understand that liquidating it would require finding new shelter. This is very different from liquidating an investment asset such as a stock, bond, or a rental housing unit. A household that sells their primary and only residence has to either purchase or rent another. Since over time people prefer to move into better and therefore more expensive housing units, inflation in the housing sector may actually hurt households.

---

[58] Recall that in economics, a house is considered a capital unit which provides a service - shelter.

For example, assume that you live in a $100,000 house and are considering moving into a bigger one, e.g. $200,000. At present, the spread between the two prices is $100,000. Let us assume you decide to postpone your decision to move by one year in the hope you will be able to benefit from the appreciation in the market value of your current home. Let us also assume that during this one year the housing market experiences a uniform price inflation of 20%. This means that all housing prices rise by 20%, making the value of your current home $120,000 and the value of the home you wish to move into $240,000. Note that home price appreciation has indeed made you wealthier by $20,000, but the appreciation also made it more expensive for you to move into a better home because the new spread in the prices is $120,000. This example shows that housing price inflation may actually make it more difficult for households to improve their housing conditions by moving into homes with greater market values.

The clear beneficiaries of housing price inflation are real estate investors and lending institutions. Both groups benefit from increases in home equity. For real estate investors the benefit is obvious as it increases the value of their assets. For lenders the benefit is a bit more hidden as they don't own housing assets directly. However, as housing prices increase, so does the equity of borrowers, which in turn causes foreclosure to decrease.

MISSING THE HOUSING MARKET: THE MONETARY POLICY OF 2006 – 2007

In the summer of 2004, the Federal Reserve shifted to a contractionary monetary policy. Rate increases continued until June of 2006, at which point the federal funds rate reached 5.25%. This reversal in monetary policy had a pronounced impact on mortgage rates. In July of 2006, the average 30 year mortgage rate in the U.S. stood at 6.76%, more than a whole percentage point above where it was in the summer of 2005 (source: Freddie Mac). This rise in mortgage rates would have been a welcomed step in correcting the housing market had it not been for the dependency of the housing market on price inflation and the wide spread use of ARMs (adjustable rate mortgages). However, given the wide spread use of ARMs and a low down payment practice, the rise in mortgage rates proved to be disastrous to the market. Instead of just moderating the demand for housing, the policy inadvertently triggered a brief rise in secondary market supply as homeowners with ARMs sought ways to avoid the resettlement of their rates by selling their homes.[59]

It is interesting to note that the residential investment component of the GDP started to contract at the start of 2006. This meant that private investors had already started to reduce their commitment to the housing market nearly two years prior to the actual crash. Furthermore, the rate of decline of the housing investment was deteriorating rapidly as seen in Table 14.5.

The Federal Reserve reversed its long standing policy on September 18 of 2007 when it began a monetary expansion aimed at reducing the impact of the housing meltdown on the economy and stabilizing the housing and financial sectors. Interestingly, the Federal Reserve chose September to be the starting point for helping a market that is seasonal in nature and is primarily active in late spring and in summer. It is also interesting to ask why the signs of the meltdown in the residential investment (see Table 14.5) did not trigger an earlier policy response (prior to the summer of 2007). The residential investment contracted sharply during the course of 2006 and in the first half of 2007. It seems that the Federal Reserve failed to preemptively address the crisis and its policy response served more as damage control.[60]

2005				2006			
I	II	III	IV	I	II	III	IV
7.5	9.6	4.2	0.1	-4.2	-16.9	-21.2	-19.7
2007				2008			
I	II	III	IV	I	II	III	IV
-16.4	-12	-24.1	-29.3	-28.5	-14.5	-20	-33.2

Table 14.5. Residential Investment Growth. Source: U.S. BEA.

As a damage controller, the Federal Reserve proved itself rather effective during the course of 2007 – 2009 when many new policy tools were quickly introduced. The Federal Reserve effectively pumped liquidity into every market that seemed

[59] Secondary market is another term for the market of existing homes.

[60] However, it is easy to criticize the Federal Reserve, but a central bank is in charge of monetary policy and does not have direct control over lending policies in the housing market. The use of monetary policy is not market specific (housing market) and can have implications across all markets (including commodity markets). For instance, a rate reduction prior to the summer of 2007 may have contributed to further inflation in housing prices.

to suffer liquidity issues and in doing so stabilized the financial system. It is important to note that as the crisis developed, the equity markets across the world rapidly retreated, creating massive wealth destruction that magnified the crisis.

Examples of emergency policy tools introduced by the Federal Reserve included: Primary Dealer Credit Facility (operational between 2008 – 2010), Term Asset Backed Securities Loan Facility (operational between 2008 – 2010), Commercial Paper Funding Facility (operational between 2008 – 2010), Money Market Investor Funding Facility (operational between 2008 – 2009), Maturity Extension Program and Reinvestment Policy (operational between 2011 – 2012), Interest on Required Balances and Excess Balances (established in 2008), and Quantitative Easing.[61]

Although many of these new policy tools have already expired, several continue to be used. One such remaining policy instrument is the interest payment on required reserve and excess balances. In its attempt to boost the nation's banks, the Federal Reserve began to pay interest to member banks on the required and excess reserves. This was a direct way to boost the revenues of member banks and therefore strengthen them. It is also interesting to point out that because these payments do not constitute purchases of assets by the Federal Reserve, their effect on the monetary policy is somewhat "hidden" from the balance sheet of the Federal Reserve.

To understand the magnitude of the monetary policy in recent years, one just needs to observe the changes in the balance sheet of the Federal Reserve. Every time the Federal Reserve acquires an asset, such as a U.S. Treasury bond or a mortgage backed security, the balance sheet increases. On September 12 of 2007, the balance sheet of the Federal Reserve included approximately 857 billion dollars in assets. By May 30 of 2013, the balance sheet expanded to about 3.352 trillion dollars. This massive monetary expansion produced some unintended results.

INFLATIONARY EXPECTATIONS

The balance sheet of the Federal Reserve shows how engaged the central bank has been in its monetary expansion since the fall of 2007. The recent rounds of quantitative easing, a sophisticated term for money printing, are in part designed

---

[61] For the complete list and a further discussion please see the Federal Reserve website at: http://www.federalreserve.gov/monetarypolicy/default.htm

to motivate businesses and households to spend money and therefore restart the circular flow of the economy. The logic is rather simple, by committing to ongoing money printing and shifting the focus of policy away from inflation, the central bank effectively sends a signal that inflation may be permitted to accelerate in the future. This signal in itself is a powerful tool because it can motivate businesses and households to start spending their monetary holdings and therefore increase the level of economic activity. However, inflation and inflationary expectations are not easy to control. There is an applicable historical analogy to this and that is the battle of Zama of 202 BC. The commander of the Carthaginian force, Hannibal, opened the battle by unleashing his war elephants on the Roman lines in the hope of scattering the enemy. However, the Romans were able to scare the elephants; many of them turned around and instead disrupted the left flank of the Carthaginian force, in the process changing the path of human history. Perhaps the moral of the story is that one should not unleash a force that one does not control.

The policies of the Federal Reserve can also be seen as attempts to create inflation in a number of markets including the housing market and equity markets. As mentioned earlier, inflationary expectations can potentially induce households and businesses to change their consumption and saving behavior. However, inflation is not a force that can be easily controlled and directed. Inflationary expectations may induce households and businesses to seek protection from inflation and move their wealth into assets that are perceived as hedges against inflation. Depending on the economy, these assets may vary. For example, at the onset of the Russian rouble crisis in August of 1998, there was an attempt by the residents of Russia to move away from the rouble and into more stable currencies such as the U.S. dollar. Unlike the Russian economy of 1998, the U.S. economy remains the largest in the world today. In the event of a global crisis, it is hard to imagine a more stable currency than that of the U.S. dollar at this time. Thus, any reallocation of assets due to a crisis impacting the U.S. dollar itself, would likely become biased towards commodities.

Indeed, one of the first consequences of the recent monetary expansion was a rise in most commodity prices. A rise in commodity prices generally is not a good factor for the U.S. economy as it means higher costs of production. The prices of some commodities, such as oil, can be perceived as a "tax" on the U.S. economy given the level of oil imports. In fact, when the price of oil peaked in 2008, the U.S. spent about a billion dollars a day on imported petroleum and petroleum based products. Interestingly, a rise in commodity prices also helps lift the currencies of major commodity exporting economies.

Energy commodities are not the only commodities that are affected this way by inflationary expectations. Agricultural commodities and farm land may also be seen as hedges against inflation. This means that inflationary expectations can cause increases in food prices.

Another consequence of the low rate policy conducted by the Federal Reserve was the inflation created in insurance premiums. This is because insurance companies tend to use bonds in their investments, and low interest rates translate into reduced income, which tends to translate into higher insurance premiums from their clients. Similarly, low interest rates lead to lower returns on fixed rate annuities and so on.

LACK OF MEANINGFUL INFLATION

The monumental expansion of the Federal Reserve's balance sheet has so far had a rather subdued effect on the overall inflation in the U.S. There are a number of factors that offer an explanation. One obvious factor is the high unemployment rate and the underperformance of the U.S. economy. Another factor is the current global economic environment. Much like in the late 1990s when the Asian Financial Crisis helped reduce inflationary pressure in the U.S., the current economic downturn in the European Union has had a similar effect. The EU downturn has caused a reduced demand for commodities across the globe. Although European economic problems have a direct impact on the U.S. economy through trade, such an impact is rather minute since the U.S. trade dependency on the European Union is somewhat small. In 2011, the U.S. exports to the entire European Union constituted 273 billion dollars, while the U.S. exports to Canada were 282 billion dollars.[62] Recessions can spread from one economy to another. One mechanism of recession transmission is through international trade; however, such a mechanism generally allows recessions to spread from an importing economy to an exporting economy.[63] In the case of the

---

[62] The U.S. trade statistics are obtained from the U.S. BEA (http://www.bea.gov/iTable/index_ita.cfm).

[63] Another transmission mechanism works through the financial markets. A recession can cause asset values in the economy to decline. This decline can impact the wealth of investors in other economies. This connection may exist for a number of reasons. One, foreign investors may hold the assets of the economy experiencing recession. Two, residents of the economy in recession may liquidate their foreign holdings. Three, a financial panic may cause markets outside of the economy to deflate. Four, foreign

bilateral US-EU trade, the U.S. has been a net importer, which reduces the likelihood of an EU recession spreading to the U.S. economy.

On the other hand, some of the indirect impacts of the European economic downturn on the U.S. economy have been positive. One such beneficial effect has been a reduced demand for commodities, which has led to reduced inflation in commodity markets. Another has been an increased demand for what might be perceived as the safe-haven assets. Generally, during a crisis the assets of large economies tend to be perceived as safer investments. The U.S. economy is the largest in the world and therefore may benefit from the demand for safety. Overseas weaknesses also induce foreign central banks to embark on their own money printing adventures that in turn further help the value of the USD and reduce the inflationary pressure in the U.S.

Combined, these effects reduce the pressure on prices in the U.S. They effectively allow the Federal Reserve to conduct a monetary expansion with little inflationary pressure although it is a short-run scenario. In the long-run, the foreign economies will eventually return to their long-run equilibrium at which point the monetary expansion in the U.S. can potentially result in inflation.

MONETARY POLICY CAN BE SELF-REVERSING

It is also important to note that monetary expansion can be self-reversing at a later point in time. For example, the preceding discussion made reference to an expanding balance sheet of the Federal Reserve. As the central bank acquires more financial assets (typically U.S. Treasury bonds), its balance sheet expands. However, to reverse this policy, the central bank can simply stop purchasing additional assets, and over time its balance sheet will automatically contract as the acquired financial assets mature. This implies that to maintain the existing level of its balance sheet, the central bank would have to rollover the maturing assets because in the absence of such rollovers the balance sheet would decline with time.

THE FISCAL SIDE

---

companies that export goods to the recession experiencing economy may see their equity prices decline.

Perhaps the most interesting aspect of the U.S. economic policy in 2008 – 2013 was not the monetary but the fiscal side. During this period, a number of massive fiscal steps were undertaken. The statement that "desperate times call for desperate measures" inevitably comes to mind. The U.S. Federal government addressed the recession that began in December of 2007 in a standard way by increasing the level of spending. As discussed earlier, there are three broadly defined categories of fiscal instruments and the U.S. government deployed all three: government spending, taxation, and transfers. Examples of the fiscal instruments used during this period include the stimulus package of 2009,[64] a temporary reduction in the payroll taxes under the Tax Relief Act of 2010 (the tax holiday was established for 2011 and later extended into 2012), and an extension of the unemployment benefits.[65] These policy actions are perfectly consistent with the Keynesian approach to stimulating the aggregate demand.

The fiscal expansion along with the downturn in the economy resulted in rising federal budget deficits. It is important to note that to a large extent, the rise in the annual budget deficits is not a consequence of the policy but a result of the economic downturn, which caused a contraction of the tax base and a rise in transfer payments. However, the discretionary expansionary policy also impacted the size of the budget deficits and contributed to the national debt.

We mentioned previously that there are three broad instrument so fiscal policy. One of these is government spending (G) generated by the provision of government goods and services. This component directly enters the nation's Gross Domestic Product. Table 14.6 shows the size and contribution of government spending to the U.S. GDP during 2002 – 2012. Table 14.6 shows that the spending by the Federal government jumped in 2008 and then continued to increase in 2009 and 2010. Even following the pullback in growth in 2011 – 2012, the level of government spending continued to remain above its long-term trend in 2012.

In addition to its direct contribution to the GDP, the public sector also plays an indirect role by redistributing income through transfer payments. Table 14.6

---

[64] The American Recovery and Reinvestment Act. For more information about the stimulus package please see www.recovery.org.

[65] Emergency Unemployment Compensation was first established on June 30th of 2008, but has been extended since then, with the most recent extension lasting until January 1 of 2014. The extension under the program is a function of the unemployment rate of the state as the program is designed to target states with higher sustained unemployment rates, see the U.S. Department of Labor (http://www.ows.doleta.gov/unemploy/supp_act.asp).

demonstrates that the value of transfer payments, which already had been on a rising trajectory, increased substantially during the recent economic crisis. In 2012, in part thanks to a pullback in unemployment compensation spending, the transfer payments declined to 16.86% of personal income, which is still considerably higher than the 14% level seen in the pre-crisis years.

The effect of transfer payments on GDP is complex. First of all, such payments allow low income households to maintain a certain standard of living and therefore help them to maintain their consumption spending. A reduction in transfer payments is likely to cause a significant drop in consumption spending by these households. Secondly, if lower income households exhibit higher marginal propensity to consume, then such a redistribution of wealth may have a positive effect on the overall consumption spending. However, certain types of transfer payments may induce higher reservation wages and therefore lead to a lower labor force participation.

Table 14.7 shows the U.S. budget deficits during the 2003 – 2012 fiscal years. The U.S. government continued to accumulate debt throughout this period, and with the outbreak of the recession, the size of the budget deficits significantly expanded. In the 2013 fiscal year, the U.S. national debt exceeded the GDP. Although this is an important mark, it is by far not the highest ratio amongst developed countries. For comparison, the national debt of Japan is about twice their GDP.

The expansion of the U.S. national debt has created further uncertainty about the future of taxation, government spending, and inflation. Any uncertainty tends to reduce investment and therefore reduce economic growth. Without significant productivity growth, the U.S. national debt may become unsustainable in the future and this has several important implications. Unless the productivity of economic resources expands drastically, the national debt would have to be addressed in one of three possible ways, or any combination thereof: increased taxation, reduced government spending, and partial monetarization of the debt. Although it is possible that all three mechanisms will be employed, the exact mix of the mechanisms is unknown at this time. Because it is unclear how the national debt will be addressed in the future, its growing size contributes to the overall uncertainty about the future. Since investment does not like uncertainty, any such uncertainty tends to deter investment into productive capital.

	2002	2003	2004	2005	2006	2007	2008	2009	2010	2011	2012
U.S. GDP (in billions of dollars)	10980.2	11512.2	12277	13095.4	13857.9	14480.3	14720.3	14417.9	14958.3	15533.8	16244.6
Government Spending (in billions of dollars)											
Government	2094.9	2220.8	2357.4	2493.7	2642.2	2801.9	3003.2	3089.1	3174	3158.7	3167
Federal Government	740.6	824.8	892.4	946.3	1002	1049.8	1155.6	1217.7	1303.9	1304.1	1295.7
State and Local Government	1354.3	1396	1465	1547.4	1640.2	1752.2	1847.6	1871.4	1870.2	1854.7	1871.3
Contribution To GDP Growth											
Government Spending	0.81	0.42	0.31	0.12	0.29	0.3	0.54	0.64	0.02	-0.68	-0.2
Federal Government	0.46	0.46	0.33	0.13	0.18	0.12	0.5	0.44	0.37	-0.23	-0.12
State and Local Government	0.35	-0.05	-0.02	0	0.11	0.18	0.04	0.2	-0.35	-0.46	-0.08
Spending as Percentage of GDP											
Government Spending	19.08	19.29	19.20	19.04	19.07	19.35	20.40	21.43	21.22	20.33	19.50
Federal Government	6.74	7.16	7.27	7.23	7.23	7.25	7.85	8.45	8.72	8.40	7.98
State and Local Government	12.33	12.13	11.93	11.82	11.84	12.10	12.55	12.98	12.50	11.94	11.52
Contributions to Personal Income											
Government Social Transfer Payments to Persons (in billions of dollars)	1246.2	1316.6	1399.9	1486.3	1588.2	1692.2	1847.3	2101.5	2234	2260.3	2316.8
Percent of Personal Income from Government Transfer Payments	13.62	13.88	13.93	14.01	13.94	14.11	14.86	17.39	17.97	17.13	16.86

Table 14.6. Source: U.S. BEA.

291

Fiscal Year	US Federal Government Budget Deficit	Budget Deficit as % of Existing National Debt
2012	1,275,901,078,829	7.94
2011	1,228,717,297,665	8.31
2010	1,651,794,027,380	12.18
2009	1,885,104,106,599	15.83
2008	1,017,071,524,650	10.15
2007	500,679,473,047	5.56
2006	574,264,237,492	6.75
2005	553,656,965,393	6.98
2004	595,821,633,587	8.07
2003	554,995,097,146	8.18

Table 14.7 U.S. budget deficits (Source: U.S. Treasury).

It can also be argued that the ongoing and significant borrowing by the Federal government positions the Federal Reserve into a difficult situation by limiting the ability of the central bank to run any contractionary monetary policy. If the Federal Reserve were to embark on a course of monetary contraction, the cost associated with financing the U.S. national debt would likely increase significantly. De facto, this leads to the central bank losing some independence in its policy.

In addition to the fiscal expansion, the U.S. Federal government introduced a number of reforms that also impacted the costs of production and the reservation wages. Examples of these include: changes in the EPA regulatory requirements, the minimum wage, the Affordable Health Care Act, and recent changes in taxation. Although some of these reforms may be desirable from the long-term point of view, their implementation during an economic downturn and a subsequent weak recovery may potentially have some adverse effects.[66] Generally, changes in regulations are disruptive to business activity. It is similar to changing the rules of chess half way into a game. The more fundamental a

---

[66] One example would be the healthcare sector. Over the course of the past two decades, the health care cost inflation consistently outpaced the overall inflation, and the cost of healthcare benefits has been one of the fastest rising components in the Employment Cost Index. However, the Affordable Care Act seems to mainly focus on the demand side of the market and therefore does not seem to promise a successful control of the costs of provision of healthcare.

change in the rules, the more disruptive it is to the business environment in the short-term.

STATE AND LOCAL

While the Federal Government embarked on a massive expansionary policy during the recent economic crisis, most state and local governments were forced to actually cut their expenditures. This pro-cyclical behavior of state and local government spending in a way helped magnify the crisis. Traditionally, economists tend to refer to the banking sector as an amplifier of business cycle fluctuations. This is because banks tend to scrutinize loans more in bad economic times and expand lending in good economic times, thereby causing lending activity to amplify the cyclical fluctuations of an economy. However, during the recent economic crisis, the same could in some sense be said about state and local governments. As seen in Table 14.6, state and local government spending produced a negative contribution to the U.S. GDP growth beginning with 2010.

The negative contribution by state and local governments is in part due to the reliance of these governments on those sources of revenue that were particularly drastically impacted by the recent economic downturn. The collapse of housing values during 2008 - 2010 directly impacted the state and local governments given their significant reliance on property taxes. According to the U.S. Department of the Census, in the fourth quarter of 2012, the property tax revenues constituted 44.6% of all tax revenue for state and local governments (U.S. Census, 2012). The property tax base declined in 2010 and exhibited virtually no growth in 2011 – 2012 (U.S. Census, 2012).

IMPLICATIONS

The crisis that began in 2007 may have very well been rooted in the stock market rise of the late 1990s. The bubble that formed in the stock market in the late 1990s may have simply been shifted into the housing market during the expansionary period of 2002 – 2007. The resulting massive financial crisis engulfed not only the U.S. economy, but through trade and financial markets, it impacted the entire world. The U.S. Federal government and the Federal Reserve deployed a number of policy responses to address the economic downturn. New monetary policy tools were developed. Historically, we are still too close to the crisis, and as a result we can't adequately evaluate the impact of the policy responses by the Federal government and the Federal Reserve. It will take years before their role will be fully understood by economists and historians.

However, we can argue that these policies, much like any remedy, tend to have side-effects. The stabilization policies themselves may contribute to uncertainty. The rising national debt is an example of such a contributing factor. The dependency of the U.S. equity markets on the monetary expansion in 2011 – 2013 is another possible example of a side effect. Such side effects tend to impact the level of composition of business investment spending, which in turn impacts employment growth. For the moment, it appears that the economy has shifted to a lower sustainable growth rate and to a higher natural unemployment rate.

An economy's business sector is like a plant, and the government is in charge of providing the proper environment for that plant to grow. This environment includes transparency of policy, a stable political system, well-defined property rights, a transparent judicial system, etc. In the right environment, the plant will produce fruits and generate enough tax revenues for the environment to be supported.

References

BBC News, 1998. "Indonesia: economic weaknesses exposed." Published on January 8, 1998 and available online at:
http://news.bbc.co.uk/2/hi/special_report/1998/asian_economic_crises/45472.stm

Miller, M., Weller, P. and Zhang, L. (2002), "Moral hazard and the US stock market: Analysing the 'Greenspan Put.'" The Economic Journal, 112: C171–C186.

NBER, 2013. "US Business Cycle Expansions and Contractions." Accessed on March 27, 2013. Available online at:
http://www.nber.org/cycles/cyclesmain.html

NY Federal Reserve, 2013. "Historical Changes of the Target Federal Funds and Discount Rates." Available online at:
http://www.newyorkfed.org/markets/statistics/dlyrates/fedrate.html

Rosen, Harvey S. 1999, *Public Finance*, 5th edition, Irwin/McGraw-Hill.

US Bureau of Economic Analysis, 1999. "Note on the Personal Saving Rate." Prepared by Daniel Larkins for *The February 1999 Survey of Current Business*. Available online at: http://www.bea.gov/scb/account_articles/national/0299cba/maintext.htm

US Census (Department of), 2012. "Quarterly Summary of State and Local Government Tax Revenue for 2012: *Q4.*" Available online at: http://www2.census.gov/govs/qtax/2012/q4_infosheet.pdf

US Energy Information Administration, 2013. "Petroleum and Other Liquids." Available online at: http://www.eia.gov/petroleum/

World Bank, 2013. World Development Indicators. Available online at: http://data.worldbank.org/

INDEX